VICTOR TAUSK'S SUICIDE

K. R. Eissler, M.D.

VICTOR TAUSK'S SUICIDE

K. R. Eissler, M.D.

With Comments by

Prof. Dr. Marius Tausk

International Universities Press, Inc.
New York

Library of Congress Cataloging in Publication Data.

Eissler, K. R. (Kurt Robert), 1908–
   Victor Tausk's suicide.

   Bibliography: p.
   Includes index.
   1. Tausk, Victor, 1879–1919. 2. Freud,
Sigmund, 1856–1939. 3. Psychoanalysts — Biography.
4. Suicide — Case studies. I. Tausk, M. II. Title.
RC339.52.T38E37   1982   150.19′52′0924 [B] 82-12725
ISBN 0-8236-6735-9

Manufactured in the United States of America

TABLE OF CONTENTS

Acknowledgments

I thank the following persons for assistance of various kinds:

Dr. Bernard Berglas

Prof. Ernst Federn

Anna Freud

Prof. Franz Gall

Prof. Martin Green

Dr. Emanuel Hurwitz

Prof. A. S. Kagan

Gina Kaus

Fritz Keller

Dr. Friedhelm Kemp

Dr. Ernest W. Kulka

Prof. Dr. Erna Lesky

Michael Meyer

Dr. Maurice Nadelman

Caroline Neubaur

Dr. Paul Parin

Dr. Ernst Pfeiffer

Prof. Dr. Marius Tausk

Camilla Ullmann

Wirkl. Hofrat Winter

The late Dr. Olga Knopf greatly assisted my inquiries.

K. R. Eissler, M.D.

I. Introduction

Victor Tausk, psychoanalyst and pupil of Freud, committed suicide on July 3, 1919 at the age of forty. This text records the results of an inquiry into the events of the last eight months of his life.

Some will raise objections to this undertaking. Since Tausk's suicide had been examined in an apparently exhaustive manner by Paul Roazen in 1969 and Tausk's prominence was not such as to require another inquiry into his tragic end within a decade, this endeavor will be considered superfluous. After all, although Ludwig Holzmann (1846–1906), a giant in physics, committed suicide, that tragedy did not precipitate comparable efforts. Tausk's position in the history of science was a minor one which does not seem to warrant in relatively short sequence two detailed inquiries into the background of his suicide.

Three passages from Roazen's book *Brother Animal*

1

(1969) will, however, make evident the importance of a renewed inquiry.

> [Tausk] wrote a Russian gypsy tale. . . .Ultimately, Husein [the protagonist] is slain by his own father. The tale was based on an actual court case, yet it foreshadows Tausk's fate with Freud as well [pp. 13–14].

> [Freud's pupils and collaborators] made [Freud's] every wish into a command. King Henry is supposed to have breathed with a sigh that Becket be dispatched; so if Freud wanted Tausk dead, it seemed perfectly in order for Tausk to oblige. Freud had such tremendous power over them because they all wanted to have it so [p. 157].

> [Tausk's] destruction at Freud's hands seemed irresistible. . . .[A] striking literary parallel appears in a story by Kafka. . . . In. . ."The Judgment," an angry father "sentences" his son to death by drowning; the son immediately complies by rushing from his father's house to a bridge from which he jumps to his death in the waters below [p. 158].

These images have in common a father (or a substitute) who wishes to cause the death of his son (or a substitute). They contain the three ways in which a murderer may proceed: he may commit a murder himself (first quotation); he may hire underlings to carry it out (second quotation); or he may create conditions which coerce the victim into death (third quotation). The third statement speaks a particularly clear language. Since Freud did not kill Tausk or hire anybody to do so, Roazen would have risked having his tale dismissed as fantasy had he claimed either of these possibilities. Therefore, he had to remind the reader that even when the police record correctly registers an incident of the sort as suicide, the incident may in truth be a murder. Roazen's book is the story, not of a suicide, not even of a manslaughter, but of a murder in which Freud is unmasked as the culprit.

The reader interested in Freud's biography may welcome the opportunity to learn about the events that were responsible for Tausk's tragic end, as they emerge from a consideration of all available documents and records. Five documents have been published that contain direct references to Tausk's death: part of his last will; his farewell letter to Freud; Federn's letter to his wife, written on the day of Tausk's death (Roazen, 1969); Tausk's obituary (Freud, 1919); and Freud's letter to Lou Andreas-Salomé (Pfeiffer, 1966) in which he informed her of the tragedy. All of these documents will be carefully discussed and evaluated. As will be seen, however, they are partly contradictory, and even though they suggest explanations and possibly point to contributory factors, they do not account for Tausk's suicide. I shall be able to add new material that makes it clear why Tausk at that particular moment in his life felt unequal to the task of carrying on. Prior to writing about the nature of the formidable stress on Tausk during the last few weeks of his life, and the traumatic misfortune of his last night, I present a reconstruction of his general psychopathology in order to make understandable his inability to withstand stress and trauma.

Next, I shall weigh various factors that have been held totally or partly responsible for his suicide and then proceed to the evaluation of a key document from which the reader will learn of an ominous complication in his life. I shall then review those events on the road to the final disaster that can be reconstructed from documents and eye-witness reports.

The subsequent discussion of Freud's obituary and historical deliberations, while perhaps not germane, strictly speaking, to a consideration of Tausk's suicide per se, help to develop the implications of this study.

I owe thanks to Prof. Dr. Marius Tausk for writing a critical appendix. It is to be expected that the historian and the loving son do not reach the same conclusions, and thus the reader has the advantage of having before him points of view that at times are diametrically opposed.

Prof. Dr. Tausk will have written his appendix after reading the text which follows. In response to my initial draft of that text, he conveyed to me his main objections in a personal meeting. Since he is not in favor of the custom of letting the author answer a rebuttal, nothing will follow his appendix. Therefore I have taken the liberty of anticipating some of his critical remarks.

Prof. Dr. Tausk has reproached me for approaching his father's tragedy, not as an understanding physician but as judge and moralist, and for selecting among possible inferences those that make his father appear in the worst light. I was struck when I found the same objection in Hurwitz's book (1979), where it was raised against C. G. Jung's psychiatric evaluation of Otto Gross, with whom the reader will become acquainted in Chapter VII. I am defenseless against a reproach such as this. Should I be guilty of that bias, it would stem from an interference by the unconscious, and an assurance that I feel free of such bias would not disprove its possible existence. Even under optimal conditions interpretations always leave a margin of uncertainty, small as it may be. I selected among possible interpretations those that carry the highest explanatory value without disagreeing with the preserved documents and eyewitness reports. But one has to agree with Freud's remark "that what is probable is not necessarily the truth and that the truth is not always probable" (1939, p. 17).

This report was made possible mainly by Anna Freud's kindly making Dr. Knopf's letter available to me and by Prof. Dr. Marius Tausk's giving me copies of his father's last will, of eight letters written by his father to Freud, of the very important letter he himself had written a year after his father's death to Lou Andreas-Salomé, and of a part of the equally important last letter of his father to Lou Andreas-Salomé which was only recently discovered in her literary estate. He also answered frequent inquiries. From Prof. Ernst Federn I received important documents by Paul Federn's hand.

What follows is not a biography but a case history aiming at the reconstruction of the proximate factors which caused the suicide of an unusually talented man. The reader will therefore hear nothing about his assets and probity but much about clinical psychopathology.

The reader will notice an unusual freedom in revealing the identity of persons with whom Tausk entertained intimate relations. But to have followed the tradition of protecting privacy would have been pointless, since the names that appear have already been made public by Roazen (1969).

II. An Outline of Tausk's Psychopathology

The following outline[1] of Tausk's life history may suffice for the reader's general orientation.

Victor Tausk was born March 12, 1879 in Sillein (Hungary). His nuclear family was composed of the following individuals: father, Hermann (1850–1916); mother, Emilie (1858–1938); and nine children — Jelka (1880–1911), Zora (1883–1971), Anka (1885–1955), Mirko (1887–1937), Vladimir (who died at the age of two, date unknown), Augusta (1891–1968), Zdenko (1893–1922), and Nada (1897 to the present) — that is, five sisters and, with Victor, four brothers.[2]

[1]See Roazen (1969); in addition, I used data obtained from Prof. Dr. Marius Tausk, wirkl. Hofrat Winter, and Prof. Franz Gall.

[2]For those concerned with family research, it is interesting to notice the vital superiority of the daughters as compared with that of the sons. Three of the latter died a violent death: Vladimir by an

6

Victor's father started as a schoolteacher, but then he became an internationally known journalist, first as an editor of a weekly and later as the publisher of a journal. He also held an important government job. He was restless, frequently absent from his home, tyrannical with his family, and unfaithful to his wife. His failure to provide adequately for his family forced his wife to accept money from her mother. He impressed women by his charm. Tausk's mother was a beautiful, self-sacrificing woman who was lenient in bringing up her children.

Shortly after Victor's birth the family moved to Croatia and in 1892 to Sarajevo, the capital of Bosnia, which Austria had occupied in 1878, carrying out a stipulation of the Berlin Congress (1878). Apparently Tausk's father tended to settle where the old Habsburgian monarchy was most endangered. As a matter of fact, in 1908 Austria annexed Bosnia and caused one of those many mini-crises that finally led to the explosion of World War I, which took its start in the very city of Sarajevo. He tried to act as a conciliator between the monarchy and its reluctant subjects. The possible effect on Tausk's growing up in a locale in which he was a minority member in two respects, namely, that of being a Jew (although his family did not observe religious obligations) and that of being a member of a German-speaking family, is not known.

In 1897 he moved to Vienna. Tausk was antagonistic to his father and in school rebelled against his teacher in religion. The rebellion probably was the reason why he had to move to Varazdin (Hungary), where he passed the

---

accident; Mirko, who joined the Spanish Republican Army, by gunshot at the hands of Communists for criticizing their excesses; and Victor by suicide. Zdenko died of generalized miliary tuberculosis.

Matura with honors in 1897. He would have preferred to study medicine, but financial considerations forced him into the study of law, which was less expensive. One had to pass three examinations *(Rigorosa)* in order to obtain the degree of Doctor of Law. Tausk flunked the first examination but eventually passed all three with the grade of "satisfactory."

The year following his move to Vienna, he met Martha, a Protestant of mixed parentage who was to become his wife (her personality will be described below). She fell in love with Tausk. From the time they met one another Tausk was on bad terms with the man who was to become his father-in-law; they hated each other intensely. Martha became pregnant. She and Tausk married in 1900, when Martha was 19 years old, and moved back to Sarajevo. The baby died at birth. In 1902 Marius and in 1904 Victor Hugo were born.

Tausk continued his career as a lawyer. He was ready to defend the poor. He succeeded in obtaining the acquittal of a woman who had killed her illegitimate child. This was an almost unheard-of accomplishment.

In 1905, when he had established himself as a lawyer, he and his wife decided to separate. They returned to Vienna, where Martha had always longed to live. After her separation from Tausk she earned a living in her father's enterprise. In 1906 Tausk settled in Berlin. He relinquished his profession and became a writer. He wrote a play that was never performed. He also wrote poetry and sketched. In order to eke out a living, he accepted assignments as a journalist although he considered them degrading. All these attempts did not solve his financial difficulties.

Tausk's morale became gradually undermined in Berlin, and he felt lonely. As a last resort he sought hospitalization and obtained a free place in a private hospital for physical and nervous illnesses, Sanatorium Ahrweiler on the Rhine. Possibly he also needed treatment for pulmonary disease, from which he suffered sporadically. At any rate, the initial diagnosis was mental and physical exhaustion. But what really drove him into the hospital was a grave frustration he had suffered in a love affair (Roazen, 1972). Initially his condition got worse at the hospital, but he recovered and after a stay of three weeks he left on October 22, 1907. He had "had enough of this life" (Roazen, 1969, p. 23). A trip to Italy seems to have gotten him out of the depression or whatever his nervous disorder may have been at that time.

After reading an article by Freud, Tausk wrote to him. Freud thought Tausk was a physician and was evidently sufficiently impressed by the communication to encourage him to come to Vienna and study psychoanalysis. Thus Tausk arrived in Vienna in the fall of 1908 and started to study medicine. At that time he and his wife were divorced "by mutual culpability" (gegenseitiges Verschulden), as the Austrian law calls it when both parties caused the failure of a marriage.

Tausk had at last found a firm prospect in his professional life. He was supported financially by Freud and four members of the Vienna Psychoanalytic Association. This made it possible for him to go through medical school. He passed the first Rigorosum in March 1911, the second in October 1913, and the third in January 1914: the first two "satisfactorily," the third with honors [ausgezeichnet]. He became an M.D. on January 23, 1914.

He did not have to wait for graduation to establish firm relations with the psychoanalytic group. Tausk was listed as a guest of the Association October 12, 1909

(Nunberg and Federn, vol. 2, p. 276) for the first time and attended their sessions from then on almost regularly. Already in the subsequent session he participated in the discussion. In the next session he was proposed as a member, and on November 3, 1909 he was elected to membership.

On November 24 he presented his first paper, "Theory of Knowledge and Psychoanalysis" (*ibid.*, p. 323), to the Society. It is noteworthy that Tausk had to stop his presentation and to declare himself unable to continue out of weariness (*ibid.*, p. 336). Wilhelm Stekel (1868–1940) wrote about the incident in his autobiography (Gutheil, 1950, p. 133): "He [Tausk] had started off excellently, but in the middle of the speech he became confused and was unable to finish. It was an uncomfortable moment for all. I tried to save the situation and continued the lecture extemporaneously." The lecture, however, was evidently good enough for Freud to say: "It would be desirable if, despite today's misfire, Tausk would make it his task from time to time to present to us single parts of this broad constellation, in a clear, detailed and elementary fashion" (Nunberg and Federn, vol. 2, p. 335).

Tausk was particularly successful in his psychoanalytic career. For several years he was the only one besides Freud to give regular lectures in Vienna on psychoanalysis. In 1912 Freud insisted "that all analytical papers should be reviewed in our journal [the *Zentrallblatt für Psychoanalyse*, the official organ of psychoanalysis] by Tausk" (Gutheil, 1950, p. 143), and he let Stekel quit the Association rather than give in on this demand.

Tausk presented at least nine full-length papers to the Association without further incidents of the kind recorded occurring again.

In 1912 Lou Andreas-Salomé (1861–1937) came to Vienna to study psychoanalysis with Freud. She was one of the most remarkable women of her time, not only because of her emancipation from the traditions the nineteenth century imposed upon women but also because of her literary, philosophical, and psychoanalytic output. The fact that Nietzsche proposed marriage to her and that Rilke was one of her lovers secured a central place for her in the biographies of these men. In 1912 she became a psychoanalyst and from then on maintained a close relationship with Freud, as their correspondence and Freud's (1937) obituary show. In the present context she is of importance because it has been assumed as certain that she had an intimate relationship with Tausk when she lived in Vienna during 1912 and 1913. Dr. Pfeiffer, who for many years was close to Lou Andreas-Salomé and whom she made the administrator of her literary estate, informed me, however, that in view of what he was told by her and diary entries that will be published by him in due time, it is certain that, notwithstanding her close relationship with Tausk, no physical relationship eventuated. Lou Andreas-Salomé is also relevant to this inquiry because her *Journal* records much material relevant to Tausk's biography.

Tausk's dawning psychoanalytic practice was rudely interrupted by the outbreak of the First World War. He served from August 1915 to November 1918, mainly as chief physician of psychiatric wards, and from the end of 1916 as neurologist in the service of the military government in Belgrade, the capital of Serbia, which was occupied by Austria during the war. Since he had worked extensively at Wagner-Jauregg's University Clinics in Vienna, he evidently had the standing of a specialist in psychiatry and neurology.

Since events following his return to Vienna will be discussed in detail, this biographical sketch can stop with these summary remarks.

Tausk was the author of 28 psychoanalytic papers, the best known being his paper (1919) "On the origin of the 'influencing machine' in schizophrenia." Certain of his poems were published in German newspapers; a verse dialogue with Spinoza was translated and published in French; and the pages of the *Berliner Lokalanzeiger*, for which he worked during his stay in Berlin, must contain a number of his essays. A specimen of his literary criticism has been translated into English (Tausk, 1973; see also Neumarkt, 1973, and Kanzer, 1973). Tausk's biography is the subject of a doctor's thesis prepared at a German university, and his literary work is at present being studied by a German scholar.

All who knew Tausk seemed to agree that he was good-looking, endowed with a brilliant mind, a splendid debater, witty, a dashing character of great passion; they were deeply impressed by the splendor of his personality. He had an almost magnetic effect on women, few of whom could resist his wooing. Almost no one appears to have suspected the extent and intensity of the psychopathology hidden behind the glitter and luster of the surface he showed to the world, to the discussion of which I now turn.

In the center of Tausk's psychopathology stands his relationship to women, which ultimately brought about his downfall. A childhood memory he told Lou Andreas-Salomé will make this clear. It reflects frighteningly the deep disturbance in the child's relationship to his mother.

[I]n an unbridled rage that demanded action, he went to the room where there was a picture of his mother in her youth and pierced it through the heart with a needle — so that for a long time he hardly dared enter the room, as if it were the scene of an actual murder. Later his mother made mention of the "scratched" picture, and he was astonished until he was able to convince himself that it really was only scratched, the penetrating thrust having been made only mentally [Andreas-Salomé, 1958, p. 107f].

Absence of conscious or unconscious death wishes against close relatives in children as well as in adults is a great rarity; that Tausk as a child harbored such a wish against his mother would not have made him exceptional. Of prognostic decisiveness, however, is the form in which this wish made its appearance. A child may throw an object against his mother when enraged or curse, but to thrust a needle into the effigy of the mother with the wish of killing her, as Lou Andreas-Salomé's report indicates, is ominous.

It may seem as if there can be no mental contents that cannot find their way into a manifest dream, and nevertheless there may be the one or the other which transgresses what human beings are able to dream. The impulse and wish to kill the mother are at times detectable in the course of the analysis of a dream, but in the dream they are hidden behind symbolic representations or dream distortions of other kinds. I have reason to doubt whether a male has ever dreamed a dream with the manifest content of killing his mother. Possibly this is a limitation imposed on the capacity of a male sleeper's psychic apparatus to tolerate unconscious imagery.

The meaning of this digression is evident. It aims at bringing into full relief the intensity and degree of the psychopathology that is expressed when a child's fit of rage carries him so far as to stage the murder of his mother in effigy. This childhood recollection not only bespeaks an unusually high degree of psychopathology in the child's relationship to his mother but must also be taken as an ominous prognostic sign with regard to his later dealings with women. Destructive outbreaks of such intensity in a child not basically damaged in his mental development presuppose an inordinate attachment to the mother.

As a matter of fact, in Tausk's life there was a biographical coincidence which must be regarded as extremely rare. The mother's and her first-born son's birthday coincided: both were born on March 12. The particular date of a birthday often has significance for a child, for example, when the child's birthday is Christmas or New Year's Day.[3] But I do not know of a report referring to the effect of identical birthdays of mother and child, a coincidence whose relevance ought not to be limited to the child's feelings but extended as well to the mother's.

There is no documentation which would affirm this relevance to Tausk's life, but primary empathy may assure the mutually intensifying attachment between both the mother who was privileged to give birth to her first son on her birthday and the son who had the privilege of being the first-born on his own mother's birthday. One may infer that this biographical oddity intensified identifications and impeded the formation of ego boundaries, besides nurturing in the child the expectation of a privileged position in the future. Indeed, there is an outward sign indicating that Tausk as an adult felt himself to hold a privileged, not to say unique, position. He signed

[3]Cf. the Wolf Man's history (Freud, 1918).

his letters simply "Tausk" without adding a given name, although other members of the nuclear family, even his father, were still living. This is unusual. Goethe and Freud, for example, had that habit. I conjecture that this practice is always an external sign of an inner conviction relating to uniqueness and irreplaceability. But as important as these factors evidently are, of equal importance is the fact that the infant was not yet one year old when his mother became pregnant. The birth of his baby sister — when the infant was at the tender age of 20 months — must have been particularly traumatic.

Indeed, the mother's pregnancies were so frequent as to give the boy no respite. Almost seven of the 18 years he had lived when the last child was born were filled with his mother's pregnancies, and there may have been even more. It is highly probable that the mother was also pregnant when the child was overwhelmed with the murderous rage that Lou Andreas-Salomé reported. At any rate, the mother's early and many subsequent pregnancies must have had a shattering effect on the growing child, who was assured every year on his birthday that a mysterious affinity and bond existed between him and the mother.

Tausk's relationship to his father was no less bizarre and disturbed. A poem written by the adult (probably around 1909) forcefully reflects this:

That I am a son, I regret,
    It always embarrasses me

When somebody, who knows my countenance,
    Still calls me with fathername.[4]

[4]Dass ich ein Sohn bin, tut mir leid./Es macht mir stets Verlegenheit/Wenn einer, der mein Antlitz kennt,/Mich noch mit Vaternamen nennt.

This poem, written during the father's lifetime, is a son's hate song against the necessity of acknowledging paternity. It is not an expression of adolescent rebellion against father, the impetuous desire to free oneself from the past, a show of strength directed toward the future. Rather, it expresses nausea and detestation at the idea of owing existence to a predecessor whose genes left an indelible pattern in the offspring's face. The nonce word *Vaternamen*, fathername, is not easy to interpret. Prof. Dr. Tausk is certain that it was not caused by a slip but was a purposeful formation. It makes of two elements that are separate, father and name, a configuration that cannot be disjoined. It becomes a fateful entity, like a ghost. It implies that no effort can ever eliminate that ghost, that the stigma of "fathername" is indelible even after a countenance has taken on its individual features.

A poet must be able to integrate opposites, and an analysis of a poem does not necessarily lead to psychological elements that are intensely active in the poet. But this poem by Tausk can and perhaps must be understood as a confession of a conflict that Tausk carried within himself. It was by no means the upshot of a momentary or transitory constellation but rather of a constant one, for Tausk's relationship to his father was miserable throughout his life, and authority in any form gave frequent occasion for conflict and attack. An unresolved hatred of such proportion against his father in an adult, who should have by then come closer to an attitude of forgiveness and tolerance, is again an ominous sign.

Having identified the general foundation of Tausk's psychopathology, I turn to its special features. I shall infer from Tausk's discussion remarks as recorded in the *Minutes of the Vienna Psychoanalytic Society* (Nunberg and Federn, 1962–1975) two symptoms from which he in all probability suffered. However, I shall first present a historical example in which an inference of the sort I propose seems cogent. Leonardo da Vinci wrote that through the contraction of the anus the penis becomes erect and urine or sperm is ejected (O'Malley and Saunders, 1952, p. 452). Since it is probable that this view was not traditional but idiosyncratic, one is permitted to infer that Leonardo reported a self-observation. Thus under special circumstances it is possible to learn from a purportedly general empirical statement a subjective feature significant of the reporting quasi-observer.

The following two inferences fall into the category outlined. In the discussion following Theodor Reik's paper "On Death and Sexuality," at the meeting of the Vienna Association on November 15, 1911, Tausk is recorded to have said:

> It may never be entirely possible for one to be completely spent by the act of love, one part of the libido (affect) is not wholly consumed, and it is this dissociated part that produces anxiety. At this point disunity arises: the affect turns the subject against himself — if it has not used up its energy in one direction. Orgasm turns itself against itself [Nunberg and Federn, vol. 3, p. 314].

The same evening Tausk took up the discussion once more and added that the sexual pleasure of the individual "can never be fully satisfied." Tausk explained this by virtue of the conflict between species and individual. The primary function of serving the species comes into conflict with the secondary one of obtaining individual pleasure.

At the meeting of February 7, 1912, he stated: "Sexual-

ity is never capable of giving complete satisfaction"
(Nunberg and Federn, vol. 4, p. 41), because it does not
have to do with one individual alone. In the *Minutes* of
October 30, 1912, one reads: "In the discussant's
[Tausk's] experience, the existence of the castration complex is betrayed by (1) an anesthesia of the penis during
coition and (2) exhibitionism" (*ibid.*, p. 111). The idea
must have been of great importance to him, for he postulated priority for it, as the *Minutes* (Nunberg and
Federn, vol. 3, p. 353f.) report: "Tausk would like to
claim priority for the thought that the sexual instinct is
not capable of providing full gratification, insofar as Professor Freud does not claim priority." There is a crescen-
do in the sequence of statements ending in a claim of
anesthesia of the male organ during intercourse, a statement which apparently included the end pleasure too.
Tausk's initial explanation was a wrong inference drawn
from the biological truth that sexuality serves a dual
function: the preservation of the species as well as the individual's pleasure gain. Why this should be an obstacle
to full gratification remains obscure.

Tausk first made a statement of this kind two and one-
half years after he started to attend sessions of the
Association in his third semester of medical studies. It is
not known when he took his first case in psychoanalytic
treatment, but whenever this may have been, his practical experience with patients cannot have been extensive
enough to warrant a law of limitations on sexual pleasure, a claim amounting to the assertion that anesthesia is
virtually universal. Moreover, the impressive sentence,
"Orgasm turns itself against itself," would have its proper
place in an existential essay, but it is not a valid empirical
statement. Freud, as far as I know, never intimated that
the potential of the sexual drive is limited with regard to

reaching subjectively adequate gratification. Just to the contrary, in fact, for if this were the case, it would imperil Freud's basic views on the drives. Consequently, Tausk's offering Freud the privilege of priority on this question is all the more puzzling.

I reconstruct here that Tausk derived from his own subjective experience a general theory. It would have served as a rationalization of a defect in orgastic potency. If Freud had been the originator of the theory, the theory would have become tellingly divorced from Tausk's subjective experience and have lost the mark of a rationalization.[5]

Another symptom which can be derived from other of Tausk's discussion remarks relates to depersonalization and knowledge of self. In the discussion of Wilhelm Stekel's paper "On the feelings of strangeness in dream and life," Tausk made the following remark (Nunberg and Federn, vol. 2, p. 539f.): "On the basis of his own experience, Tausk suspects that the sense of estrangement is combined with a feeling of guilt. Perhaps the feeling of strangeness means nothing but this: 'If I recognize myself, then I must kill myself.'"

[5]Complaints about anesthesia of the penis are rather seldom heard, and the analysis of sensations in the penis usually meets with strong objections by the patient. It is my impression that far more males than are actually aware of it experience a retrenched orgasm. The defective sensation is not brought to attention because men in general equate orgasm with ejaculation. Indeed, ejaculation per se may be followed by tranquility and absence of excitation, which may easily obscure the fact of reduced penile pleasure. Anesthesia of the penis must be of a considerable degree before it becomes an explicit complaint, and then it is accompanied by the urge to cohabit with many women. In one instance of marked anesthesia of the penis, a patient reported the ability to maintain an erection indefinitely after ejaculation. (My clinical statements in this context, it should be noted, are based on observations of only a limited number of instances.)

Feelings of strangeness are difficult to analyze, and Tausk at that time had been a member of the Association for about six months. Again one must ask, from where did Tausk derive this knowledge? Why should self-recognition ever lead to self-annihilation? Clinical experience does not confirm this, and again I feel compelled to interpret Tausk's discussion remarks as a reflection of what was true of himself.

In this instance I am able to go beyond the *Minutes* and can refer to one of Tausk's poetical creations. Its title is "Of Living and Knowing" (Vom Leben und vom Wissen). It was written in December 1907, but in January 1915 Tausk added: "Every word in this dialogue has retained its validity for me to the present" (Jedes Wort in dieser Schrift gilt mir auch heute noch). It is "a spoken scene between the *exalted Spinoza* and a man known to me" (Eine gesprochene Szene zwischen dem *Erhabenen Spinoza* und einem mir bekannten Menschen). The man, of course, was Tausk himself. The dialogue between Spinoza and Tausk is written in verses. The language is at times obscure and susceptible of various interpretations. Spinoza offers an instrument he has formed with which one can see into far-off countries and learn what is going on among human beings, "to ferret out the traces that point the ways between man and woman" (den Spuren nachzuspüren, Die Zwischen Man und Weib die Wege weisen).[6]

---

[6]It is noteworthy that Spinoza as presented by Tausk is somewhat reminiscent of Freud, whom Tausk met after the dialogue was written. One may conjecture from this piece that Tausk met in Freud a personality that came close to an ideal image he had formed previously. Oddly enough, the invention he ascribes to Spinoza is suggestive of the psychoanalytic method.

Spinoza then offers another instrument that is far more potent and would carry vision to the stars and show "the purity of law" (die Reinheit des Gesetzes). The man refuses. He carries a load which Spinoza should remove: "liberate my wings" (befreie meine Flügel); then, if Spinoza does this, perhaps he would follow him. He fears dying. The burden he would have to carry when he looks through Spinoza's magnifying glass would become greater. If he looked through Spinoza's giant telescope, "how should I be permitted to think that I am [existing] in the sight of what I am viewing. When I am not [existing] how should I make an effort to exist" (Wie soll ich denken dürfen, dass ich *bin*. Im Angsichte dessen, was ich *sehe*. Und bin ich nicht, Wie soll ich mich bemühen zu sein). And later the decisive verses follow: "Exalted one, I feel that I am living, Yet I live only in the mirror of alien life and measure my death by the death of others" (Erhabener, ich fühle, dass ich lebe. Doch leb ich nur im Spiegel fremden Lebens und messe meinen Tod am Tod der anderen). Here a profound depersonalization is described as a general quality of life's experience. Indeed, a function of this global depersonalization is intimated by the reference to death. It seems to say: "My death is depersonalized, I can understand it only in terms of that of others." Apparently depersonalization serves the denial of one's own mortality. Here Tausk is close to what he had said years later in the discussion of Stekel's paper: "If I recognize myself, I must kill myself." The dialogue suggests that this was not a chance remark but an apparently fairly constant structural element in Tausk's personality.

Prof. Dr. Marius Tausk finds in another part of the scene the essence of his father's conflict.

Man: You bow me heavier than reality

For if you speak truth, I am the lie.
The exalted one: Who are you that you may
feel contempt for yourself?
Man: I know about myself, therefore I must feel
contempt for myself,
When I am conscious of myself under me.[7]

Prof. Dr. Tausk may be right. These verses would demonstrate another aspect of inherent dangers which might have become activated in Tausk when exposed to the process of acquiring knowledge of self.

How did Tausk deal with such formidable psychopathology? Even though subtle mechanisms cannot be inferred from the data at hand, some general conclusions can be drawn. As I have indicated above, the father was authoritarian and tyrannical, often absent from home, and unfaithful to his wife; he was also hypermoralistic in his demands on the children (Roazen, 1969, p. 9f.). Starting as a schoolteacher, he worked his way up and became an internationally known journalist. Tausk wanted to study medicine, but the family could not afford it, and he had to become a lawyer. He disliked this profession and later switched to journalism. Evidently, he identified with the father.

Further, he did to others what he had to suffer from his father as a child. He deserted his family by moving to Berlin, the equivalent of the father's frequent absences, and was a poor provider, as his father was; in Tausk's

7Der Mensch: Du beugst mich schwerer als die Wirklichkeit./ Denn sprichst Du die Wahrheit, dann bin ich die Lüge./Der Erhabene: Wer bist Du, dass Du Dich verachten därfst?/Der Mensch: Ich weiss um mich, drum muss ich mich verachten/Wenn meiner ich bewusst bin unter mir.

case, however, being a poor provider was the result of financial exigency. As will be seen below, he also was quite demanding of his children. His original desire to study medicine may be hypothetically interpreted as an attempt at avoiding rivalry with the father. When he was forced to study law, he, too, discontinued his original profession, as his father had˙done, and took up the latter's profession. Unfortunately, it is not known why he did not continue to pursue his career as a journalist. He certainly had the talents that made such a career a promising one. After his death, the *Neue Wiener Journal* (July 4, 1919, p. 7), a Viennese daily on whose staff he had served, published an obituary full of praise. I infer — again hypothetically — that he was unable to continue in a position in which rivalry with the father was inescapable — or did he fear lest he would not exceed his father in accomplishments and regard?

Episodically, he got involved in battles with authority, whose injustice and arbitrariness he passionately unmasked. As mentioned, he succeeded in obtaining the acquittal of an unmarried mother who had killed her newborn child (Roazen, 1969) — an accomplishment which at that time was a veritable *tour de force*. From the aforementioned obituary one learns that he had terminated a beginning career in the judicial system when he refused to sign a death judgment after a trial in which he had been active. From his military service during World War I several instances are known in which he rescued civilians from unjust arrest. The Austrian Army was extremely brutal in occupied territories, and its proceedings were marked by utter injustice. It is highly probable that Tausk rescued a number of people from the firing squad and in so doing did not shun risking his own life.

Prof. Dr. Tausk rightly called my attention to the dangers his father exposed himself to when he protested against the way deserters were treated during World War I (V. Tausk, 1916b). In these instances the old father conflict led to highly constructive actions. Government authorities and courts are genetically derivatives of the authority the father holds in the child's life. Tausk had been a rebellious youngster, and his rebelliousness continued to be manifested in his adult years. It is remarkable that an attitude of this kind did not become sublimated into a systematized outlook. He was not interested in politics and was neutral in that area, Prof. Dr. Tausk told me. This is surprising since the prevailing atmosphere among intellectuals in Central Europe of those years was one of defiance against government control, and Tausk would have found a wide area of activity. The instances recorded suggest that what was necessary for Tausk to initiate an attack against the overbearance and injustice of authority was direct sense perception. Those highly constructive episodes of social action that are reported seem to have been momentary flashes that were never organized into a consistent program. Furthermore, it was the contact with a murderer, with deserters — that is, with individuals often regarded as conspicuously mutilated victims of blind, cold-hearted society — that aroused his empathy.

His father-in-law, a printer, was a Social-Democrat of strong conviction who actively fought in the ranks of the party. Prominent members of that party who held liberal, progressive views went freely in and out of his home. He himself was one of the owners of the printing firm that brought out the Social-Democratic daily *Arbeiterzeitung* (Magaziner, 1975). He must have been a courageous man for it was no easy matter in those days to be prominent in the labor movement. One might have expected that the young anti-authoritarian student of law would find a wide area to share, even to admire in that man. But the opposite occurred, and there were severe altercations that separated the two. Perhaps it was just the well-organized, determined way with which his father-in-law dealt with society's injustices that provoked Tausk. From these observations one may infer a deficit in Tausk's sublimation of aggression. It remained fixated to a concrete fight with father figures.

By joining Freud's group Tausk not only gained professional stability at last: he was able to enter a field in which he no longer had to rival his father. Furthermore, in Freud he apparently found for the first time an acceptable authority. But even when dealing with an acceptable and idealized authority, a father conflict of a proportion like Tausk's cannot be expected to come to rest, and as soon as he had established himself professionally in his own right, it was bound to flare up.

The form in which the conflict found expression was surprising. As several witnesses reported, Tausk had repeatedly claimed that some of his ideas had been used by Freud without acknowledgment of their true source. To be sure, Tausk was known to have repeated in his lectures what Freud had lectured the day before. Thus identification was at work again but compensated by what seemed a rebellion in the form of the accusation of plagiarism committed at the expense of the son by the father-substitute. The functions of that illusion are easy to divine: it created a particular closeness to a father-figure; it made him superior to his colleagues (siblings); it provided superiority over a father-representative, even though only in a limited area, but thus discharged pent-up aggression against a paternal figure. Be that as it may, the illusion made it possible for Tausk to function for several years as a respected, productive, and successful psychoanalyst. Thus he was able to partake in Freud's greatness and at the same time lay claim to part of it.

I shall now outline Tausk's relationship to women. The first object-choice I know of was that of his eventual wife, Martha Tausk (1881–1957). It was a splendid one, the best he possibly would ever make. An outline of this extraordinary woman's career appeared in a memorial article (Magaziner, 1975). From 1911 on she was a member of the Social-Democratic party. She was apparently a most effective organizer and orator. She became a member of the Upper Chamber of the Austrian Parliament, a great honor. From 1928 on, she was in Zurich as a member of the executive committee of the Socialist Workers' International, a position which by itself is sufficient to prove her to have been a person of superior abilities. A booklet (Martha Tausk, 1930) conveys the charm, the depth, the solidity and honesty of her personality. It contains some of her short stories, two of which include autobiographical material.

One story, "Fernambuk," the story of a bow and a fiddle, dedicated "to women of great men," is written with such excellence and is so moving that one can hardly doubt that this woman would have become one of Austria's best female story writers if she had had the leisure to devote her life to writing. But her life was for years one of penury and hard work to achieve survival and an adequate upbringing for her two sons.

Despite her grave accusations against society and her fate, there is nowhere self-pity or bitterness about the life destiny had meted out for her. On one occasion, she calls the years after Tausk had left her, without reference to the event: "... my gravest years, when I was suffering from privations and disappointments..." (...meine schwersten Jahre, als ich in Entbehrungen und an Enttäuschungen litt...) (Martha Tausk, 1930, p. 63). Not one word more. No line of sentimentality can be discovered, only deepest gratitude for the friendship and kindness she occasionally received from others: she was a woman who experienced existence as tragic without caving in or despairing. I could add much to illustrate the greatness of her personality, but shall end this profile with the report of a trait that is hardly ever met. Her son told me that she never said one bad word to the children about their father; precisely to the contrary, she supported the sons' idealization of him. With that attitude she made possible their healthy development: the father's physical absence was compensated by the mental representation of an ideal one. I have never observed such a healthy and magnanimous attitude in divorced mothers who had been treated with iniquity by their husbands.

As a rule children have to pay for their father's sins by experiencing the impact of the mother's accusations against their absent progenitor. They evolve self-destructive ambivalence against the father, whereas in this unique instance, as Marius Tausk's paper (1973) shows, unswerving affection, love, and loyalty tied the son to the memory of his father, who had gravely disappointed him as a little boy.[8]

Tausk's wife, as we have seen, was a woman who was autonomous, self-sufficient, and undefeatable. It has been suggested that Tausk could not tolerate a relation with a woman after she became dependent on him (Roazen,

[8]This interpretation has been negated by Prof. Dr. Tausk. However, in Chapter III, under the heading "Tausk's written messages to Freud...," I shall refer to Tausk's own remarks about his son which seem to confirm my interpretation.

1969). But his separation from Martha Tausk would show that the problem of dependency was not relevant (see Neumarkt, 1977), for although she had preserved her own convictions and independence, the marital situation had become intolerable for Tausk. I conjecture that Tausk was aware of her superiority and possibly for that reason maintained a correspondence with her for the rest of his life. The specimens which Roazen (1969) published and which Prof. Dr. Tausk let me read suggest strongly that he used her as a receptacle for his pains and complaints. Roazen maintained that Tausk wrote pitiful letters from Berlin at a time when he was carrying on a happy love affair. It seems to me that he was quite dependent on Martha Tausk and tried to maintain a bond by frequent arousals of her pity. His decision to separate from her was probably the most consequential of his life (prior to the final one).

His subsequent dealings with women necessitate the assumption that he was driven by most unruly passions. Roazen gives the names of at least ten women with whom Tausk had affairs. There were three or four broken engagements, if not more. After the publication of his book, Roazen received letters from other sweethearts who congratulated him for having written about their former lover and conveyed memories. Thus the exact number of women is not known, but it must have been considerable, for it was not probable that each of them found documentation. When I met Felix Braun (1885–1973), a sensitive Austrian writer, and he heard of my profession, his first question was whether I was familiar with Tausk's love affairs: "they were the talk of the town." Since he himself hardly knew Tausk personally, his knowledge was second hand. But this, in turn, would indicate, in my estimation, that Tausk conducted his love affairs in an exhibitionistic, flamboyant way. One may be inclined to conjecture that he wanted the town to know of his many liaisons.

A fellow-student of his, Olga Knopf, reported that when he gave a private course in hypnosis, he abused female participants in hypnotic experiments by seeking to find out who among them would be inclined to go to bed with him. As another incident that illustrates Tausk's lack of discipline and discretion, Roazen's report (1969, p. 118) may serve. At a public clinic, he stimulated a woman's genitalia with electric current in order to find out whether she was sexually excitable after her ovaries had been surgically removed.[9]

If my reconstruction of Tausk's relative anesthesia of the penis is correct, it would fit into the impulsive meandering from one woman to another. The urge to find a satisfactory release at last may have created the illusion that the intensity of sexual pleasure depended on the qualities of the lover, the symptom thus forcing him to be constantly searching for a new object that would redeem him. Important as this psychobiological factor might have been, the situation was far too complex to be reducible to this one issue.

A number of women were depressed for a long time after their relations with Tausk had been terminated (Roazen, 1969). It even seems that some were emotionally injured for the rest of their lives. Roazen quotes a letter to him by a woman who had an affair with Tausk during "his psychoanalytic period in Vienna," that is, during his more mature years:

> Now I am surrounded by the ghosts of yesteryear. After all those years, I now start understanding so

[9]Prof. Dr. Tausk believes that this could have been a creditable experiment in the field of endocrinology.

much, which was not clear to me then. I understand why his nickname for me was 'dear it,' as compared to him I was indeed only it, who did not know why he could be so kind and lovable, and then again aloof and a thousand miles away. I also understand why one day, out of the blue sky, he left me standing on the street (I'll never forget the place), telling me that he could not see me anymore, he was just following the direction of his tormented mind. He said, "for reasons I would not understand..." [Roazen, 1972, p. 584f.].

This manner of taking farewell from a lover is remarkable since the *modus operandi* was brutal and traumatic to the victim. In dim outline this can be seen already when he separated from his wife.[10]

Tausk was forced to desert wife and children in his early manhood, one may conjecture, by his inner destiny. He may have thought that he had to fulfill a mission in life that would have been threatened by absorption in the daily battle for the support of a family. But the incident Roazen reports concerned a decision of lesser conse-

---

[10]Quite aside from the anguish she had to suffer, he left her and his children almost destitute. She wrote (Martha Tausk, 1930, p. 12f.): "I lived...in a very primitive apartment..., worked half days (five and a half hours)...and developed great abilities in economizing. Otherwise, I would not have been able to raise my children....I always walked to work, the daily bus would have cost back and forth four guilders [per month]" (Ich wohnte...in einer sehr primitiven Wohnung, arbeitete halbe Tage (fünfenthalb Stunden)...und entwickelte grosse Fähigkeiten im Sparen. Anders hätte ich wohl meine Kinder nicht grossgezogen.... [D]enn zu Fuss ging ich immer, der Omnibus hätte täglich hin und zurück 4 Gulden ausgemacht).

quence. To be sure, amorous relations are volatile; should a girlfriend become obnoxious many a man must face the necessity to separate. In Vienna, there were a huge number of coffee-houses in which love relations were started and ended, and minimal courtesy would have been to take the girl to the nearest one and let her gradually know that this would be the last tryst. To tell a woman on the street out of the blue sky that she will have no opportunity in the future to meet the man to whom she evidently was tied by strong affection and simply to walk away, is more than discourteous. It is a procedure which necessarily is traumatic to the deserted woman, as is evident from the repeated (and haunting) recollections of the place where she had been mentally brutalized. The persistence of such recollections is indicative of a permanent injury, small as it may have been, that had been inflicted on the deserted girl. Moreover, no word of regret, excuse, or gratitude for past ecstasies was offered, and the humiliating comment that the understanding of the event transcended her mental capacity was added. Did the departing lover understand why he was compelled to desert one woman after another? Further, it should not go unnoticed that he had called the lover "it." I take it this is a translation of the German word *es*, which at that time had not yet acquired the alluring meaning it gained after it had been incorporated into psychoanalytic terminology but meant something impersonal, thing-like.[11]

Tausk must have been the ideal lover. His hypothesized penile anesthesia may have provided him with inexhausti-

[11]Prof. Dr. Tausk suggests a possibly affectionate implication of the allocution. Yet the reduction — as reported by the informant — in feeling of self-value as compared to the lover would prove the correctness of the above interpretation.

ble potency; his wit, his dazzling personality, his passionateness, his poetic imagery — all these qualities must have given women unforgettable hours of extreme pleasure. He must have noticed that women became profoundly and passionately attached to him. The same sequence must have occurred repeatedly: the woman gradually becoming helplessly dependent on him, followed by abrupt and unexpected separation. From the episode reported the inference may be drawn that he carried out an inner urge, for there was no external necessity visible that would have forced the lover to proceed in such a way when separation had become inevitable. The pattern definitely carries the earmark of a sadistic attitude toward women. This is partly confirmed by Prof. Heinz Winnik. Lea Rosen, a former sweetheart of Tausk's, told Prof. Winnik that Tausk spoke to her without inhibition of intimacies with his lovers and in one instance boasted to her of the pleasure he had derived from humiliating one of them.

Thus his exhibitionistic, narcissistic personality with all its great assets attracted women, and, as can be reconstructed on good grounds, he showed his very best face when he strove toward taking possession of a woman. He was not only a great lover but also a great seducer without giving a signal of the destructive potential that later would reveal itself.

Do I go too far when I conjecture that in his narcissism he did not want ever to be forgotten by a woman he had loved? He had succeeded in that in the instance of the lover who could not forget the details of the place at which she had seen Tausk for the last time. Another example would be that of Kosa Lazarević, a Serbian aristocrat whom Tausk rescued from arrest by Austrian soldiers. She became his mistress and they became engaged, but Tausk broke off the relationship. Rescue, love, desertion followed here — in a typical fashion, I am inclined to conjecture — but Kosa Lazarević remained faithful and after Tausk's death she came, according to Roazen (1969), every year to take care of her former fiancé's grave.

Human memory has a strange aspect. If somebody asked me what to do in order never to be forgotten by a certain person, I would not advise showering that individual with kindness and gratifications. Rather, my advice would be, "Humiliate the person publicly. He will think of you for the rest of his days." Profoundly injured narcissism leaves a smarting wound that not even revenge can heal. And that is what Tausk apparently did. He took his farewell from women in a way that caused trauma. Revenge was practically not possible for those he deserted, perhaps not even desired. The woman left deserted on the street was told at the end how worthless she was. She believed it, and the image of her fickle lover persevered, overtowering, incomparably superior to the little nothing she had been made to believe herself to be. Of course such sequences were particularly consequential to masochistic personalities. It is feasible that Tausk unconsciously selected predominantly masochistic women.

But another feature of Tausk's relationship with women must be kept in mind: his own narcissistic vulnerability when a relationship did not proceed in accordance with the pattern that was of such importance for him. Two such instances are documented in Roazen's book (1969). During his stay in Berlin after his marriage broke up, he went through the aforementioned crisis. Kanzer (1971, p. 563), following Roazen, stated that Tausk was hospitalized "for treatment of his recurrent pulmonary condition and for a mental disorder. . . .

When the doctor made a diagnosis of hereditary psychopathy, Tausk readily concurred. . . ." I mention this because subsequently the event that had led to the manifestation of "hereditary psychopathy" became apparent. "Tausk's stay in a sanatorium had been precipitated by a frustrated love affair" (Roazen, 1972, p. 585). Thus when events defied the sequences of the usual pattern and ended in narcissistic frustration by the love object's independence and maintenance of autonomy, they amounted to an unbearable injury that led to crisis and collapse.

Another example of this pattern is documented. Edoardo Weiss (1970, p. 11) recalled that he met Tausk during the First World War in Poland. "I was shocked by his state of deep depression." Tausk expressed pessimism about a good many things. "He also spoke of unhappy personal experiences. The woman he loved, to whom he had been engaged, had betrayed him with another man." Roazen (1969) amplified this report: Tausk's fiancée had been unfaithful with one of the patients he treated at Lublin, where he was stationed during World War I. He "expressed very pessimistic ideas about life and. . .felt he could no longer trust anyone." Here again the same pattern is encountered. This time it was a depressive, paranoid reaction to a love object's asserting herself in a way contrary to his expectations and wishes. It is noteworthy that after the "defeat" in Lublin, a kind of flight into a sanatorium recurred. After having served eight months in Lublin, he spent four months in "Sanatorium Grimmenstein" in Lower Austria (see below). It is likewise noteworthy that the disillusionment he had suffered was again followed by a tubercular involvement, and further, that such severe reactions are not reported as being prompted by conflicts with men but, so far as the available documentation goes, are referable to frustrations imposed by women in situations in which he had lost control of them as love objects. Apparently he refused to submit to that to which he submitted others regularly.

The necessity of submitting a woman to a brutal farewell after having aroused her maximal love suggests that as a child he had been traumatized in a similar way. Psychoanalytic experience suggests that with each birth of a younger sibling he felt brutally abandoned by his mother, whom he must have loved intensely prior to her unfaithfulness.

I have discussed Tausk's relationship to women in such detail because, as will be seen later, it became his undoing.

In general, it is not possible to find a common denominator of the whole spectrum of a personality's psychopathology. Nevertheless, a few general features, as observed in Tausk, may be cited. There is foremost the enormous distance between the demands of his superego and the ideals toward which he strove and the demands of drives and passions. An ability to reach bearable compromises between the two extremes was evidently stunted. Thus he must have been in a state of permanent restlessness and deep discontent. Consequently, words must be taken with a grain of salt in his instance. There is no doubt that he felt affection for his children and wished them the best. Prof. Dr. Tausk showed me letters which express these sentiments strongly and impressively. Roazen also stressed this. One even gets the impression that Tausk was constantly haunted by feelings of concern for his children's welfare. His words express the intensity of the demand his conscience put on him.

But what were his actions? He deserted them when

they were at a tender age and left them with their
mother, who had to struggle hard to provide them with
necessities. Other signs of his ambivalence toward one of
his sons will be further documented below.

This inner contrariness, which was stronger than the
usually encountered ambivalence, shows up in other life
situations. He loved women excessively and hurt them
excessively. He admired Freud and defended him with
greater vigor than others when Freud was attacked and
criticized (Roazen, 1969) but also detracted from him by
claiming to have been plagiarized by him.

The discrepancy between words and actions, reflecting
the distance between superego, conscience, and ideal, on
the one side, and the passionate wishes, on the other,
conveys the impression that here was a personality that
was not ready, was perhaps unable, to make a real
sacrifice but at the same time insisted on the narcissistic
gratification derived from the conviction of being a person of high morality.

Tausk's life history as presented is replete with instances of acting out. One may say that one of the main
symptoms which reduced his analyzability was acting
out. Instead of internalizing a conflict and sublimating it,
he resorted to action. Consequently, his aggression was
unusually strong. In his relationships to women this became conspicuous but was likewise present in relationships with men. Many discussion remarks reported in the
Minutes were abrasive. Lou Andreas-Salomé's *Journal*
also gives instances of his rudeness. Yet these instances
do not seem to have had serious consequences; they
probably were forgiven quickly in view of his many
assets.

However, there might have been an uncanny connection between his professional activity and his psycho-

pathology which I shall tentatively present. I have reported above Tausk's distrust of self-recognition and his even equating it with self-destruction under certain circumstances. Now, an analyst's basic goal and activity are to help others on their road toward self-recognition. He is constantly engaged in providing others with insight into self. Yet in view of what insight into self, that is, self-recognition, meant to Tausk, his professional activity might have had an aggressive, destructive meaning to him. Here again we would run into a similar dynamic situation as before, and he would have done to others what he did not want to have done to him. This mechanism was deeply rooted in him. Lou Andreas-Salomé reported in her *Journal* (1958, p. 107) that Tausk as a child "helped himself when his mother punished him severely, silently answering her scolding epithets 'That's just what you are, you are!' and, how, finally, it came to be an automatic reactive discharge that pacified him. . . ." This defiant defense once got him into trouble when he forgot himself and uttered the words openly.

Inasmuch as Tausk felt threatened by self-recognition, his making it possible for others, I conjecture, was for him an act endowed with a highly aggressive meaning, possibly also "a discharge that pacified him."

After having drawn a rather somber picture of Tausk's psychopathology, I want to remind the reader of Tausk's assets: his superior intellectual gifts, the brilliance and charm of his appearance, the pleasure and bliss he was able to give others, the courage and energy with which he was prone to rescue others on the spur of the moment.

III. The Possible Reasons for Tausk's Suicide

In searching for the reasons that have induced or compelled a person to commit suicide, one has to distinguish, principally, between two groups of suicides. There are those of whom one can be reasonably certain that they would not have committed suicide if certain circumscribed events had not taken place in their recent past, and those by whom the deed would probably or even certainly have been accomplished unless they had been protected by hospitalization or exceptionally favorable environmental conditions.

The most convincing instance of the first group I know of was the following.

A middle-aged Viennese physician, baptized a Catholic though born of Jewish parents, a bon vivant, successful, and enjoying life in full measure, was ordered shortly after the German occupation of Austria in 1938 to one of the barracks which the National-Socialists had taken over. He had never engaged in politics, having always been apolitical in his attitudes. His denunciation was an act of revenge by an employee whom he had dismissed. At the barracks he was subjected to a most humiliating treatment. In the evening he was dismissed and told to appear the next day. He went home and committed suicide with his wife. From what I heard, the way he was maltreated, though not outrightly tortured, makes the decision understandable.

It is reasonable to conclude that this man would never have committed suicide if he had not been made a victim of grave abuse. (However, I must note that this man's mother had committed suicide after she fell into the hands of a blackmailer who threatened to expose a sexual indiscretion.)

Likewise, it is not probable that most of those Jews who committed suicide following the occupation of Vienna would have done so, had their future not become utterly hopeless. To this group belong also those who know that they suffer from an incurable fatal disease or any other disease that would reduce them to permanent helplessness. To be sure, as in the instance of the Viennese physician, one may find in the histories of those who commit suicide under the impact of intolerable, or at least excessive stresses, signs or events which are suggestive of a predisposition. However, it is reasonable to assume that this predisposition would not have led to concretization without the burden of a trauma or a series of traumata that gravely undermined morale.

The other group contains those whose histories make it

understandable that their lives ended in acts of self-destruction. To be sure, this is often ascertained retrospectively. Such individuals may have successfully camouflaged the tendencies which finally conjoined toward their self-defeat.

A group which one may assign to either of these two types is that composed of those who suffer from a major psychosis, such as melancholia. Melancholic patients are susceptible to suicidal impulses, particularly through the inception of recovery, but their suicide can be prevented by continued and vigilant attention during the acute phase.

As in so many other instances, here too Freud's complementary series are found, a group in which internal factors outweigh the external ones and vice versa. But one must search for the precipitating factor that makes it understandable that the suicide occurred at that particular point in time in both groups.

Thus I shall first inquire into environmental factors, of which two have been suggested as possibly having precipitated or caused Tausk's suicide.

(A) Tausk's Financial Situation at the Time of His Suicide

The financial conditions under which Tausk lived at the time of his death have been suggested to have had a bearing on the suicide. As a matter of fact, in 1919 Tausk was called upon to build up his career for the fourth time: previously he had done so, first as a lawyer in Bosnia, second as a journalist in Berlin and Vienna, and third as an analyst before 1915 when he joined the Army. Freud wrote (1919, p. 274) about Tausk:

He was faced...in his state of mental exhaustion

[brought about by "the stresses of many years' service in the field"] with the hard task of building up a new existence— this time under the most unfavourable internal and external conditions.

Also in a letter of August 1, 1919 in which he informed Lou Andreas-Salomé of Tausk's death, Freud referred to "the necessity of building up under the most unfavourable circumstances the practice in Vienna" (Pfeiffer, 1966, p. 98). This factor, however, was only one among several Freud took into consideration. From a letter by Paul Federn (1872–1950]), a colleague of Tausk's, to his wife on July 3, 1919, one learns that the economic factor came first to his mind when he heard of Tausk's death, but he relegated it to a secondary place. He wrote: "Destitution and the impossibility of borrowing money to satisfy his hunger were only the last straw" (...die Noth und die Unmöglichkeit, sich Geld zum Sattessen auszuleihen, der letzte Anstoss).

Even though it is not possible to ascertain accurately Tausk's financial situation at the beginning of July, it can be reconstructed. In order to appraise the validity of financial difficulties as a leading element in the causation of Tausk's suicide, one must have knowledge both of Tausk's income and expenses around July 1919 and of the general economic situation in Vienna at that time. Some insight into the former can be gained from Tausk's correspondence with Freud and from his last will.

From six letters Tausk wrote to Freud which Prof. Dr. Tausk put at my disposal, one learns the following: two patients are acknowledged in a letter of January 22, 1919. They had been referred by Freud: an engineer who would not stay long in treatment according to Tausk's prognostication, and patient L, "a good case" (ein guter Fall), who according to the patient's mother's description, suffered from a manic-depressive psychosis, and according to Tausk's impression, from a depressive hysteria. Aside from these two patients, he had one from his own circle of acquaintances. He reported having three full-paying patients in all, each paying 30 Kronen, and two who paid 20 Kronen each; he also had a patient in analysis at no charge.

A week later (January 29) he thanked Freud for referring a patient suffering from compulsive neurosis who paid a fee of 40 Kronen, "the highest fee so far attained" (das höchste, das ich bisher erreicht habe). In a letter of March 1, he reports having had three sessions with "young R." This is a patient whom I have interviewed. He told me that he paid a fee of 40 Kronen per session. Thus for a while Tausk earned approximately 3,000 Kronen per month. On March 30, Tausk asked Freud to take his older son into treatment. "When I have 6 full-paying cases, I am in a position to pay the full, normal fee" (Wenn ich selbst 6 Fälle vollbezahlt habe, bin ich in der Lage, das volle, normale Honorar zu bezahlen).

On May 31 Tausk reported that patient L had gone into an acute state of excitement and had to be transferred to a private hospital. "Since bad events like to obey the law of series" (Da die schlimmen Dinge gern dem Gesetz der Serie gehorchen) two other patients told him the same day that for financial reasons they would have to discontinue treatment in a few days or a few weeks.

Tausk apparently felt quite discouraged. He wrote:

> I see my labile existence again threatened, although I have gotten mentally as far as to be able to endure it. When you have again a case to spare, I beg you to think of me. I deeply regret to have to come to

you over and over again as one who needs help. But it is stronger than I.[1]

Since young R, as he told me, went for his session on the very day on which Tausk had committed suicide in the morning, it is assured that he kept at least one of the two patients who paid the highest fee. If the best-paying among his other patients had left treatment, he would have earned about 2,600 Kronen per month and if those who paid the lowest fee had left, his income would have been about 3,300 Kronen. The average between the two extremes would have been about 3,000 Kronen per month.

From Tausk's last will written and signed at 1:30 a.m. on the day of his suicide, one learns that his estate comprised, among other possessions, ten suits, six pairs of shoes, and four overcoats (one for each season); 3,600 Kronen in cash, a bank account of 2,100 Kronen, and a credit from a woman who owed him 2,000 for a typewriter he had sold to her. The fees of three patients, among them young R, were outstanding — that is, the payment of at least 2,000 Kronen was still be be expected. He owed a lady friend 5,000 Kronen and ordered their payment. He also instructed that the cook be paid her monthly salary of 300 Kronen for July.

A list of his creditors was attached to his will; who they were, I do not know. He asked them to renounce repayment of their claims on the estate in favor of his

[1]Ich sehe meine labile Existenz neuerlich bedroht, trotzdem ich psychisch ebensoweit gekommen bin, sie aushalten zu können. Wenn Sie wieder einen überschüssigen Fall haben, bitte ich Sie darum, an mich zu denken. Es tut mir sehr leid, immer wieder als Hilfsbedürftiger zu Ihnen kommen zu müssen. Aber es ist stärker als ich.

children. I presume this list referred to debts that had accumulated during the years of his medical studies when Freud and four of his colleagues had supported him.[2]

Thus on the day of Tausk's death his cash and receivables probably amounted to 9,700 Kronen. It is not to be assumed that his friend would have expected repayment of the debt of 5,000 Kronen in the near future, since he could have taken the loan only a relatively short time before. Thus one may say that in absolute terms his financial situation was not alarming at the time of his death. Whatever errors I may have made in calculating his income, the last will proves that 5,700 Kronen were at his immediate disposal, an amount which would have amply sufficed to provide him with food—if food had been available, as I shall discuss presently. Federn was mistaken when he assumed that Tausk was living in a destitute state.

By culling data from newspapers, one obtains an approximate picture of what prices were at that time in Vienna. The monthly salary of a typist was between 300 and 800 Kronen; room and board for one month in the country for vacationers was between 400 and 750 Kronen; luncheon in a restaurant cost between three and ten Kronen.

For a working class family of four members the monthly expenses for food were 2540.99 Kronen in July 1919 (Klenner, 1951). The earnings of other professional groups in July 1919 are also pertinent. From the *Bundeskanzleramt* (Vienna) I received the following data: The monthly salary of a government employee just beginning his service was 800 Kronen; that of a secondary school teacher, up to 1,400 Kronen; that for the principal of

[2]Apparently this request was fulfilled. See Roazen (1969, p. 198).

such a school, 1,800 Kronen; that for a university professor, 1,800 Kronen; and that for an officeholder at a high ministerial level, 2,500 Kronen. However, these salaries were "hunger salaries," and half a year later they were increased by 150 percent.

Mr. Fritz Keller, to whom I owe the following information, made the important suggestion that at that particular time money was of secondary importance because the city was exhausted of merchandise. Black market purchases were out of the question for members of the middle classes. Hunger was general and the main effort was directed toward obtaining food. More important than money was a connection with a person who had access to food. From a letter to be discussed below, it is known that Tausk had received a substantial food package from abroad shortly before his death.

Also relevant was the inflation of that day. Three years after Tausk's death, the working class family that had spent 2,540.99 Kronen for a month's food needed 296,734 Kronen—that is, food became 1160 times more expensive during that period. Even though Tausk expected prices to fall, as he wrote in a letter to Freud, everyone felt insecure about the economic future.

Further, in order to understand the economic situation in Vienna around July 1919, one has to consider that at that time war rationing was still in full swing, as the Federal Department of Business, Trade and Industry was kind enough to inform me. Bread, flour, meat, milk, fat coffee, potatoes, sugar, gasoline, coal, electricity, cigarettes, and soap were all rationed. One person was entitled to one loaf of bread per week. At the end of June, the newspapers announced that high-quality beef had been imported from Yugoslavia. Its price would not be subsidized by the government; rather it would be sold at cost, that is, at a charge of 35–45 Kronen for one kilo (2.2 lbs.). As another illustration, the price of the very popular daily, the *Illustrierte Kronenzeitung*, was raised on June 30 from 12 to 14 Heller. The only alleviation for consumers was the rent control law of October 26, 1918,[3] which oddly enough is still in force. In brief, the disastrous inflation which led to a devaluation of the Krone in the proportion of 1:14,400 and to the currency reform of February 12, 1924, in which the Schilling (1 Schilling = 10,000 Kronen) was introduced, was in its initial phase.

At the time of Tausk's suicide, the problem was where and how to get food. Shortly thereafter merchandise became available, but the vast majority of the population did not have the means of acquiring it. As mentioned, the prevailing stress was an alarming insecurity. No one knew what the next day would bring. Political conditions had not settled either in Austria or in her neighboring countries, and as I conjecture, the mood was ominous, as if at any time new disasters could befall the tiny, newly established republic.

When Tausk returned to Vienna, he moved into the same apartment which he had left when called to the Army in 1915. Thus he probably did not have to spend much on transition to a civilian existence. The wardrobe he left may sound extravagant and was, I believe, unusual in quantity. It was probably an accumulation of prewar purchases. Apartment, wardrobe, housekeeper, and the cash balance—all together evoke the image of relative economic ease rather than of want of the means of existence, but certainly he did not belong to an economically favored group that could look into the future

[3] I owe thanks for this information to the Austrian Federal Department of Justice.

with relative ease. He must have felt worried about what his financial situation would be in the long run.

Tausk had financial obligations toward his two sons, at that time 17 and 15 years old, respectively. As many letters document, he always tried his utmost to provide for them. A letter of January 7, 1919 to his divorced wife shows that he intended to provide 1,000 Kronen a month for them. Shortly thereafter it may have become questionable whether he would be able to continue his support on that scale. But he knew — from prior experience — that his sons, by virtue of their mother's devotion and efficiency, would never be exposed to serious want. She had recently received a high appointment in the Social-Democratic party, which had just come to power. Thus her financial future and that of his sons were half-way assured. As a matter of fact, as Prof. Dr. Tausk told me, his father's death did not delay or damage their academic progress or preparation for a career, even though they had to struggle hard to get through secondary school and university.

Nevertheless, considering all factors, one may infer that even though worries about his financial future preyed on Tausk's mind, he was objectively in a better position than many other intellectuals. He was not subjected to the constraints on government employees, for example, teachers at secondary schools or professors at the University. The outlook for the future contained bright spots. He had a chance of becoming a *Dozent*, a kind of university instructor; to be named a *Dozent* was a great honor and gave the recipient a considerable opportunity of attracting patients.[4] Being a *Dozent* would

[4]There is no record in the Archives of the University of Vienna that would indicate Tausk's prospective *Dozentur*. The first step in the rather complicated process of acquiring the status of a *Dozent*

have provided Tausk with a position superior to that of other members of the Psychoanalytic Association, none of whom was connected with the University. Since Freud had stopped his University lectures, Tausk was in the last few months of his life the only person in Vienna who gave lectures on psychoanalysis, a fact which must have been a source of considerable narcissistic gratification. If his financial situation and outlook on the economic future should have carried any weight in Tausk's final decision — a supposition for which there is no evidence — then it would have been due to a depressive reaction precipitated by feelings about the economy or other psychopathology. To be sure, the delusion of impending starvation is frequent in mental disturbances of old age, but Tausk was still far from that life period. Furthermore, it is known that in the great depression millionaires, even though they possessed the means with which to live comfortably, even in luxury, nevertheless committed suicide when they lost part of their fortunes.

That dynamic situation is also not applicable to Tausk in 1919. He was in the same boat as the overwhelming majority of the population. No stigma was attached to being in financial straits, and Tausk was by no means exposed to humiliation; nor was there reason to expect it. Moreover, in none of his farewell messages is there any reference to financial plight.

It is well justified to say that there is neither specific evidence nor a general probability that such factors drove Tausk into suicide, even though there is no reason

---

was an application to the University College of Professors. Tausk apparently had never filed such an application. When Freud and Lou Andreas-Salomé referred to Tausk's *Dozentur*, they apparently had only Tausk's ambitions in mind, rather than any concrete steps he might have taken. The only realistic alternative — that Wagner-Jauregg, who was Chief of Psychiatry at the University Clinics, had given Tausk the go-ahead to make an application — is a remote possibility.

to doubt that he felt distressed about the economic situation, as did practically everyone in Vienna of that time, unless he was a member of that minority of racketeers and grafters who profited from speculation as well as exploitation of the contemporary economic scene. Thus, it can be considered proved that he was not preoccupied by his financial plight in July 1919. However, that an entirely different sort of preoccupation held him can be documented, as will be seen below.

To be sure, common sense might suggest a preoccupation with the general economic situation, in conformity with the mood prevalent at that time in Vienna, and as Federn's letter testifies, those who felt puzzled by his action thought first of that situation. In view of this, and in view of Freud's writing of "generally deteriorating conditions in Vienna" and his powerlessness to further Tausk's career, it may be doubted that the picture I presented and the inferences I drew are in accordance with historical reality. It is true that sources I have used, such as letters, do not always convey that which is psychologically relevant in this context. Yet the possibility of having been misled notwithstanding, I thought it useful to survey the available documentary evidence and assess the objective economic situation at the time of Tausk's death.[4a]

(B) Tausk's Relationship to Freud in 1919 Prior to July

Aside from the economic factor, considerations growing out of Tausk's relationship to Freud have been sug-

[4a]After the manuscript had been submitted for publication, I discovered that I had ignored two letters by Freud that are pertinent in this context. On October 3, 1919, he wrote to Abraham that he earned 500 Kronen a day through the analyses of five patients. On December 2, 1919, he informed Eitington that he earned 900 to 1,000 Kronen a day in this manner. I regret that I cannot discuss these figures and show that they do not necessitate changes in the conclusions I have drawn in the foregoing.

gested as causes of Tausk's suicide. I shall first describe
events as they evolved after Tausk's return from the
Army and assess them as possible causes, and then present documents that have been neglected and assess their
value as evidence of the way Tausk felt about Freud during that period.

(1) Tausk's psychoanalysis and its termination

In December 1918, about a month after he had settled
down in civilian practice, Tausk asked Freud to take him
into psychoanalytic treatment. It is not known what
Tausk told Freud as to why he was in need of it. Freud
declined but arranged for Tausk's treatment by Helene
Deutsch.

There were, as we shall see, decisive considerations
that made it impossible for Freud to accept Tausk as a
patient, and it is even remarkable that Tausk asked and
expected to be analyzed by Freud. Tausk had told several
people for years that Freud had used ideas of his without
acknowledging him as a source (Roazen, 1969; H.
Deutsch and E. Weiss, personal communications). Why
would an analyst who is convinced of having been de-
spoiled want to be analyzed by the alleged despoiler? In
an analysis he would lay bare every nook and cranny of
his creative potential; thus, by going into analysis with
the despoiler he would make himself purposefully a victim of further despoliation. According to this conviction,
had Freud complied with his request, Tausk would have
exposed himself throughout his treatment to the loss of
his intellectual treasures to the freebooter. In Tausk's request to be analyzed by Freud one meets for the first time
a sign of impairment of judgment or sense of reality, a
kind of defect that will be discussed in a broader context
below.

Tausk, at that time regarded as an experienced analyst, should have known that there was a psychoanalytic reason that obviated his being analyzed by Freud. He had formed a negative transference to Freud even before starting his treatment. A hostile transference to the analyst almost regularly evolves during a psychoanalytic treatment, and usually it can be dissolved by using the proper technique of interpretation. Yet when it has been formed before the inception of treatment, as a conviction allegedly derived from observation of reality to boot, the psychoanalytic process cannot be initiated and the treatment is bound to founder.

Here it is necessary to digress in order to discuss whether Tausk had perhaps been correct in his claim that Freud plagiarized him, as Roazen (1969) suggested. Freud's and Tausk's papers are published, as are the *Minutes* of the Vienna Psychoanalytic Association, in which every discussant's remarks during the relevant years are singled out in summary form. From these three sources it should be possible to determine at least the instances in which there would have been the possibility of theft. No one, however, so far as I know, has presented an instance in which Freud mentioned an idea that possibly came from Tausk without acknowledging it. This alone banishes Tausk's claim into the realm of illusion.

However, a careful examination of Tausk's papers leads to a passage that may allow a glimpse into the way Tausk occasionally coped with Freud's discoveries. In his paper on war psychoses (Tausk, 1916a) Tausk wrote: "I found the answer to the problem [the reduction of self-esteem in melancholia] *in an observation made some time ago and confirmed by Freud* to the effect that the melancholic's self-reproaches are only seemingly directed against himself: they are really intended for the love ob-

ject he has abandoned [emphasis added]" (*ibid.*, p. 395).
Can one say anything about the time of Tausk's conversation with Freud?[5] Yes, it must have taken place, if at
all, prior to December 30, 1914, since on the evening of
that day Freud mentioned to the Vienna Association his
view on the origin of the melancholic's self-reproaches.
This occurred in a discussion remark following Tausk's
presentation "Contributions to a psychoanalytic exposition of melancholia," a summary of which is reported in
the *Minutes* of the Association (Nunberg and Federn,
vol. 4, p. 272ff.). Tausk's presentation contains no reference to the mechanism.[6]

[5]Prof. Dr. Tausk objected to my taking this passage to mean that
his father had had a conversation in which he told Freud of his observation and in which Freud confirmed its correctness. Prof. Dr.
Tausk maintains that his father's remark amounts to the statement
that he and Freud made the observation independently of each
other — that is, Tausk made the observation, and subsequently it
turned out that Freud had made the same observation. It is true that
an author may refer to the findings of another person as confirming
his own. But then he cites the work done by the other person.
Freud's work on melancholia was not published at the time Tausk
wrote and published his paper, and if he had wanted the term "confirm" understood the way Prof. Dr. Tausk wants it to be understood, a reference to where and when Freud had confirmed Tausk's
findings would have had to be added. Since Tausk referred in that
article to conversations with Freud, I do not see how a reader could
understand Tausk's remark except as referring to a conversation.
The sequence of documented events does not confirm Tausk's independent discovery of the origin of the melancholic's self-reproaches.

[6]To be sure, a summary of a paper published in the *Minutes*
necessarily contains only an abbreviated version of a presentation.
Yet the summary makes it clear that Tausk was concerned with
quite different aspects of melancholia. He explained the self-accusa-
tions in melancholia by the intactness of the melancholic's intellect
and his refusal to adapt to an early libidinal phase. Aside from that,
if Tausk had said what he claimed in the quoted passage of 1916, it

Freud, however, is reported on that occasion to have said in the discussion: "The self-reproaches of melancholia are aimed at other persons and are merely turned onto one's own person" (*ibid.*, p. 275).[7] Freud's explanation of the melancholic's self-reproaches goes back to 1897 (see Strachey, 1957, p. 240, and Freud, 1950, p. 267). In December 1914, Freud must have had already fully conceptualized his paper on melancholia (1917), since Jones recalled that Freud "had expounded the theme of it [the paper on melancholia] to me as long ago as January 1914" (Jones, 1953–1957, vol. 2, p. 329). Freud finished the essay on May 4, 1915. War conditions delayed its publication for two years. It is plain from the documentary evidence that Tausk's claim to have told Freud about the origin of self-reproaches in melancholia or of having made the observation prior to December 1914 must have been a paramnesia.[8]

Further arguments can be raised in favor of this inference. Since he allegedly had told Freud about the explanation of self-reproaches, Tausk would have had the right to publish his discovery. Why did he not publish a paper on the origin of self-reproaches in melancholia but

---

would have struck everyone present as so original and revealing that it would have found a place in the summary

[7]Freud's remark would have been reported differently if he had elaborated on an assertion which Tausk had made in his presentation.

[8]Another statement by Tausk in his paper on the psychology of deserters (1916b) must be ascribed to paramnesia. He wrote of "a not yet published conjecture of Freud (which I feel free to use here with [Freud's] specific permission)," namely, the predisposition to melancholia in individuals who follow narcissistic patterns in their object choices. Yet in his paper of 1917 (p. 249) Freud *expressis verbis* stated that he had no title to this discovery, since Rank (1911) had made it.

wait over a year until he included it as a short remark in a paper that was not published in a psychoanalytic journal and whose title, "Diagnostic considerations concerning the symptomatology of the so-called war psychoses," would not suggest to anyone that it contained a theory that opened a new vista into the psychopathology of melancholia and a striking explanation of a problem that had puzzled psychiatrists since yore?

In addition, it must be noted that the passage is ambiguous insofar as it does not make clear whether Freud had made that observation prior to Tausk's communicating it to him, or whether he had confirmed it *a posteriori*. Since Freud's paper was published after Tausk's and Freud did not refer to Tausk, one might have reconstructed an instance of plagiarism.[9]

Freud's explanation of self-reproaches in melancholia is so striking because upon hearing it one has instantaneously the feeling that it cannot be otherwise, and one wonders why the idea did not come to one's own mind. I conjecture that Tausk might have had a similar reaction and therefore felt regret, since he had spent much thought on that disorder. Thus I see in the passage an attempt at rehabilitation, as if he wanted to say: "Even if I have no priority to an observation which is so clear, I have at least had it in my mind before I heard about it from Freud." I feel justified in this conjecture, since there is a precedent of that sort in the *Minutes*. In his dis-

[9]This, of course did not occur. It is questionable whether the published paper came to the attention of psychoanalysts at all. Tausk had presented it to the Association in January 1916, and an essential part of the theoretical argumentation was the result of the discussion that followed his presentation, as he lets the reader know. But he neither named the discussants nor specified the debt he owed to them.

cussion of Freud's paper "On the two principles of psychic happenings" (Oct. 20, 1910), Tausk said that "some time ago he himself arrived, by entirely different paths, at some minor theses. . ." (Nunberg and Federn, vol. 3, p. 30). The text is not quite clear but it seems certain that Tausk claimed a kind of "priority of thought" regarding the very new ideas Freud presented on that occasion.

Circumstantial as this digression has been, it may have been worthwhile to make it clear that Freud never infringed on Tausk's rights and that Tausk's conviction that Freud had abused him was a manifestation of a negative transference. Freud had no choice but to refer Tausk to a colleague.

Before turning to a discussion of Tausk's treatment by Helene Deutsch, I shall quote from Tausk's letter to Freud of March 30, 1919, since it contains a remark that permits a comment on that critical moment when Freud was compelled to transfer Tausk to the care of another therapist. I shall discuss the letter at length in the subsequent section and limit myself here to a comment on a remark Tausk made in conjunction with his request that Freud should take his older son Marius into analytic treatment. He wrote: "Since in this instance you cannot possibly have the hesitations which have determined you to decline me [as your patient]. . ." (Da Sie in diesem Falle unmöglich die Bedenken haben können, die Sie bestimmt haben, mich abzulehnen. . .).

The two words of importance in this context are *Bedenken* and *ablehnen*. The former is a weak word signifying objections that have not crystallized and do not permit a final decision; that is to say, one feels disinclined to do something but does not know whether one should accept or reject this disinclination *qua* final decision.

Ablehnen is a strong word, though not as strong as "reject." It is somewhere between "fail to accept" and "refuse." I go into these details because they provide a glimpse into the atmosphere surrounding Freud's negotiations when he tried to reach an understanding with Tausk.

Tausk's use of the word *Bedenken* permits the inference that Freud discussed the situation in detail with Tausk, stating the reasoning that led him to conclude that it would be unwise to accept him as a patient. Evidently no outright rejection had occurred; rather, a discussion took place that led to Freud's convincing Tausk of the validity of his *Bedenken*.

The word *Bedenken* would have made one expect a term milder than *ablehnen*. The choice of the latter would reflect Tausk's feeling of pain on being rejected by Freud. But the fact that Tausk could write calmly to Freud about the incident, implying, as one may suggest, understanding and acknowledgment of Freud's *Bedenken* strongly militates against the assumption that Freud's recommendation of Helene Deutsch as therapist had any bearing on Tausk's suicide. If Tausk had harbored resentment and a feeling of having been unjustly treated, it is hardly conceivable that he would have turned toward Freud in so delicate a matter as the analytic treatment of his son. It is difficult to imagine that a man of Tausk's sensitivity and temperament would entrust his own child to the care of a man who, in his opinion, had shown a hostile bias three months earlier. Tausk's request that Freud analyze Marius proves that he was convinced of Freud's professional integrity.

I shall now turn to Helene Deutsch, who was in a training analysis with Freud when she became Tausk's analyst in January 1919. Helene Deutsch's reputation as one of the foremost analysts was at that time still a matter of the future. She was elected a member of the Vienna Association on February 13, 1918. Six years later she became director of the Association's newly established Institute. The fact that she had been a senior resident of the University Psychiatric Clinics for many years as well as her eminent talents would make Freud's choice seem appropriate.

Since it has been claimed that Freud's refusal to analyze Tausk, Tausk's alleged humiliation by being sent to a junior analyst, and the premature termination of his analysis contributed to Tausk's early death (Roazen, 1969), all these circumstances have to be discussed.

There is no direct documentary evidence regarding details, but Helene Deutsch provided extensive information when I interviewed her in 1954 and 1970, and she deposited a summary in a private memorandum. According to her, Freud did his utmost to ensure Tausk's analysis by the best analysts in Vienna, but Tausk rejected all suggestions and insisted on receiving help only on his own terms, that is, from Freud. Finally he accepted Helene Deutsch as a therapist because she was in analysis with Freud at that time. He foresaw correctly that Helene Deutsch would bring up in her own analysis what her patient had to tell her. Indeed, to let Freud know what he had against him was the principal reason for Tausk's seeking treatment at all. Thus it happened that Tausk did not talk in his analysis about anything else but his accusations against Freud. The motive for going into analysis was, as Helene Deutsch stated, not the desire to be analyzed, to change, but to fulfill a wish, and that wish was that Freud should know about his grudges. In his analysis it became clear that he did not stop at the normal identification of the pupil with an admired teacher but that he wanted to be like him, indeed that he wanted to be him. He had in the end the feeling that Freud's teaching was a plagiarism of his own ideas; he had incorporated Freud's ideas as his own—all this according to Helene Deutsch.

Thus his wish was fulfilled, and Freud became informed of all his charges, Helene Deutsch having been the intermediary. She stated, in my opinion quite rightly, that Tausk's analysis was doomed to failure. She attributed this mainly to the fact that Tausk's only motive for going into analysis had been the gratification of a wish and not a serious striving for a cure. But she also remarked that Tausk's pathology possibly was not accessible to psychoanalytic treatment. Roazen (1969, p. 17) wrote that Tausk had a symbiotic relationship to Freud. I wonder whether he did not go too far in this, but this is clearly at least a possibility, and if Roazen were right, it would confirm Helene Deutsch's doubt as to Tausk's analyzability. A symbiotic relationship in a man of 40 is an ominous symptom and can hardly be expected to be corrected by a classical psychoanalysis, if at all.

In a letter Tausk wrote to Lou Andreas-Salomé as late as March 26, 1919, only part of which is available to me, there is a sentence that possibly throws some light on Tausk's psychoanalysis. He wrote: "Since the Congress of 1913,[10] I have hardly spoken any more with a human being" (Seit dem Kongress 1913 habe ich kaum mehr mit einem Menschen gesprochen). At the time he wrote that sentence, Tausk was still in psychoanalysis with Helene Deutsch. Would one ever expect such an avowal from a

[10]The 4th International Psychoanalytic Congress took place in Munich from September 7 to 8, 1913 (see Andreas-Salomé, 1958, pp. 168–170), and Tausk spent there the last days of his association with Lou Andreas-Salomé.

person who is in analysis or, at best, had just terminated one? The difficulty with some of Tausk's letters is that one does not know when he seeks to convey the truth and when he pursues another intention, such as manipulating the feelings of the recipient. Roazen touched upon that point when he discussed the wretched letters Tausk wrote from Berlin to his wife when he had a happy love relationship (Roazen, 1969, p. 18). In a letter to Lou Andreas-Salomé he definitely wanted to arouse pity, and therefore the sentence does not necessarily reflect the true situation. But if he conveyed the truth, this would be a final proof that Tausk's analysis was lacking in any seriousness of motive on his part to speak of.

When it became apparent that Tausk's analytic treatment was hopeless and when Helene Deutsch's own analysis with Freud became greatly impeded by her treating Tausk, Freud and Helene Deutsch agreed upon the termination of his analysis (March 1919), as stated in Helene Deutsch's memorandum.

The assessment of that termination should not cause difficulty. Tausk had not used the treatment situation for evolving the psychoanalytic process; that is, Helene Deutsch never became the so-called "mirror" for him but remained a means to a nontherapeutic end, and therefore it is doubtful that he developed a transference to her in the proper meaning of the word. More cautiously, one may say that since Tausk centered on his grievances against Freud in his analytic sessions, not much could be observed of what his transference to his therapist might have been. Yet it is relevant that he neither reacted negatively nor remonstrated or complained when Helene Deutsch told him that she would terminate his treatment. If Tausk had been serious about his analysis, one consequence would have been that he would have turned to

Freud and consulted him about what to do next. But no such step is known. He seemed unperturbed by the termination, as Helene Deutsch told me. This would be in keeping with the primary intention that brought him intc psychoanalysis. By now, so he must have thought, Freud had to have been fully informed of his imputations. To all external appearances at least, he seemed satisfied that his main purpose had been fulfilled.

I should not like to close this section without adding a comment. I do not feel satisfied with the prevalent explanation of Tausk's relationship to Freud. I have a strong suspicion that Tausk operated on the assumption that he had fertilized Freud's ideas without Freud having been aware of it. He possibly experienced this not as an active process of insemination but rather as having passively contributed to the work of Freud, who without noticing it used ideas put into his head by Tausk's originality. Thus the impulse to be analyzed by Freud might have been based on the wish that Freud at last should find out that Tausk all along had been a loving and generous son-like person who voluntarily had surrendered his best for the glory of a father figure, a gift he at long last wanted acknowledged. It is unnecessary to repeat that this construction is a mere conjecture on my part.

Although it is almost certain that Tausk felt hurt by Freud's unwillingness to accept him as a patient — as patients who wish to be analyzed by a particular analyst inescapably feel frustrated when the analyst is not ready to comply with their request — there is no evidence that this rejection had relevant consequences. It is, indeed, not probable that a man of 40, unless he is pathologically sensitive, would commit suicide six months after he had been told by Freud that it would be more suitable for him to be treated by another therapist. Likewise, Tausk's behavior subsequent to the termination of his treatment with Helene Deutsch did not show signs that would suggest that he had been traumatized by the termination. This will become even clearer in the next section.

I shall now turn to the available documents in a search for evidence of what Tausk's relationship was to Freud from the time of his return to Vienna in November 1918.

(2) Tausk's written messages to Freud in the first half of 1919

In the preceding section I had to rely on indirect evidence culled from Tausk's behavior as reported by an eyewitness or other incidentals, but now I shall turn to documents that contain direct evidence regarding Tausk's relationship to Freud. These documents consist of six letters written by Tausk to Freud in the first six months of 1919 which should permit an assessment of at least one aspect of Tausk's feelings about Freud during those crucial months preceding his suicide.

Letters are under all circumstances an important, even though often ambiguous, source material in any biographical study. As is known, a letter may be deceitful, even outrightly mendacious; it may be pragmatic or expressive of a hidden sentiment the writer exposed only on this one occasion and never again. A letter may betray unconscious contents which the writer would deny passionately. Someone commented on the double aspect of a letter: on the one hand, it conveys less than conversation with its huge mass of nonverbal signals — e.g., in modulation of voice, gestures, and facial expression. On the other hand, a letter usually compels the writer to be more precise in formulation than he may be in conversation, precisely because he can rely only on words as his communicative medium.

The golden age of letter writing was the eighteenth and nineteenth centuries (see Benjamin, 1977). Its tradition, still alive in most of Freud's letters, had greatly declined by the early years of the twentieth century. Thus, most of the letters to be discussed are sober and mainly devoted to practical purposes. The July letters written by Tausk shortly before the suicide and to be discussed in the next section are of a different structure. Yet at least one of the pre-July letters contains an important lead regarding Tausk's relationship to Freud. The six letters to be examined are dated January 22 and 29, March 1 and 30, April 12 and May 31, respectively.

As an introduction and for completeness' sake I shall start with a letter Freud wrote Tausk regarding a patient on December 7, 1918, a month after Tausk had started his practice. Freud asked Tausk "to take an interest, in the meantime, in this precocious, very strange 15-year-old boy who will reward your interest not only personally but [also] theoretically as a model of juvenile neurasthenia" (sich unterdes mit diesem frühreifen sehr merkwürdigen Jungen von 15 Jahren zu beschäftigen, der nicht nur persönlich, auch theoretisch als Vorbild einer juvenilen Neurasthenie Ihr Interesse lohnen wird).[11] The patient was apparently impecunious, because Freud assured Tausk at the beginning of the message that "Whereas I usually do not impose on you non-paying patients..." (Obwohl ich Ihnen sonst Gratis-patienten nicht zumute, bitte ich Sie doch...), he nevertheless asked him to do it in this instance. He closed with: "Next time more from your Freud" (Nächstens mehr von Ihrem Freud).

[11]Quoted with the permission of the Sigmund Freud Copyrights, Ltd.

Freud seems to have been somewhat embarrassed about being compelled to ask Tausk, who was in the process of building up a new practice, to spend time on a gratis patient. He evidently did not expect him to analyze the patient, for he limited his request by using the word "to take an interest," which probably meant to devote only a minimum of time to this patient. It is not known whether this was the first patient Freud referred after Tausk had resumed practice. The fact that Freud felt free to take the liberty of asking Tausk for a favor of that kind would, if anything, suggest that there were no tense feelings between them at that time.

Tausk's two January letters are devoted mainly to professional matters. The first letter expresses optimism and gives a report on the status of patients, as cited above when I discussed Tausk's financial situation: "Thus everything looks very auspicious and if existence becomes a bit cheaper I shall be able to maintain my standard of life" (Es sieht also alles sehr zuversichtlich aus und ich werde, wenn die Existenz nun etwas billiger wird, meinen Standard of life halten können). He expressed surprise that no one had yet registered for his courses, but this, as he indicated, might have been due to the fact that only one daily paper had as yet published the announcement.

The second letter is brief and contains thanks for the referral of a patient. Tausk wrote, "I owe to your kind solicitude..." (Ich verdanke Ihrer gütigen Fürsorge ...). It should be noted that Tausk used *gütige Fürsorge* in both letters. This, I believe, is not merely a cliché but a strong expression of appreciation. I emphasize this because these two letters were written shortly after Freud had declined to function as Tausk's analyst. If this had caused resentment in Tausk, one would not have expected a term of such personal warmth but rather a sign of coolness.

In the letter of March 1, Tausk briefly reported about a patient Freud had seen in consultation. He had now all in all seven patients in treatment. He was able "to cope with the great quantity only with great effort and as it seems to me inadequately" (. . . bewältige die grosse Quantität nur mit grosser Mühe und wie mir scheint unvollkommen). He "had always to wonder how you manage even more cases in addition to everything else" (. . . muss immer daran denken, wie Sie es fertig bringen noch mehr Fälle neben allem anderen zu beherrschen). He proposed that some meetings of the Association might be devoted to the discussion of actual technical problems. "Certainly also others would be glad to be able to set forth their woes" (Gewiss wären auch andere Herren froh, ihre Kümmernisse vortragen zu können). He apologized for the new grievance.[12] To analyze seven patients would not be considered nowadays as too burdensome and was not at the time when the letter was written. How much time Tausk had spent in full-time psychoanalytic practice before he was called into the Army is not known. Much of the time was spent at the University clinics. It is possible that he did not respond well to the constraints of analytic practice, which grants little outlet and discharge of activity to the practitioner. On the other hand, his feeling of insufficiency may have to be connected with the effects on him of his years of Army service. Tausk's sober remark of admiration about Freud's superiority in handling a large workload should be noted.

The next two letters are in many respects of great importance. They give a glimpse into Tausk's relationship to his children as well as into Freud's skill in dealing with a precarious clinical situation.

---

[12]"Ich bitte Sie für die neue Querulation um Entschuldigung."

In his letter of March 30, Tausk asked Freud to take his older son Marius, who was 17 years old at that time, into psychoanalysis. Tausk had published the analysis of two of the boy's dreams seven years earlier and enclosed a reprint (Tausk, 1913).[13] He enumerated the symptoms he had discovered "to my consternation in an abnormal degree and have tried at the end 'of the paper to abate my apprehension with theoretical comforting considerations" (zu meiner Bestürzung in abnormen Masse entdecken müssen und meinen Schrecken mit theoretischen Trosterwägungen am Schluss der Arbeit abzuschwächen versucht).

Then Tausk presented an outline of Marius's development in the last ten years. His mentality and morality are high. The picture he offers is that of "a noble human being" (Edelmensch). He has "unusual discernment in all things that can be subject to theoretical abstraction" (beweist einen ungewöhnlichen Scharfsinn in allen Dingen, die sich theoretisch abstrahieren lassen). Tausk described him as writing surprisingly talented novelettes. Only two negative observations were mentioned: the boy had a tendency toward rumination (Grübelsucht) and his stories were formed along the lines of anxiety dreams.

A complication occurred by virtue of the following events:

> He got spontaneously into psychoanalysis after he was carried with impetuous momentum into the inside of things last year owing to conversations and

[13]In his letter Tausk erroneously gives 1912 as the year of publication. Kanzer (1971, 1972) has discussed Tausk's paper extensively and drawn broad conclusions regarding Tausk's relationship to his sons as well as his psychopathology. See Marius Tausk (1973) for some corrections.

suggestions I made. I had not meant it that way and had structured my communications deliberately and sparingly.[14]

In order to satisfy the youngster's curiosity, Tausk let him read only Freud's *Psychopathology of Everyday Life*. Yet the boy recalled the previous analysis of his dreams and obtained a reprint of his father's paper. He started to analyze his dreams in secret. Tausk enclosed a manuscript and letter of his son as the first specimen of such activity. "Now," he continued, "I intimated to him that he apparently was still in a fight against masturbation and has to suppress incestuous wishes" (Nun deutete ich ihm an, dass er sich wohl noch im Kampf gegen die Onanie befinde und Inzestwünsche zu unterdrücken habe). To these interpretations Marius responded with "an unusually talented short story, a source, precious for psychoanalysis, of insight into the artistic mechanisms representing the unconscious wish [to commit] a sex murder. Thereupon I called the boy's attention to sadomasochism" (Als Antwort kam eine ungewöhnlich begabte Novellette, eine für die Psychoanalyse kostbare Quelle für Einsichten in die künstlerische Mechanik, den unbewussten Lustmordwunsch darstellend. Darauf machte ich den Buben auf den Sadomasochismus aufmerksam). The letter with which Marius answered "shows that I have scarcely to say anything to the youth which he had not already found with impressing sharpness and far and away radiant intuition" (. . . zeigt, dass

---

14Ist voriges Jahr spontan, durch Gespräche und Andeutungen von mir mit stürmischer Wucht ins innere der Dinge getragen, in die Psychoanalyse geraten. Ich hatte es nicht so gemeint; hatte auch meine Mitteilungen mit Bedacht und Sparsamkeit eingerichtet.

ich dem Jungen kaum etwas zu sagen habe, was er nicht schon mit imponierender Schärfe und weitausstrahlender Intuition gefunden hat). Tausk thought that the boy's fate hung in the balance: "It should not become his father's fate" (Es soll nicht das seines Vaters werden). It was a matter of saving from ruination not only his son "but a fine human being and an eminently endowed psychoanalyst" (Es ist nicht nur mein Sohn, sondern ein feiner Mensch und ein hervorragend begabter Psychoanalytiker vor dem Verderben zu retten).

Then follows the above-quoted sentence that Freud "cannot possibly" have in this instance the doubts which made him decline Tausk's analysis and therefore "I shall permit myself to beg you urgently to take over the analysis of my son with the beginning of the next school year [September]" (erlaube mir nun Sie inständigst zu bitten, die Analyse meines Sohnes mit Beginn des nächsten Schuljahres...zu übernehmen). Freud should determine the fee. Since Tausk had six patients paying the full fee, he would be able to pay the full, normal fee. Freud was supposed to give him an answer at the next meeting of the Association, since he would have to prepare immediately for the boy's move from Graz[15] to Vienna.

The letter is remarkable for a variety of reasons. As noted, since it was written after Freud had declined to accept Tausk as a patient and after the termination of his analysis with Helene Deutsch, it proves that neither event had caused Tausk to feel alienated from, or hostile to, Freud. It bears repetition: it is hardly imaginable that a father would have entrusted a son as dearly loved as Marius to the care of an analyst by whom he was an-

[15]Graz, the capital of Styria, an Austrian province. Marius lived there with his mother and younger brother.

gered, rejected, or humiliated, and only a short time before, to boot. It is a rule that parents respond to their children's analysts with particular sensitivity, and one of the many difficulties which those who analyze children and adolescents run into is to curb parental acting out caused by an unfavorable bias against the therapist. Tausk's spontaneous turn to Freud for help must be taken, whatever the secondary motives for his so doing may have been, as a far-reaching indication of his basically good feelings about Freud and the trust he placed in him.

Marius, as one learns from Tausk's publication (1913), had been disappointed by the birth of his brother. He felt neglected by his mother and turned toward his father, "who gave him unrestricted tenderness and herewith offered homosexual substitute for the ungratified love of mother" (der ihm uneingeschränkte Zärtlichkeit und somit einen homosexuellen Ersatz für die unbefriedigte Liebe zur Mutter bot). Two years later the father left the home for a long time, and Marius took over the father's role toward the brother and met him with love and affection. His role as protector went so far that he could not bear it when his brother, who was jealous and therefore aggressive and violent toward him, was punished for such misdemeanors.

Evidently the boy possessed an unusual degree of flexibility and a high adjustment potential: the trauma of the brother's birth, the reduction of the mother's affection, and the desertion of the father who had aroused all his affectionate tenderness—all these stresses were apparently borne without neurotic symptoms to speak of.

From the dreams Tausk reported and their analysis one becomes acquainted with a boy eager to grow up, curious about the riddles of the world, alert, intelligent, and enjoying an excellent relationship to his environment.

Both in 1919, when Tausk turned toward Freud, and earlier, in the paper of 1913, one is surprised because his request for treatment of his son was not based on any manifest symptom that would give cause for concern.[16] I wonder with what sentiments Freud read this communication. Here was one of his most talented pupils who practiced what probably was already acknowledged at that time as "wild analysis." In Tausk's paper of 1913 one does not find anything that would have justified the apprehension of which he wrote in his letter to Freud. Tausk must have noticed seven years later that he had been mistaken because the boy had developed into an *Edelmensch*. Nevertheless, he became alarmed once again and communicated to his son deep, global interpretations of the unconscious.[17] A dangerous dwindling of ego boundaries announced itself between son and father when the latter saw in his progeny already an "eminently endowed psychoanalyst." Tausk's suggestion that his son should move from Graz and come to Vienna one year before he was to take his University entrance exams

[16]It is debatable why the father started to analyze his son's dreams when the latter was ten years old. Kanzer (1971) suggested that Tausk may have responded to a request by Freud (Strachey, 1955, p. 4). But Freud asked that analysts collect certain of their patients' dreams from which the inference could be supported that they had witnessed sexual intercourse as infants.

[17]To be sure, at that time many analysts still neglected the distinction between symptom and developmental manifestations, but the information at hand does not include any evidence of overt psychopathology in Marius. It seems to me that Tausk was more inclined toward deep interpretations than was customary at that time. Thus he reports (1916–17) having interpreted a patient's death wish against the mother on the basis of a slip of the tongue in what seems to have been the first interview.

(*Matura*) was impractical and would have been justified only by an emergency. Freud probably knew about the adolescent's past, his parents' divorce, the boy's attendance at boarding school, and frequent long travels to see the father (Marius Tausk, 1973). In Graz he had apparently taken root at last for two years.

Tausk's letter substantiates the son's high creative potential. Whenever the father gave a deep interpretation, the youngster replied with a creative achievement. Otherwise, one may conjecture, he would have been led into acting out. The son shows here an asset that was lacking in his father, as will be seen later. Did the father envy the son in whom he discovered unusual endowment and solidity of character (see Kanzer, 1971, 1972)?

At any rate, to take this adolescent into psychoanalysis would have been a misapplication of the psychoanalytic treatment. Marius was in an anabolic crisis, if it can be called a crisis at all. His defenses operated constructively and led to high sublimations. A weakening of defenses, as was partly unavoidable in adolescent analysis as conducted at that time, would have constituted a poorly calculated risk. An interference by psychoanalysis would have interrupted a highly promising development, not to speak of the upheaval a move to Vienna would have caused. If Freud had fulfilled Tausk's request, he would have endangered Marius, if anything.

What Freud told Tausk at their next meeting is not known, but Tausk's letter of thanks is preserved. I shall reproduce it in full, first outlining hypothetically what the preceding events must have been, in view of this letter.

It seems that Tausk did not wait for what Freud would have to say but communicated with Marius about his intention of moving him to Vienna in order to have him undergo an analysis. Freud and Tausk then apparently met, and Freud explained to Tausk why an analytic treatment of his son was not feasible, if for no other reason than that it would endanger the adolescent's autonomous development. All one had to do for the time being was to let that promising adolescent grow and find his own way. Shortly thereafter Tausk apparently received a letter from his son in which he rejected the entire project and insisted on his personal independence.

On April 12, 1919 Tausk wrote Freud the following letter:

Hochverehrter Herr Professor,
The enclosed letter of my boy concurs with your views unreservedly. The fact of his using even your words in order to safeguard his right of independent development I want to emphasize to my son's credit. For this price I do not mind having made a fool of myself in this instance. I thank you for this great service. Have also the kindness to return the letter [of Marius] at the Wednesday meeting.
Mit herzlich ergebenen Grüssen, Ihr
Tausk[18]

It is noteworthy that Tausk after termination of his own analysis immediately tried to establish a new link with Freud, using this time the projection of his self-image as messenger. A clinging attitude and persistence

18Der beiliegende Brief meines Jungen gibt Ihnen in uneingeschränkten Masse Recht. Dass er sogar Ihre Worte gebraucht, um sich das Recht auf selbstständige Entwicklung zu sichern, will ich zum Lobe des Sohnes hervorheben. Um diesen Preis bin ich gern der blamierte in diesem Falle. Ich danke Ihnen für diesen grossen Dienst. Haben Sie auch die Güte mir den Brief Mittwoch bei der Sitzung wiederzugeben.

can hardly be overlooked. But no sign of impatience or brushing aside can be observed on Freud's part. He used his clinical acumen and apparently understood Tausk's son well even though he had never met him. During his conversation with Freud, Tausk may have received a glimpse of what was going on between him and his son and he felt indebted to Freud, so much that he did not mind "being made a fool."

At any rate, the two letters seem to prove that Tausk bore no rancor against Freud after his own analysis by Helene Deutsch had been terminated. His praise of Freud does not sound fulsome but to the point. Indeed, Freud did him a great service by averting a crisis in his relationship with his son.

The letter of May 31 was reported above. It concerned mainly the professional reversals that had recently occurred.

"I very much regret," he wrote, "that I must approach you over and over again as one who needs help. But it is stronger than I" (Es ist mir sehr leid, immer wieder als Hilfsbedürftiger zu Ihnen kommen zu müssen. Aber es ist stärker als ich). He evidently felt embarrassed by the necessity of turning again to Freud as a supplicant and therefore, perhaps, he closed with a particular flourish: "Meanwhile accept my thanks in advance from your still very much thanks-owing Tausk" (Nehmen Sie indessen vielen Dank voraus von Ihrem noch sehr viel dankschuldigen). Unless one assumed that Tausk was going out of his way to pretend, one cannot overlook the cordiality and affectionateness of his words.

Nevertheless, one may perhaps believe that these letters should not be taken at their face value. Tausk had to survive; and survival depended on the referral of patients; and Freud was the most promising, if not the only, source of such referrals. So what else should he have done but do his utmost to keep up optimal relations? But against the interpretation that the emotional tone of these documents had been dictated basically by utilitarian pragmatism, one may raise the argument that Tausk did not hesitate in his analysis to pour out his negative thoughts and feelings about Freud, even though he knew they would reach Freud's ear. From the utilitarian point of view, he should never have gone into psychoanalysis with a person who was in analysis with Freud himself. Does one observe here a feature that is characteristic of Tausk's psychopathology: the isolation of contrary trends which by being kept separate do not interfere with each other?

On the other hand, one may surmise that Tausk, when confronted with that apparent contradiction, would have countered that he acknowledged Freud's greatness as well as his benevolent attitude for which he repeatedly expressed gratitude, but that he had to protest against Freud's not acknowledging that he, Tausk, had made a substantial contribution toward that greatness and that many an idea which had gone to Freud's credit had had its true origin in Tausk himself. Thus it may have appeared to Tausk that it was not a lack of friendliness on Freud's part that caused tension between them but merely Freud's apparent denial of what he owed Tausk; independently of whether this debt might have been large or small, it seemed to him to have been a debt that remained unacknowledged.

One may conclude that the letters Tausk wrote Freud were an honest exposition of one aspect at least of the way he felt about him. This is confirmed also by Tausk's letters of July 2 and 3, which will be discussed below. Here I must emphasize that they do not contain a shadow of any alienation, disappointment, or negative feelings that might have separated Tausk from Freud. Just the opposite. Tausk's farewell letter, written shortly before his death, is a panegyric about Freud. For certain, he would have had at long last an opportunity to express any ill feelings or grudges he might have harbored against Freud.

The six letters discussed prove that the panegyric with which Tausk parted was not a final sudden rush of deepest gratitude meant to compensate for a preceding period of hostility, rivalry, and frustration that now would be ended by death. The farewell letter was the expression of feelings that are characteristic of Tausk's relationship with Freud from beginning to end, as evidenced by the rest of the letters that have reached posterity and, to a certain extent, by the *Minutes*. Nevertheless, all this would not refute the argument that Tausk also felt hostility and rivalry to Freud and at times felt frustrated by having to stand in Freud's shadow, as Adler frankly admitted about himself (Freud, 1914); but the documents do prove that negative feelings were outweighed by far by positive ones.

Ambivalence is hardly avoidable between a great scholar and teacher and his pupils. The question can only be in what form that ambivalence expresses itself. It may be deeply repressed and leave the friendly feelings uncontaminated; or it may lead to sporadic outbreaks of hostility; or it may find an isolated channel of discharge. At any rate, considering the letters Tausk wrote to Freud in 1919, one does not find the trace of a conflict that may have been aroused by his relationship to Freud and may have been among the factors that precipitated the suicide. The letters prove the noteworthy fact that between his return from the Army and his suicide Tausk made four requests to Freud at short intervals, each of no minor range. He requested that Freud: (1) take him into analysis; (2) send him patients; (3) take his son into analysis; (4) organize technical sessions in which he would discuss the difficulties he met with in his practice.

Freud did his utmost to meet Tausk's requests. He arranged for his psychoanalysis;˙ he sent him, if I am not mistaken, a new patient almost every month; and he did his homework, unhurriedly reading the father's reprint, the son's short stories and letters in order to give counsel in a hazardous family situation. To what extent he satisfied the fourth demand is unclear. In any case, on April 18 Tausk read a paper entitled "Unresolved problems of psychoanalytic technique" to the Association (Fragestellungen aus der psychoanalytischen Technik).[19]

---

[19]Documentation of the period in Tausk's life that followed his return to civilian life disproves Edoardo Weiss's statement (1970, p. 8): "Gradually he [Freud] lost some of his compassion. . . . For example, when after the First World War Victor Tausk was destitute and had fallen into a deep depression, Freud could not give his old friend the moral support he needed." One wonders as to the source of this misinformation. No sign was reported of a deep depression in Tausk after his return to Vienna, and Tausk had never been a friend of Freud's. Furthermore, it is strange to hear that Weiss was not surprised when he learned of Tausk's suicide. "I realized that he must have felt abandoned by persons close to him, perhaps particularly by Freud" (ibid., p. 11). What made him think that Freud had abandoned Tausk? He had seen Tausk earlier in "a deep depression" (ibid., p. 11) owing to his having been betrayed by a lover (see Chapter II). Consequently, one might rather have expected Weiss to surmise that Tausk had been abandoned by a woman. Weiss allegedly called Freud Tausk's "murderer" (Roazen, 1977). Roazen does not report on what grounds Weiss made that remark. Quite a few signs of ambivalence against Freud can be found in Weiss's writing. To quote a minor one: he complained to Roazen (1969) about what he had already intimated in print (Weiss, 1964),

In Tausk's letter of March 26, 1919 to Lou Andreas-Salomé from which I quoted above, there is a passage that summarizes Tausk's feelings about Freud at that time: "Freud shows respect, but little warmth. After all, the relations [between us] are better since the time I [stopped] pursuing them. Much better, I guess, they cannot become; he excludes now as ever anything personal. But I am at last also cured of the wish for it."[20] The question is whether a reliable assessment can be made of Tausk's feelings about Freud on the basis of this statement. The facts Tausk reports sound plausible. The absence of personal warmth was correctly observed by him, as confirmed by the letter of Paul Federn that will be discussed in the next section; Freud probably felt irritated by him. That their relations improved when Tausk diminished the intensity with which he sought contact would make good sense.

Was Tausk reconciled with that outcome? In the beginning of the letter, as I shall indicate below, Tausk expresses his longing to meet Lou Andreas-Salomé. As Dr. Maurice Nadelman suggested, the fact that the expression of this longing is followed by his avowal that he no longer seeks personal warmth in his relation with Freud indicates that his longing for closeness to Freud was only

namely, that Freud had omitted to cite him when he described derealization as a defense (Freud, 1936). Indeed, Weiss had published a remark to that effect in 1932, but he ignored the fact that Freud had presented derealization as a defense five years earlier (Freud, 1927) and that he, if anything, should have cited Freud (Eissler, 1978). Thus, this man was victimized in his old age by ambivalence to Freud, as happened not infrequently to aging analysts who had been in personal contact with Freud and owed him a great debt.

[20]Freud zeigt Achtung aber wenig Wärme. Die Beziehungen sind immerhin bessere, seit ich sie nicht suche. Viel besser können sie wohl nicht werden, er schliesst nach wie vor alles Persönliches aus. Ich bin aber endlich auch vom Wunsch danach geheilt.

denied or suppressed but still active. It is relevant that Tausk records Freud's respect for him. It would be important to know from what time Freud was lacking in personal warmth, for it is not probable that Freud did not feel personal warmth for Tausk at the very beginning of their acquaintance. It is possible that this warmth subsided when Tausk began to complain that Freud was making an unfair use of his ideas. At the time when the letter was written, Freud was having to listen to a long list of incriminating complaints which Tausk directed at him through Helene Deutsch. Since Tausk knew that these complaints would reach Freud, one wonders why he expected that Freud would respond with personal warmth.

At any rate, it seems that at least at that time the intensity of his conflicts with Freud had abated and reached a bearable level — at least externally.[21] However, whatever Tausk's subjective feelings may have been, Freud's consistent heedfulness of Tausk's needs, as can be inferred from Tausk's letters to him, is remarkable, since Tausk at the age of 40 hardly had to cope with more intense worries than Freud had to cope with at the age of sixty-three. In March 1918 his wife fell gravely ill with influenzal pneumonia (Jones, 1953–1957, vol. 3, p. 8), and Anton von Freund, to whom he felt so close, showed signs of fatal disease around that time. His children's future was questionable and his own financial future discouraging. On March 28 he wrote to Jones: "I can't remember a time of my life when my horizon was so dark. . ." (ibid., p. 6f.).

It also must be kept in mind that Tausk was not the only person who asked Freud for help. In 1919 there was

[21]Very probably Tausk's opportunity to ventilate his feelings about Freud in his treatment with Dr. Deutsch lessened the intensity of his reproaches against Freud.

probably a situation comparable to that of 1938, when after the occupation of Austria, a huge number of people turned toward Freud for counsel and practical help. At that time, too, Freud was indefatigable, even though his health was severely undermined. In 1919 the demand put upon him by colleagues' and outsiders' requests and pressures was probably not quite as intense as two decades later, but such external pressures must have been grave enough (see Jones, vol. 3). Thus, from the six letters Tausk wrote to Freud one becomes acquainted with only a narrow sector of what Freud had to cope with at that time. Further, Tausk did not belong to those who were close to Freud's heart. It is highly probable that Freud felt irritated by Tausk, as noted above and as discussed in the next section of this chapter. Nevertheless, nothing of his personal feelings interfered with a friendly, benign, helpful attitude. When Tausk asked Freud for a consultation regarding his son, anyone else burdened by a sea of troubles, as Freud was at that time, would have felt entitled to pass the new demand on to a colleague. In his April letter Tausk expressed appreciation for Freud's great service on his behalf. Little would he suspect that fifty years later a biographer would reward this act of service on the part of Freud with the following comment: "But Freud did not heed this [Tausk's] plea for a surrogate analysis [i.e., of Marius in the place of Tausk], and Tausk must have seemed a greater nuisance than ever. Freud was through with Tausk, no matter how difficult it might prove for Tausk to accept the rejection" (Roazen, 1969).

(3) Paul Federn's letter of July 3, 1919

Among the available documents that contain clues as to Tausk's motives for committing suicide is a letter by

Paul Federn to his wife, written on the day of Tausk's suicide.[22]

In determining the degree to which one may accept inferences about the objective state of affairs in a writer's environment on the basis of a letter such as this, one must take account both of the writer's emotional perspective, that is, his mood and conflicts at the time of writing, and of the range of facts he was in a position to know at that particular moment. Once these and allied circumstances are clarified, one may be able to distinguish those of a writer's statements that contain references to facts from those that represent interpretations of facts. An interpretation may contain important clues, but the vantage point from which it was made must be ascertained in order to determine the probability of its correctness, since interpretations even under optimal conditions contain a margin ever so small of uncertitude.

Federn was terribly shocked by the news of Tausk's tragic end. Common sense alone would assume such a response. He made several *lapsus calami* in his letter, as will be seen, and the letter contains many contradictions. He did not apprise his wife immediately of the tragedy but delayed communication of the principal news, as Freud did in his letter to Lou Andreas-Salomé (see below). Federn's letter began: "Worries oppress because the present state is such that indeed one often cannot go on any further" (Die Sorgen drücken, weil es jetzt so ist, dass man wirklich oft nicht weiter kann). After this preparation, he continued: "I must write you the worst. Tausk has shot himself today." Fortuitously, a colleague, Eduard Hitschmann (1871–1958), had called Tausk by telephone while the ambulance was there. I quoted above

---

[22]Federn, an early follower of Freud, became an eminent analyst.

Federn's supposition that Tausk's financial plight (which apparently was the first thing to come to his mind) was only "the last straw" (der letzte Anstoss).[23]

Then follows the sentence which was used as a proof that Freud was responsible for Tausk's suicide and that a break had occurred between the two (Roazen, 1969, 1972). "The motive was 'Freud's turning away" (Das Motiv war die Abwendung Freuds). Further on, Federn writes: "Had Freud treated him with humaneness [warmth of feeling], not merely recognizance and assistance, he would have borne the martyr's existence still longer" (Hätte Freud ihm die Menschlichkeit gegeben, nicht nur Anerkennung und Unterstützung, hätte er das Martyrerdasein noch weiter getragen.)[24]

What did Federn have in mind in referring to Freud's failure to treat Tausk with humaneness? Very probably he referred to knowledge he had obtained in conversations with Freud. That Freud had confidence and trust in Federn is evidenced by the fact that he became Freud's deputy in the Vienna Psychoanalytic Association four years later, at a time when illness prevented Freud from discharging some of his administrative duties. It is almost

[23]The patient of Tausk whom I interviewed continued his treatment with Federn. He was told by Federn that Tausk's financial condition was the reason for suicide.

[24]This statement alone establishes that no break had occurred between Freud and Tausk, as has been claimed, for recognition and assistance exclude a break. As Prof. Ernst Federn called to my attention, the word Unterstützung would not necessarily signify the referral of patients but might imply monetary contributions. It is possible that Freud had resumed his earlier pecuniary gifts to Tausk after December 1918. Prof. Federn informs me that among his father's papers, an undated visiting card of Freud's was found with the inscription "advance fund for Dr. Tausk, June–July" (Vorrat für Dr. Tausk Juni–Juli).

certain that Freud spoke to Federn about Tausk. I infer
this from a sentence about Tausk in Federn's letter that
puzzled me for a long time. He wrote: "In the end he
[Tausk] literally drove the psychic cases away (from himself), obviously out of ill-will against Freud in order to
expose the ineffectuality of the [psychoanalytic] method"
(Er hat zuletzt die psychischen Fälle direkt von sich fort-
getrieben offenbar um die Nutzlosigkeit der Methode zu
demonstrieren aus Rancune gegen Freud). Since Tausk
did not treat neurological patients, the reference to
Tausk's psychic cases hardly makes sense. However, if
Federn had committed a *lapsus calami*, omitting two letters and writing "psychic" when he intended "psychotic"
(psychotisch), the sentence makes sense. The reader may
recall that Tausk informed Freud on May 31 that for all
practical purposes two patients would be leaving and
that he had hospitalized one of his patients. Today, when
a patient suddenly terminates his analysis, the first question is: what mistake has the therapist made? The termination of treatment by a patient of his own accord is
usually referred to the analyst's acting out. Rightly or
wrongly, in view of the simultaneous occurrence of two
such instances and Tausk's hospitalizing one of his patients, this thought must have crossed Freud's mind.
Since Federn and Tausk were, as will be seen, not on
friendly terms and therefore Federn was in no position to
obtain this information from Tausk, I must infer that it
came from Freud.[25]

Withal Federn got caught in a contradiction. First he

[25]Weiss, in turn, must have been informed by Federn, unless he
saw Federn's letter in later years. Demonstrating again his own ambivalence to Freud, he wrote: "To demonstrate the usefulness [*sic!*]
of Freud's therapeutic procedure, Tausk dismissed many patients
after a short period of treatment" (Weiss, 1970, p. 14).

ascribed Tausk's "martyrdom" to external economic conditions and then he described a behavior pattern in Tausk that would make his "martyrdom" appear as self-inflicted by his uncalled-for dismissal of patients. A therapist who dismisses his patients arbitrarily necessarily suffers loss of income.

An even more surprising contradiction is found when one holds the disastrous character profile Federn presented of Tausk side by side with his criticism of Freud. He wrote: "Had I been able, I certainly should have helped him [Tausk], even though he always pricked the hand that was extended to him for help" (Hätte ich gekonnt, hätte ich ihm sicher geholfen, obgleich er immer die Hand gestochen hat, die ihm zur Hilfe gereicht wurde).[26]

On all occasions Federn met "vanity, envy and indifference when [he] approached [Tausk] in a friendly manner. . . . [Tausk], it is true, has made enemies for himself everywhere and always" (bei jeder Gelegenheit. . . nur Eitelkeit, Neid und Teilnahmlosigkeit fand, wenn ich ihm freundlich entgegenkam. . . . Er hat sich allerdings überall und immer Feinde geschaffen). Why, one asks oneself, should Freud have treated Tausk with "humaneness" under such conditions? That a highly talented person suffers from a severe character defect is not infrequent, and Federn's evaluation of Tausk's character might or might not have been correct. But there is a contradiction when he reproaches Freud for having given *only* recognition and assistance to a person who was ungrateful, allegedly was out to spite Freud by damaging his own pa-

[26]Federn presents the cliché of the dog which bites the hand that feeds him, but he uses the verb "to prick." Federn might have recoiled from completing the metaphor — appalling in this context — of the ungrateful dog and therefore slipped into a catachresis.

tients, and aroused enmity "everywhere and always." Federn reported about himself that he "had forgiven him [Tausk] internally, but was no longer fond of him" (Ich habe ihm innerlich verziehen gehabt, aber ich hatte ihn nicht mehr lieb). To forgive insults is a great virtue[27] but certainly not a duty. Did Freud have no reason to complain about Tausk, who had discredited him with the reproach of plagiarism? Had Tausk not also "pricked" Freud's hand? It is my impression that Federn demanded or expected saintly behavior from Freud whereas indeed nothing was further from Freud's mind than to act as a saint or to pretend saintliness. It is surprising that Federn, having presented a dark profile of Tausk's character, did not appreciate Freud's continuing to give Tausk support and recognition. At the risk of repetition, from his vantage point Federn should have been perplexed if Freud had extended "humaneness" to a man who allegedly made enemies everywhere and always and was profoundly ungrateful.

Was Federn right in his character profile of Tausk? He did not spare words in commending Tausk — for example, "exceptionally gifted" (überlegen begabt), "*grosswollend*"[28] — and he regretted the loss of "this great mind and the artistic power" (schade um den grossen Geist und die künstlerische Kraft). Yet the negative appraisal prevails. I doubt that it was generally valid but may have described correctly the way Tausk behaved toward Federn, as we will now see.

Federn certainly was entitled to respond ambivalently

---

[27]True forgiveness, however, ought to lead to restoring of a former state of love and friendship.

[28]*Grosswollend* is a nonce word that may be understood as "desiring the great" but with a shade of pretense, as in "wanting to act like a great one."

to Tausk, for Tausk had been provokingly ungrateful to Federn. Federn was one of the analysts who had helped to finance Tausk's medical studies, but Tausk had caused Federn embarrassment by trying to seduce his wife (Roazen, 1969). It can hardly be expected that under such complex conditions Federn would be able to be objective in his assessment of the total situation. Furthermore, one must account for the subjective responses that are evoked by suicide. On hearing of a suicide, those who were close to the victim respond with a feeling of guilt. The first reaction, as far as I have observed, is almost regularly one of self-reproach for not having given greater care to the deceased. Federn evidently responded with a self-reproach, since he wrote: "That we were unable to hold Tausk [among us] is a shame for us" (Dass wir Tausk nicht halten konnten, ist eine Schande für uns). But he was in a peculiar position, for he would have done his utmost for Tausk had Tausk not responded to his advances with hostility. Thus he could not well regret having been negligent. It is significant that his reasoning became quite contradictory. He wrote: "But *he* [Tausk] was *not* good as little as Freud was good" (Federn's italics)[29] (Aber *er* war *nicht* gut — so wenig Freud gut war). Yet he quickly contradicted this reproach: "Freud has so much love for human beings that he can be good" (Freud hat soviel Liebe für Menschen, dass er gut sein kann), only to contradict himself once more: "But in old age he became always more hard [unfeeling]" (aber im Alter ist er immer mehr hart geworden), which, in turn, is partly undone: "and that is understandable in Freud because he too has to lead a life that is unworthy of his greatness" (und das ist bei Freud begreiflich, weil auch er

[29]Perhaps more idiomatically: "But he [Tausk] was *not* good; he lacked this attribute as much as Freud did."

ein Leben führen muss, dass seiner Grösse unwürdig ist). Thus one observes a criss-crossing of arguments and counterarguments. Tausk's suicide created temporarily a crisis in Federn as a result of which he was led to have doubts in the psychoanalytic method: "The rigor of the method which Freud teaches hardens human beings and alienates them from their fellow-beings" (Die methodische Härte, die Freud lehrt, macht die Menschen hart und entfremdet sie den Mitmenschen). These are strange words for Federn, who never uttered anything of its like in print or in his teachings. It is hardly to be assumed that he made a secret of his criticism of Freud and of psychoanalysis, since he wrote and taught for many more years and his was not a type of personality that would conceal his convictions. His harsh words about psychoanalysis must have been a momentary reaction to the distressing news he had received.

That Freud—as stated above—felt irritated and annoyed by Tausk is highly probable, and he apparently had expressed his negative feelings to Federn, but it is unclear why Federn felt resentment about Freud's emotional response to Tausk, particularly since he had to acknowledge that Freud continued to act affirmatively toward Tausk.

Oddly enough, there is no evidence that Tausk himself may have taken exception to Freud's response to him,[30] aside from the passing regret that he was not accepted as a patient, a decision which Federn apparently did not have in mind when he was critical of Freud. What Federn possibly meant was that *for a person like Tausk* Freud's alleged withdrawal of "humaneness" was too much to bear. It is possible that Federn projected his own feelings

[30]Unless Tausk's letter to Lou Andreas-Salomé of March is taken as such.

into the situation. The unconscious background of Federn's interpretation of the motive that lea to Tausk's suicide might have been: "If Freud should ever lower his opinion of me, I would not be able to tolerate it."

The other question to be answered concerns what Federn actually had known about Tausk when he wrote the letter. Direct communication between the two had been stalled for many months. Moreover, he had not yet read Tausk's farewell letter to Freud. This letter alone must later have convinced him that it was not Freud's alleged turning away that motivated Tausk. In addition, he did not know of some of the changes that had recently taken place in Tausk's personal life, which will be discussed in the next section. Two days after Tausk's funeral, that is, on July 8, he wrote his wife: "I am thinking often of him [Tausk] and do not dare to visit his folks. Also because I cannot talk openly about everything" (Ich denke oft an ihn und traue mich nicht seine Leute zu besuchen. Auch, weil ich nicht offen über Alles reden kann). In the first letter he had been quite frank with his wife. In the second, however, he did not share with her the knowledge of what he wished to leave undiscussed if he had occasion to pay respects to Tausk's family. Evidently he had been apprised of something he did not consider fit to be discussed with his wife, much less with Tausk's family.

Thus, one is forced to conclude that Federn's letter of July 3 can be used more as a source of information regarding his own reaction to Tausk's suicide, as well as regarding the recent patterns of Tausk's behavior toward him, than as information about the possible motives that led Tausk to suicide (see Neumarkt, 1977).

IV. A Proximate Cause
of Tausk's Suicide

In his last will, written at 1:30 a.m. shortly before his suicide, Tausk gave a reason for the act he was about to take. The cause was purportedly his certainty that if he married his fiancée, Hilde Loewi (1895–1976), he would be bound to cause himself and her nothing but conflicts and torments.

The letter presently to be reproduced, however, gives evidence that Tausk's personal situation at the time of his suicide was more complex and graver than his words would make the reader believe. In particular, it explains why Tausk, in view of his forebodings, did not simply break off the engagement, as he had done several times after his divorce (Roazen, 1969).

The letter was sent by Dr. Olga Knopf (1889–1978) to Anna Freud. I reproduce it in full; it provides information which brings the reader an important step closer to an explanation of Tausk's suicide.

(A) A Letter Concerning Tausk's Suicide[1]

June 12, 1970

Dear Miss Freud:

Ever since Paul Roazen's book, "Brother Animal," appeared, I have wanted to write to you and set the record straight about the circumstances that precipitated Dr. Tausk's death. It may be that you know about the events as they occurred. If such is the case, please forgive me for taking your time. I read in the book that Miss Loewi, his fiancée, was instructed by Dr. T to see your father. I do not know whether she did so or when she came to see him. Not having been connected with psychoanalysis in Europe, Paul Roazen did not include me in the list of sources for his book.

Yet, I was involved in the circumstances of Dr. T's death and I want you to know from me what had occurred. Mr. R plans to write a book about the early psychoanalytic years and will undoubtedly repeat some of his insinuations and accusations. Since I am advanced in years, I can no longer postpone recording the facts as they occurred.

I have been a member of the New York Psychoanalytic Society since 1940. I was born in Vienna and received my medical degree there in 1916. After having worked for almost two years in the clinic of Prof. Wagner von Jauregg (*Secundararzt*), I transferred to the Women's Clinic (*Frauenklinik*), whose chief at that time was Professor Schauta, in Decem-

[1] I owe thanks to Anna Freud for her permission to publish the letter. "T" stands for "Tausk," "R," for "Paul Roazen," and "L," for "Hilde Loewi."

ber 1917, and remained there until July 1920. In 1918 I was promoted to resident (*Internarzt*).

In the spring of 1919 I opened my own office and a few weeks later Dr. T came to see me. I had known him slightly from student days. He was accompanied by a young woman whom he introduced as his sister-in-law, the wife of his youngest brother, living in Graz. The young woman suspected she was pregnant. Not being able financially to have a family at that time, his sister-in-law had come to Vienna to seek help. She was under medium height, slender, good looking in a quiet way. Upon examination I found her to be six or seven weeks pregnant. She made such a pitiful appearance that I agreed to try everything I could to produce a miscarriage short of surgery, but I did not succeed. Slight bleeding ensued, and I saw her a few days later at the office of Dr. T, where she was staying. The young woman did not open her mouth during these two meetings; she seemed terrified and depressed. Dr. T was present both times and he, too, seemed to be downcast. Needless to say, there was no remuneration of any kind involved since the patient was the relative of a physician.

To my surprise, Dr. T telephoned me at the clinic two or three weeks later. He informed me that he and the young woman would get married in a day or two. His voice sounded strained, almost forcibly gay. I took this strain as a cover-up for his embarrassment for having prevailed on my pity under false pretenses. The next morning I learned about his suicide. All this came as quite a shock since I had taken the story of his sister-in-law at its face value. Moreover, having done something unlawful, I was afraid what might happen afterwards.

Two or three months later a Miss Loewi was admitted to the ward for pathological pregnancies, where I was in charge. She was referred by the then interim chief of the Women's Clinic, Prof. Ludwig Adler. The patient was four to five months pregnant. The pregnancy had to be interrupted because an aseptic tumor had developed at one side of the uterus. A vaginal Caesarean was performed by Dr. Adler. Recovery was uneventful.

I had never known Miss Loewi's real name and had not recognized her in her hospital outfit. It was she who revealed her identity to me as I was taking her history. Miss Loewi and I became acquainted during her stay in the hospital and it was then that she talked about the events that had taken place prior to her first consultation with me.

Miss Loewi had been a promising pianist. She consulted Dr. T professionally. He seduced her during the first consultation. She assured me that she had been a virgin to that time. He proposed marriage only after the efforts to induce a miscarriage failed. I saw her a few times after her discharge. If I recollect correctly, she left Vienna soon afterwards and eventually married. I never learned her married name.

In the light of these events, Dr. T's suicide invites a different interpretation than the one given by the author, though he may not be able to appreciate its validity since it does not fit into his preconceived ideas.

It looks to me that the suicide was precipitated by conflicts that long antedated his "competition" with Freud. If Dr. Deutsch terminated Dr. T's analysis after such a short time she must have come to specific conclusions concerning Dr. T's analyzability which, for obvious reasons, could not be divulged. No such prohibition exists in my understanding of the precipitating factors. Dr. T's relationship to women was his greatest problem, as described in R's book and the rumors that had flown around campus when we were students bear ample witness to these conflicts. There was no future in a second marriage that was entered under duress and so long as he was not able to keep his impulses under control. There was also no future for his career should his inclinations become public knowledge. The manner of the suicide comes closer to an execution than to a self-inflicted death.

All this may not fit into R's ideas about his hero and do not make Freud into the villain that R depicts him.

I have postponed making this statement for obvious reasons, especially because R saw fit not only to name Miss L by her full name but he also gave her exact address, as if he wanted to be sure there would be proper identification. And, for all I know she may have survived the Hitler regime and still be living.

If there is no need to make these facts public, I would appreciate their simply being incorporated into the archives, at least until after the death of his sons, that of Miss L and my own.

If you wish to have the deposition in affidavit form, I shall be glad to comply.

Sincerely yours,

[Signed] Olga Knopf, M.D.

Dr. Knopf later limited the restriction of publication to her own lifetime. Of those to whose lifetime Dr. Knopf's original restrictions were bound, only Prof. Dr. Marius Tausk is still living.

This letter, as will be seen below, is a key document that explains why Tausk felt powerless to continue. It is to be expected that those who propounded the thesis of Freud's responsibility for Tausk's suicide will consider its content unbelievable and raise doubts as to the reliability of both the document and its author. I therefore shall discuss both.

(B) THE RELIABILITY OF THE DOCUMENT

The genuineness of the letter cannot be doubted. It was written spontaneously by Dr. Knopf, and she confirmed its content in a subsequent interview. The most convincing confirmation of a statement whose content sounds unbelievable is always, of course, the number of those who corroborate it. Yet in this instance, all those who might have been in a position to corroborate the central event in Dr. Knopf's report are gone. The record of Hilde Loewi's surgery is no longer available at the Vienna University Hospital. Thus, I have to limit myself to an examination of the document's inner consistency, the correctness of details accessible to corroboration, and the motives of the informant.

In checking the peripheral data in Dr. Knopf's communication, I shall follow the sequence in which they appear there. The roster of the American Psychoanalytic Association lists Dr. Knopf as having been an active member since 1940. The Archives of the University of Vienna indicate that Dr. Knopf was born on November 20, 1889 and graduated in medicine on June 22, 1916.

The Archives do not contain any record of her post-graduate training, but there is evidence of her work at the psychiatric clinic under Wagner-Jauregg. She was called as a witness in an investigation against Wagner-Jauregg. Her testimony is contained in the unpublished record of the War Archives in Vienna (138/19–42). The content of her deposition makes it clear that she had worked extensively at the psychiatric clinic of the University of Vienna.

I was unable to obtain evidence regarding Dr. Knopf's training in gynecology and obstetrics. She reports that she worked at Schauta's clinic. Friedrich Schauta (1849–1919) was professor at the University of Vienna and chief of the *I. Frauenklinik* at the *Allgemeine Krankenhaus* (1889–1919) (Lesky, 1965, p. 476).[2]

Dr. Knopf's report that she opened her own office in 1919 is confirmed. In the Viennese telephone directory of 1919 one finds the following entry (the preceding directories do not contain it): "Olga Knopf, Frauenärztin (ord. 2–3), II, Blumauergasse 2," which meant that she was a physician for women and her office hours were from 2 to 3 P.M. Further, she reports that Dr. Ludwig Adler (1878–1958) performed the gynecological operation in 1919. The Archives of the University of Vienna show that Adler graduated in medicine in 1900, became a *Dozent* in gynecology and obstetrics in 1912, and was given the title of professor extraordinary in 1919. He was the acting chief of the *I. Frauenklinik* from 1919 to 1920, evidently temporarily filling the vacancy after Schauta's death. He came to this country in 1938 and became chief of the gynecological department at Beth Israel Hospital in New York. The correctness of these peripheral data at least confirms that Olga Knopf had the opportunity of obtain-

[2]Most of the University Clinics in Vienna were divided between two chiefs.

ing the material testimony. There is, furthermore, one detail which strongly speaks in favor of her veracity. She reports that Tausk introduced his later fiancée as the wife of a brother who, as Prof. Dr. Tausk confirmed, lived in Graz, the capital of the Austrian province in Styria. Even though the confirmation of this detail is not conclusive proof of Dr. Knopf's veracity, it vastly increases the credibility of her testimony. At the same time it would prove the reliability of her memory, at least for some details of events that had occurred about half a century earlier.

Only recently one of the more improbable details in Dr. Knopf's report was confirmed in an interview that Prof. Dr. Tausk granted Thérèse Neyant-Sutterman (1978, p. 748): he recalled that Hilde Loewi told him on the only occasion that they met, shortly after his father's death, of how she became acquainted with him: "She had gone to consult him about neurotic difficulties. At the end of the conversation, she asked him if she should come back, and Tausk, as she claimed, answered, 'You must come back, you belong to me,' and then allegedly — according to her — he took her into his arms" (Elle était allée le consulter pour des difficultés neurotiques. A l'issue de l'entretien, elle lui avait demandé si elle devait revenir et Tausk lui aurait répondu, 'tu dois revenir, tu m'appartiens,' puis il l'aurait serrée dans ses bras). Thus it seems proved, unless Hilde Loewi did not tell the truth, that the professional barrier between therapist and patient was stepped over at their first meeting, as Dr. Knopf had reported.

(C) The Reliability of the Author

A possible point of doubt may be found in Dr. Knopf's insistence on anonymity. Indeed, the problem of anonymity is challenging. Does it speak against the reliability of an informant that he insists on anonymity (cf. Roazen, 1972)? I doubt that the question can be answered in principle with a straightforward "yes" or "no," since the surrounding circumstances will make the one or the other more likely to be correct. Anonymity for obvious reasons is often used by persons who write letters to make denunciations. The quest for anonymity in the case of a document like the one presented above falls into a different category.

Dr. Olga Knopf found herself in a difficult situation. She did not hesitate to associate her name with a report (videotaped at the Mt. Sinai Hospital) on the observations she had made of Tausk during her student days. But with regard to the content of the letter, she was in a rather precarious situation in two respects. She revealed information she had received in her medical capacity. There are quite a few who insist that such information remains privileged even after the patient's demise (although I believe that that restraint has not yet found general acceptance). Furthermore, in the Vienna of those days and also in the United States at the time the letter was written, an attempt at abortion was a criminal act. Dr. Knopf admitted in her communication that she had made herself guilty of that very action. Thus the two relevant factors are sufficient to make her request for anonymity during her lifetime understandable. If anything, an attempt by Dr. Knopf to gain publicity through her very surprising knowledge would have aroused my suspicion.

Thus one has to say that a request for anonymity in itself speaks neither for nor against an informant's reliability. Only context and circumstance may make one more probable than the other.[3] In the instance under consideration, I do not find any reason to view Dr. Knopf's request for anonymity as a signal to question the reliability of her information.

It also may be asked what Dr. Knopf's motives were in sending the letter to Anna Freud. There was a time when adherents of psychoanalysis raised the argument, in discussions with opponents, that an unanalyzed person was in no position to weigh objectively the pros and cons of Freud's theories. Even though this argument has not lost its theoretical validity, one hardly ever encounters it at present. Indeed, its force may have been overrated at the time when it was used, and it is preferable to discuss theories exclusively on their own merits. Yet, oddly enough, as if contemporary analysts should be punished for the "sins" of the older generation, they are called "orthodox" when they express the belief and conviction that Freud was by and large correct in his observations and theories and was an honest, admirable person. In that moment they are in danger of losing credibility in the public eye. At present the fact that an analyst has no serious objection to Freud's opus is taken as proof of "orthodoxy" and makes him *ab ovo* biased, that is, a person whose judgment is not to be trusted.

Dr. Knopf was not an "orthodox" analyst. She belonged to the Adlerian school for a long portion of her professional career. I do not know why she switched to the psychoanalytic group. Her writings do not represent an "orthodox" view. In her book, *Successful Aging: The Facts and Fallacies of Growing Old* (1977), she referred

[3]I wish to emphasize what may easily be overlooked — readiness to be identified as a source of information should sometimes be a warning against its reliability.

only once to Freud, and erroneously at that.[4] She was certainly free of the stigma of so-called orthodoxy. As far as I know, she never met Anna Freud. Thus she did not belong to any inner circle and one can hardly ascribe to her a desire to "whitewash" Freud. She incurred no favors or other advantages by her communication. Nor can one detect the possibility that she received narcissistic gratification by doing so, since she insisted that she be identified posthumously, if at all. Indeed, if she had published what she knew about Tausk in 1971, she might easily have caused a sensation similar to that occasioned by Roazen's book. There was no indication that she wished to move into the limelight. Her aversion to publicity and her insistence on anonymity, if anything, support my belief that her information deserves full credence.

Errors of memory cannot, of course, be excluded in a report of events that occurred five decades earlier, and as will be seen, there is a puzzling detail in the report.

All in all, one has to conclude that it is assured that Hilde Loewi became pregnant by Tausk, that Tausk wanted her to abort, that Tausk committed suicide knowing that he left her with an illegitimate pregnancy, and that the pregnancy was interrupted only after his death. The circumstances of that interruption will be discussed in the following.

(D) Circumstances of the Termination of Hilde Loewi's Pregnancy

Tausk's suicide confronted Freud with two immediate issues: how to deal publicly with a tragedy that gravely

---

[4]In discussing mastery of traumata by active repetition, she gives as a source Freud's *Three Essays* of 1905 instead of *Beyond the Pleasure Principle*, which was published fifteen years later.

compromised psychoanalysis in the community (an issue I shall take up in discussing Tausk's obituary), and an even graver and more difficult problem, that of Hilde Loewi's tragic situation.

Hilde Loewi was a close friend of a late analyst, a woman to whom she confided the whole story of her relationship with Tausk. However, Hilde Loewi had demanded from her friend that she bind herself by oath never to reveal anything to anybody of what she had communicated to her, an oath the colleague kept. I met Hilde Loewi's husband after she had died in 1976. She herself adamantly refused to be interviewed. Her husband knew next to nothing about his wife's relationship to Tausk. He told me only that the few times she mentioned him she called him "the madman" (der Wahnsinnige). The only pertinent fact he reported was that his wife met Freud several times after Tausk's death. My analytic colleague had written about a single visit. The number of meetings is irrelevant, as long as one knows for certain that Freud was informed about the state of affairs in which Hilde Loewi found herself. Hilde Loewi could not have waited too long before turning to Freud for advice and help. I conjecture that she held psychoanalysis, that is, Freud, responsible for her desperate situation. Even today, when psychoanalysis is a profession shared by a large number of practicing physicians, an individual analyst's indiscretions are laid at the door of psychoanalysis. This makes it all the more probable that this must have happened in the Vienna of 1919, when only few practiced it and Freud's name was identified with the field. Hilde Loewi would have been justified in inveighing against Freud. Freud had recommended Tausk to patients and Tausk had been an outstanding, officially acknowledged and recognized representative of the small group to whom the practice of psychoanalysis was entrusted. Under such circumstances, Hilde Loewi should have rightly expected that the group would feel responsible for what one of its prominent members had done to her.

The alleged fact of her virginity at the time she met Tausk seemed to prove her innocence and Tausk's full responsibility. To let that poor woman struggle on her own and refuse to take any further responsibility was hardly feasible. Despite the free sexual mores which I presume were prevalent during a period that followed the collapse of the monarchy, when society was in a state of reorganization and burdened by deteriorating economic conditions, an illegitimate pregnancy was a grave matter in the social group to which Hilde Loewi belonged. I further conjecture that Freud discussed the whole situation with his closest collaborators. In that case the necessity of helping Hilde Loewi must have been an important consideration in their deliberations, and it may well have led to a strategy of how to proceed.

It is clear from Dr. Knopf's letter that the "aseptic tumor" appeared like a *deus ex machina* at the end of a Greek tragedy. It made possible the resolution of a complex situation which otherwise would have been bare of a tolerable termination.

Dr. Knopf's letter reports an unlikely combination of diagnosis and treatment which may even seem contradictory. She reports that "an aseptic tumor had developed at one side of the uterus." Dr. Bernard Berglas, whom I consulted not only because he is a noted gynecologist but also because he worked at the *I. Frauenklinik* until 1928 and was therefore familiar with the Viennese scene, pointed out that an extrauterine tumor would have required a laparotomy. Furthermore, a tumor in the adnexa would not have been an indication for terminating the pregnancy. Dr. Knopf apparently took the history, and we do not know the final diagnosis that was attached to the patient in order to make the interruption of pregnancy legal.

At any rate, the patient was referred by the Chief of Service and surgery was performed by him, which Dr. Berglas tells me was against routine and custom. Under ordinary circumstances, a member of the staff would have operated. It is evident that Hilde Loewi was supported by favoritism that came from the top. Dr. Berglas reports that the statement of the Chief of Service was treated like gospel, whatever it may have been. It was not feasible to contradict it.

I also had an opportunity to obtain Dr. Ernest W. Kulka's opinion. He was well acquainted with Dr. Adler, since Dr. Kulka regularly assisted at Dr. Adler's operations after the latter's arrival in the United States and after Dr. Adler's death took over his practice.

He describes Dr. Adler as a warm-hearted person who was ready to help patients in stressful situations. Thus he treated poor patients free of charge. Dr. Kulka says that it would have been in keeping with his character to resort to all available means to help a patient under the desperate circumstances in which Hilde Loewi found herself after Tausk's suicide. He is certain that Dr. Knopf recalled the terminology incorrectly when she mentioned the diagnosis of "aseptic tumor," since this term was not in use.

He suggested that the diagnosis may have been that of a benign tumor such as uterine fibroid or benign ovarian tumor. It is extremely rare for such a condition to be an indication for interruption of pregnancy. Dr. Kulka confirmed that the Chief of Service had undisputed power to resort to any operative procedure which he declared to be medically indicated. Thus Adler probably declared — more or less arbitrarily — that a benign tumor adjoining the uterus made an interruption of pregnancy desirable.

Since at that time an abdominal approach presented considerable risk, a vaginal approach was preferable. This pseudomedical justification of an abortion, which at that time was considered a crime, suggests strongly that Adler, who was an excellent diagnostician, used his all-powerful position as chief to help this unfortunate patient, using a fabricated diagnosis to protect himself against legal consequences.

Michael Meyer calls to my attention that Olga Knopf, whose English was not perfect, may not have been aware that the description "at one side of the uterus" could be understood as referring to an extrauterine tumor. She may have had in mind a laterally situated intrauterine tumor. He also suggests the possibility of a hydatidiform mole. But this would have led to hemorrhage and Dr. Knopf would not have spoken of a tumor. I am inclined to ascribe the unusual reference to an "aseptic" tumor to Olga Knopf's desire to make sure that her previous attempt at an abortion had not led to an infectious process and that the condition that allegedly enforced termination was unconnected with her earlier intervention.

Thus it is probable that someone of Freud's inner circle, if not he himself, established a connection with Adler and received a promise to solve Hilde Loewi's desperate plight.[5] An interruption of pregnancy was a crime, but

---

[5]How Hilde Loewi came to Adler is not germane in this context. For whatever it might be worth, it can be added in favor of my conjecture that Hilde Loewi's sister told me that Adler was not a family friend, and that she never heard his name mentioned.

evidently the Chief of Service was able to carry it out under the proper pretext.

Dr. Berglas as well as Dr. Kulka could not tell me whether it was customary in the twenties, as at present, to have any surgically removed tissue examined histologically. Thus it is possible that the incriminating matter was made to disappear as soon as it had been brought to light and that Adler felt free to dictate into the record whatever was suitable.

If the hypothesized meeting of Freud and his collaborators took place in fact, then the collaborators must have then decided to preserve the strictest silence. The reasons are rather obvious. If the truth had become a matter of public knowledge, the consequences would have been disastrous for all concerned. The standing psychoanalysis held in the opinion of the majority would have deteriorated even more, and there would have been agreement that not only psychoanalytic theories but psychoanalysts as well were immoral. Further, at that time, men were still sufficiently Victorian to be protective of a woman's reputation, and the concern to maintain Hilde Loewi's reputation unharmed should have been considerable. Also it should be taken into consideration that the solution found was not entirely without legal jeopardy. Last but not least, an indiscretion would have imperiled Tausk's reputation. It may be taken for granted that maximal precautions were taken against adding any possible aggravation to the terrible shock the family had suffered merely by the fact of suicide. The strategy was well thought out.

Indeed, had a gynecologist who was in the know not turned psychoanalyst and had Roazen not published the book that forced her hand, the true background of Tausk's tragedy would have remained buried forever.

On the other hand, Roazen claimed throughout the book that there was a secret attached to Tausk's suicide that analysts close to Freud held back, allegedly in order to protect Freud's reputation. Even though he did not present evidence and all surviving analysts supported his research, he possibly sensed a factor that found no documentation but actually may have had a bearing on those analysts who knew the details surrounding Tausk's tragedy. Dr. Knopf's letter then would at long last bring to light that which those analysts had been reluctant to reveal.

V. Tausk's Suicide

I have given a general outline of Tausk's psychopathology in Chapter II. Here I report events that are possible signposts on the downhill course his life was taking. In this context I think of an annotation Tausk wrote under a compilation of his poems:

> The poems here collected originated in decisive times of my life and reveal the true state of my emotions. This compilation represents the termination of a precious mental activity that was earlier very dear to me. For a long time I have been unable to write the metrical language. Now I do not have any longing for it. Vienna, January 1915.[1]

[1]Die hier gesammelten Gedichte sind in entscheidenden Zeiten meines Lebens entstanden und verraten meinen wirklichen Gemütszustand. Diese Zusammenstellung stellt den Abschluss einer mir früher sehr lieben und wertvollen geistigen Betätigung dar. Ich

In a man of delicate mental balance like Tausk creative outlets are of inestimable importance. Whether the poems he wrote were of great or minor value is not the question. The act of composing poetry per se might easily have been a safeguard against the deleterious effects of conflicts for Tausk. According to Prof. Dr. Tausk, his father never took up writing poetry again. It is not known whether the blockage of this channel was voluntary and may have had secondary consequences or whether the block itself was the result of a change in personality structure leading to a general reduction of the creative potential.

Be that as it may, it remains now to reconstruct, using the documentation and eyewitness reports that have reached posterity, the proximate happenings that ended in the catastrophe of July 3.

(A) Tausk's Recent Psychopathology and Adjustment to Civilian Life

In the foregoing, I have referred to signs suggestive of a structural impairment in Tausk's personality. His request that Freud analyze him, and possibly the difficulties he met with in his practice, seemed to me to point to such an impairment. An early sign of it was his pathological behavior at the Fifth International Psychoanalytic Congress, which took place in Budapest September 28 and 29, 1918. In Tausk's obituary Freud wrote: "[There] Dr. Tausk who had long been suffering from physical ill health was already showing signs of unusual nervous irritability"[2] (Freud, 1919, p. 274). From a passage in

kann schon seit langer Zeit nicht mehr in gebundener Sprache schreiben. Nun habe ich auch kein Bedürfnis danach. . . .

[2]In this context it is worthwhile to remind the reader that Tausk had earlier shown signs of emotional lability. When he presented

Federn's letter to his wife, one receives an inkling of what the manifestations of that irritability may have been. In that letter Federn refers to the insults he had been subjected to by Tausk. The context makes it clear that this had happened in Budapest. The word Federn used was *beschimpfen*, which means "to insult by the use of offensive words." Tausk apparently lost his temper during the Congress and burst into a rage. A public display of rage was, of course, unusual. It was explained as a consequence of Tausk's experiences during the war. However, so far as one can determine from the official records, Tausk's war experiences were not arduous. According to the Austrian War Archives, Tausk started his military service on August 2, 1915. Two months later he was assigned as senior physician of the psychiatric ward at the military hospital in Kowel, now in the western Soviet Union, twenty miles from the Polish border and ninety miles east of Lublin; Tausk was transferred to the latter city on December 5, 1915 with the same function. From August 10, 1916 to December he was treated for tubercular pulmonary apicitis at the sanitarium in Grimmenstein (Lower Austria). From December 1916 to the end of the war he was assigned as neurologist to the military government of Serbia in Belgrade. The transfer to the Balkans occurred because of his health. He was decorated with the *Franz-Josefs-Orden*. The last two years as neurologist in Belgrade were spent under relatively comfortable conditions. He was well provided for, as he wrote his former wife. He was joined by his sons and maintained a relationship with Kosa Lazarević (Roazen, 1969).

Can one reconstruct the basis for Tausk's aggressive

---

his first paper to the Vienna Association in 1909, he reached a point where he "declared that he could not go on" because of weariness (Nunberg and Federn, vol. 2, p. 336).

behavior? Federn, as mentioned above, had been one of his financial benefactors, and Tausk had previously attempted to seduce his wife. In 1914 he started an argument with Federn about a question of priority (Nunberg and Federn, vol. 4, p. 225). One obtains the impression that Tausk had been particularly abrasive in discussions of Federn's papers. Thus, in the Minutes of the discussion following Federn's paper of March 14, 1914, one reads that "Tausk considers only topic and title to be of value; he cannot accord any recognition to the exposition" (ibid., p. 242). One wonders whether Federn's paper was really that bad, since "Prof. Freud characterizes the paper as a valuable achievement, even if it was lacking in ultimate clarity" (ibid., p. 242).

I conjecture, however, that Federn was not the sole object of Tausk's anger in Budapest. Obviously the Congress stood under the hallmark of the ongoing war.[3] War neuroses, which were considered to be traumatic neuroses, occupied the center of attention, and everyone must have spoken of trauma. Ernst Simmel (1882–1947) had worked out a method to cure traumatic neuroses based on psychoanalysis, and I suppose that he was (like Grinker, who during World War II developed a psychopharmacological treatment of war neuroses) celebrated like a newly discovered star. Tausk, I conjecture, was irate that an upstart who had been an unknown among psychoanalysts should earn laurels and be spoken about by everyone. It must have stung him that he had missed

[3]Representatives of the German and Austrian Army were delegated to the meeting, which was an extraordinary event in the history of psychoanalysis. The reason for that interest in psychoanalysis had to do with the psychiatric disorders that had become rampant among soldiers and which official psychiatry did not seem to have been able to cope with satisfactorily.

the boat. His contribution to war psychiatry was a paper (Tausk, 1916a) to which I have referred above and which could not compare with Simmel's contribution. It was devoted to a peripheral question of moderate interest. The importance of Tausk's lasting contribution to war psychiatry, his article "On the psychology of the deserter" (Tausk, 1916b) was probably not recognized and therefore not acknowledged at that time. Furthermore, the paper Tausk presented as the last one on the second day of the meeting concerned the topic "Psychoanalysis of the function of judgment" [Psychoanalyse der Urteilsfunktion]. The audience cannot have been either large or enthusiastic about an abstract subject after the excitement of the preceding day, which had been devoted to the psychoanalysis of the war neuroses.

Thus Tausk must have felt isolated and discouraged. Previously he may have reconciled himself halfway with the fact that Freud, the leader, earned all the glory even though that glory was based, as he thought, partly on his own role of adding momentum and content to Freud's ideas. But, then, he should at least be the first among Freud's followers. It is also possible that at the Congress there was an announcement (or at least a rumor) regarding the psychoanalytic papers for which the newly created prizes would be awarded. The selection covered the period 1914–1918 and was made by Freud, who gave the prizes to Simmel, Abraham, and Reik. To Tausk it must have meant losing a contest and being officially and publicly moved to a secondary place. Thus he probably felt seriously threatened in Budapest, possibly even forever deprived of a favored position close to Freud.

In view of his ambitions and sensitivity, it also may have meant to him that he was the victim of an injustice. All this is hypothetical, but it would explain the outbreak of uncontrollable rage against a scapegoat such as Federn, who, as a matter of fact, became Freud's deputy five years later and stood closer than Tausk to Freud already in 1918. Tausk's condition of acute irritability in Budapest strongly suggests that a weakening of structure had occurred, that pent-up energy was explosively discharged in disregard of the reality situation and, as is often described, that the ability to postpone discharges in conformity with the reality principle was weakened.

This manifestation undoubtedly reflected a temporary disturbance, since no evidence of acute irritability was reported by those who met him after his discharge from the army (which occurred shortly thereafter), and his objectionable behavior in Budapest was held against him neither by Freud nor by his colleagues.

The transition to civilian life was no predicament, at the beginning. In a letter of November 7, 1918, he let his former wife know that he was starting his practice. However, he was concerned lest his military suitcase that contained "my entire work of eight years" (meine ganze Arbeit von acht Jahren) be lost. He had sent her recently 470 Kronen, evidently for support of the children.

Four days later he answered her letter that had arrived in the meantime. Apparently he had sent her provisions before his military discharge, since he assured her that they were for her and the children. "I myself do not need anything. . . . I am eating expensively and well in restaurants" (Ich selbst brauche nichts. . . . Ich esse teuer und gut im Gasthaus).

In a letter of December 4, he promised her to send 150 Kronen more than before per month:

> Indeed, it flutters in my head, I have not yet earned anything; the patients Freud sent did not come, also

people do not want to spend money, because they need everything for food.... The other physicians, too, have nothing to do. Further, the people who came from the provinces of the former monarchy are missing....[4]

On January 7, 1919 he wrote apparently in reply to his former wife's complaint that she did not have enough money: "That all money is too little, I unfortunately know from my own experience, no elucidations are necessary.... Still no change in my practice for the better" (Dass alles Geld zu wenig ist, weiss ich leider selber, da bedarf es keiner Erläuterungen.... Meine Praxis ändert sich noch immer nicht zum besseren); in the same letter he mentioned that her brother, too, was having difficulties and looking in vain for a job.

The letter of February 13 sounds triumphant: "Money problem already settled, from now on 1000 Kronen monthly as long as the practice continues well.... No time for Lucy, aversion to literature, particularly female [one].... Nothing else of consequence, only inordinately much work" (Geldfrage schon erledigt, von nun an 1000.-K monatlich, so lange die Praxis so gut geht.... Für Lucy keine Zeit, Literaturabneigung bes. feminine. ... Sonst nichts von Belang, nur enorme Arbeit).

The reader will recall that this propitious situation did not last. Tausk might have derived narcissistic compensation from the fact that he was appointed again as before the war by the Psychoanalytic Association as lecturer.

[4]Freilich schwirrt mir der Kopf, ich habe noch nichts verdient, die Patienten die Freud geschickt hat, sind nicht gekommen, auch will das Volk kein Geld ausgeben, weil es alles fürs Essen braucht. ... Auch die anderen Ärzte haben nichts zu tun. Dann fehlen die Leute aus den alten Bestandteilen der Monarchie....

Tausk's doubts regarding attendance of the course he had announced, mentioned above, were not realized. The official *Zeitschrift* of 1919 (p. 138) reports that the first course in elementary psychoanalysis was finished in March. The summer course would start in the middle of May and if enough participants registered, an advanced course would be added. Further, inasmuch as Tausk had been the speaker of the evening before the Association on two occasions within the eight months between his return to Vienna and his suicide, his official *persona* had become quickly rooted in the prewar functional setup.

Yet it is possible that this was only a screen which covered serious professional problems. I think here of his letter to Freud communicating considerable difficulties with his patients, using the word "woes" (Kümmernisse), a strong term which calls forth pity, and further the reference in Federn's letter to Tausk's having acted out with his patients. Thus there are hints that Tausk's adjustment to civilian practice did not proceed optimally.

(B) Tausk's Last Meeting with His Elder Son

The last person to see Tausk before his death who is able to let us know about it was his elder son Marius, who gave a brief description of the supper he shared with his father in a restaurant before returning to Graz on July 2 (Marius Tausk, 1973). Prof. Dr. Tausk's recollection is relevant because it conveys an important clue regarding not only Tausk's last evening but also his relationship to his son. He teased Marius, who was a teetotaler, for not drinking beer, and they parted with his saying to his son: "Never mind about me" (Kümmere Dich nicht um mich) (*ibid.*, p. 332). The exact parting words and their correct interpretation are not unimportant. Prof. Dr. Tausk took them to mean "Don't follow my example, you must find your own way. Don't take me as an authority." I doubt the correctness of this opinion. Tausk must have known the importance of teetotalism as an ideal for the adolescent boy, who was a member of the "Workmen's League Against the Use of Alcohol." Teetotalism was an important movement among Socialist youth against indulgence in alcohol, as propagated by nationalistic student fraternities. From his clinical work Tausk knew of the dangers of alcoholism, a disease that filled psychiatric clinics and institutions. By insinuating that Marius should take a drink of beer, Tausk tried to induce his son to accept his own way of life and value system. By so doing, he risked interfering with the adolescent's spontaneous formation of ideals which could protect him against a widespread disorder. If Prof. Dr. Tausk should be right in his interpretation of his father's parting words, it would reveal a basic contradiction. The admonition was spoken shortly after the father's intervention of tempting the son to infringe upon the very ideal the youngster had evolved.

I am not certain that Prof. Dr. Tausk is right. *Kümmere Dich nicht um mich* means: "Do not spend a thought on me," a strange thing to tell a son. Whatever the import of these enigmatic words may have been, they are expressive of ambivalence. It goes without saying that a father's relationship to a son is not unambivalent. But such ambivalence may be well warded off and of no consequence, or all too visible and active. I believe that more than the unavoidable traces of ambivalence toward Marius can be documented. Traces of it can be discovered as far in the past as in two letters the father wrote to his seven-year-old son. Both letters were affectionate. They were written in August 1909, when the children were on vacation. Nevertheless, Tausk wrote that it seems to him that Marius does not do any school exercises (Aufgaben) and that his letter is so poorly written as to suggest that he did not practice (keine Übung). Two and a half weeks later he apologized for not having written. The letter ends with an expression of dissatisfaction with Marius's handwriting. This may sound all right. Why should a father not worry about his son's penmanship and admonish him to improve it?

When Marius was about 15 years old, he sent his father a letter of condolence "in which I must have used some cliché language and when reproached for it, gave as a (poor!) excuse that I had not given it much thought, when I wrote it" (*ibid.*, p. 330). This confession was not rewarded by the father, who believed it to be correct, "but it does not please me that you write without thinking. This does not indicate great friendship. I hope we have to say to each other more than thoughtless and ready made phrases" (*ibid.*, p. 330f.).

To write a letter of condolence is not an easy matter even for adults who are happy when the right clichés come to their minds on such an occasion. One might have expected a letter of thanks and appreciation, but not an expression of doubt about the son's friendly feelings for his father. When Marius was 16 or 17, he told his father "something to the effect that certain things, such as Darwin's *Origin of Species*, had to be taken for granted, and he replied, 'What would you have done if you had lived in the time of Copernicus?'" (*ibid.*, p. 332).

In this last episode the ambivalence comes openly to the fore. The adolescent found a system of thought which apparently gave him security and orientation, an achievement which should have given the father, who himself was scientifically minded, pleasure and have made him optimistic regarding his son's future. After all, it was a good sign that the boy, who was baptized and grew up in the provincial environment of a Catholic country, despite the years of great political turmoil formed an outlook on the world that was rooted in science. What could be the rationale of asking the adolescent what he would have done in a prescientific era? One hears here again Tausk making statements that inadvertently might have the tendency to undermine the boy's morale, as was observed when Tausk tried to induce his son to drink beer. The nagging started with his son's handwriting, continued with the sharp reprimand for the letter of condolence, and now turned even against the boy's belief in science and finally aimed at endangering a self-chosen ideal. And yet despite all this unwisdom, the son evolved an excellent relationship to his father, preserving an ideal view of him and a heart full of love and affection (Marius Tausk, 1973, *passim*), and made a brilliant career. It is important to stress that Tausk as an absentee father apparently did not cause damage. If the son had grown up with his father, the upshot might have been different. There were short reunions which made the father and the son very happy. But the tendency to disappoint the son, to establish a very close relationship, and then to abandon him, to nag, to criticize, is unmistakable.

In his relationship to his son one discovers Tausk's tendency to disappoint those who loved him. (Of course, it should not be supposed that this tendency manifested itself in all relations.) Be that as it may, it is important to hold fast the details of his acting out toward Marius, because they were contrary to his words. As mentioned before, he was almost constantly worried about his sons and preoccupied with their welfare, particularly with that of Marius. Therefore, Prof. Dr. Tausk is convinced that his father was a very good father (Marius Tausk, 1973). And indeed, if words were reliable indications of goodness, he would be right. Yet when there is a gap between word and action — and this was certainly present in Tausk's relationship to his elder son — then the negative attitude has won over affection and care. Jekel's apposite statement that only a good son can be a good father is also applicable to Tausk. Rarely has a father disappointed a more loving son than Tausk did. If love of his child had been strong in him, he would never have contemplated suicide.

It is noteworthy that Tausk did not tell his son that he intended to marry the next day, although he told him that he would attend his fiancée's concert that evening. As a matter of fact, he never introduced Marius to his prospective stepmother. Did he know that this was the last time he would see his son, whom he so dearly loved? It is not probable, for one would expect a more intense display of emotions in a moment of heartbreaking tragedy.

In later years Prof. Dr. Tausk had feelings of guilt "for not having sensed the magnitude of the conflict that must have raged inside him" (*ibid.*, p. 332) on that occasion. Recently a letter of 1920 was found that Marius Tausk had written to Lou Andreas-Salomé, who tried to gather information about his father's tragedy. I shall come back to this letter and here quote only the following:

> About 6:30 P.M. we ate supper. Then father said he had to change now for the concert (his fiancée accompanied on the piano). I had to go to the station, and said goodbye to him. He just stood there in [his]

shirtsleeves to put on his jacket and was cheerful
and laughed.[5]

Thus one can be certain that Tausk himself was not
aware that he was torn by a grave conflict. There is no
reason to doubt the correctness of his son's recollection
that his father was serene at the moment of farewell;
this view is affirmed by a letter Tausk had written the
same day to his sister, which will be introduced presently.

(C) The Last Four Communications
Written by Tausk

Two letters addressed to Freud, a letter to his youngest
sister Nada, and his last will written at 1:30 a.m. shortly
before committing suicide have reached posterity. Since
they encompass less than the last 24 hours of his life,
their importance can hardly be overrated.

(1) Tausk's letter to his youngest sister

Tausk's sister Nada lived in Bosnia. The letter reached
her after Tausk's death. It must have been written and
mailed on July 2. It read:

Dear Nada,

Yesterday I was visited again by Mr. K., who de-
livered your package. Many thanks. The wonderful

---

[5]Um 1/2 7^h ungefähr assen wir das Nachtmal. Dann sagte Vater
er müsse sich nun unkleiden fürs Konzert (seine Braut hatte die
Klavierbegleitung). Ich musste zur Bahn gehen und nahm von ihm
Abschied. Er stand eben in Hemdärmeln da, um sich sein Jacket an-
zuziehen, und war heiter und lachte.

bacon is a highly welcome addition to my meager meals. The box with 100 oriental cigarettes is a veritable blessing.

I have become engaged. My fiancée is 24 years old; her name is Hilde Loewi, she is an extremely talented pianist and a particularly superb and understanding human being. Tomorrow we are going to the civil ceremony office. I hope I shall be much happier in my second marriage than I was in the first. Inform our dear mother.

Herzlichst
Victor[6]

This letter[7] permits the inference that Tausk felt certain — at least consciously — that he would marry on July 3, and he let his sister know that the marriage ceremony would take place the following day.[8] The letter is striking by its utter calm. It is well composed and does not betray any signs of excitement or doubt. It is, however, remark-

---

[6]Liebe Nada,/Gestern hatte ich wieder einen Besuch von Herrn K, der mir Dein Packet überbrachte. Vielen Dank. Der wunderbare Fleischspeck ist eine hochwillkommene Zubusse zu meinen kargen Mahlzeiten. Die Schachtel mit 100 Orientzigaretten ist ein wirklicher Segen./Ich habe mich verlobt. Meine Braut ist 24 Jahre alt, heisst Hilde Loewi, ist ein hochbegabte Pianistin und ein besonders feiner und verständnisvoller Mensch. Morgen gehen wir zum Standesamt. Ich hoffe, dass ich in meiner zweiter Ehe viel glücklicher sein werde als ich in der ersten war. Benachrichtige unsere liebe Mutter./Herzlichst/Victor.

[7]The original letter has not been preserved. Tausk's sister vouched for the correctness of the text since, as it happened, she had learned it by heart before it was lost.

[8]Since Tausk was converted and Hilde Loewi Jewish, the marriage had to take place at the *Standesamt*, a secular institution.

able that Tausk had waited to the last day to notify his sister and did not address himself to his mother directly. He must have known for at least three weeks that he would marry Hilde Loewi, for this was the interval that had to pass after the publication of bans, which were required by law for marriages outside the Church as well as within it.

The emotions Tausk expressed in the letter were adequate to the situation. The receipt of a food package was quite an event in those days, and Tausk was able to enjoy it. The intensification of expression when thinking of the cigarettes testifies to a differentiation which would eliminate the assumption that the letter was written perfunctorily. One might have possibly expected more passionate words about the fiancée. The reference to his first marriage might give occasion for interpretation. External circumstances were similar. Tausk's first wife, too, was pregnant when she married. The letter reflects a quiet, serene mood. There is no trace that would indicate that the writer was approaching a cataclysmic upheaval.

(2) Tausk's letter of apology to Freud

The second letter to be discussed, which was written, as I conjecture, after that to Nada, manifests an entirely different climate.

It is a key document of relevance for the explanation of Tausk's suicide. Ostensibly, it is a letter of apology for missing the next day's meeting of the Vienna Association, which Tausk had attended so faithfully. The letter may appear to have been in conformity with local custom. Yet the letter was by no means a routine letter of apology: it contained a personal message and apparently was written mainly for this purpose. After asking to be excused, he told Freud that "I am occupied with the solu-

tion of decisive concerns of my life" (Ich bin mit der Lösung meiner entscheidenden Lebensangelegenheiten be-
schäftigt). In this instance, the reader obtains evidence of
what preoccupied Tausk's mind during the day preceding
his death. It was not financial worries or resentment
about the way he was treated by Freud but an attempt at
solving a basic concern of his life. "I do not want," he
continued, "to let myself be tempted through contact
with you to want to engage your help" (Ich will mich
durch den Kontakt mit Ihnen nicht in Versuchung bring-
en lassen Ihre Hilfe in Anspruch nehmen zu wollen). The
sentence is clumsy in German as well as in English and
quite different from Tausk's usual style. It sounds heavily
laden with emotion and must have puzzled the recipient,
as also the next two sentences: "I hope I shall indeed very
soon have the freedom of being able to approach you. I
suppose [I shall] then appear with a minimum of
neurosis" (Ich werde wohl sehr bald wieder die Freiheit
haben, mich Ihnen nähern zu können. Ich gedenke dann
mit einem Minimum von Neurose aufzutreten).

Tausk was in general not reluctant to ask Freud for
help. Why did he suddenly fear the temptation of asking
for it? For what would he have had to ask Freud's help? It
must have been something extraordinary, since he had to
go so far as to avoid Freud's presence in order to fight the
temptation. What might it have been that deprived him
temporarily of the freedom of exposing himself to Freud's
presence? And what could possibly happen in the near
future that would reduce his neurosis to a minimum? The
letter is replete with references to what came to pass in
Tausk's mind at that time, but it is couched in vague,
almost mysterious insinuations.

But all the puzzles raised by this communication are
solved at one swoop when one takes cognizance of his
intention to marry Hilde Loewi the next day. When he

wrote Freud about the solution of a concern, he meant marriage. He was, when writing the letter, apparently aware of internal objections which he would have liked to discuss with Freud but thought wiser to leave unspoken. Aside from the fact that Hilde Loewi gave a concert that evening, and Tausk for that reason alone would have had to be absent from the Association, he knew that if he had familiarized Freud with the hesitations and doubts he might have harbored about the impending marriage, he would have been advised to postpone it. Tausk would then have had to admit that postponement was impossible owing to Hilde Loewi's pregnancy. Freud would have suggested abortion, which was performed frequently in Vienna, and we know what Tausk would have had to reply. It was clear to Tausk that Freud could not have contributed anything to the solution of the dilemma he was facing. It also must be considered that Tausk was temporarily determined to go ahead with his intention and any expression of his doubts would have weakened his determination. The prospect of appearing "with a minimum of neurosis" after his marriage—puzzling at first hearing—suggests two possibilities: once married, the usual conflicts about women would come to rest, or marriage would undo the feelings of guilt.

Why did Tausk not simply write: "I shall marry soon and my fiancée is giving a concert tonight. Forgive my absence." Why did Tausk conceal from Freud, as he did from his son, the fact of his impending marriage? From the fact that Federn did not know about it (he would have mentioned it in his letter to his wife), one can infer with certainty that Tausk had not told Hitschmann either, although he entertained friendly relations with him. Why this consistent secrecy about the whole matter?[9] Why did he postpone informing his youngest sister and his mother to the last possible moment?

Whereas virtually all of Tausk's letters to Freud were written in concise language, this one, if only by its unusual style, may suggest that his relationship to Freud was temporarily subdued. Since Tausk's cryptic language revolved around the impending ceremony, it is rather clear that the unusual ambiance surrounding this letter was not precipitated by anything Freud might have done to disappoint Tausk but must find its explanation in Tausk's attitude toward the event that was to take place on the following day. Biographers have overlooked the peculiarities of this letter to Freud. Only an explanation of the suicide that takes them into account can be considered satisfactory.

(3) Tausk's farewell letter to Freud

In the early hours of July 3 Tausk's intention of committing suicide had crystallized. I shall first comment on his last letter to Freud and then on his last will. It is not known in which sequence they were written. Contrary to the foregoing, the style of this letter is clear and precise The salutation "Dear Professor" (Lieber Herr Professor) was unusual, differing from his usual, more formal manner. In the first sentence he asks Freud to "stand by" (beistehen) his fiancée, whose name and address he gives. He describes her as "this most precious woman who ever stepped into my life" (dieser teuersten Frau, die je in mein Leben getreten ist). She will not ask much of him because — and this may sound almost like an inadvertent *double-*

9As far as is known, Tausk had let only Olga Knopf know of the marriage (see above), and according to Roazen (1969) his oldest sister, who was living in Vienna.

entendre — "she herself has great possibilities of happiness in herself" (sie selbst grosse Glücksmöglichkeiten in sich hat). "But she is," Tausk continued, "strongly inclined toward compulsive symptoms and identifications. She is noble, pure and good; to give her good advice is worth the effort" (Aber sie neigt stark zu Zwangssymptomen und Identifikationen. Sie ist edel, rein und gut, es lohnt die Mühe, ihr einen guten Rat zu geben). How should one interpret Tausk's telling Freud that Hilde Loewi would not ask for much of him although he must have known what her main complaint and worry would be after her fiancé's death?

One might assume that in his last letter to Freud Tausk would write the full truth. But it is highly probable that in the state of tension and excitement in which Tausk was at that time, denial was activated to its maximum, and he refused to be confronted with the grave face of reality. Thus no other channel was open than to appeal to an omnipotent father figure in the hope that he would provide solutions, as he had done so often in the past. Consequently, one of the most beautiful tributes ever written about Freud follows:

> You I thank for all the good you have given me. It was much and has filled out the last 10 years of my life.
>
> Your work is authentic and great. I am leaving life with the conviction that I was one of those who has [*sic*10] shared the course of conquest of one of the greatest ideas of mankind.11

10It may be niggling when I interpret this grammatical error. Since Tausk used the plural relative pronoun "die," the singular "has" is more offensive in German than appears in the translation. I believe the erroneous singular betokens Tausk's conviction of uniqueness in the psychoanalytic movement.

11Ihnen danke ich für alles Gute, das Sie mir gegeben. Es war viel

That in the end a father image arose uncontaminated, almost as if surrounded by a halo, requires an explanation. For in their simplicity covering the general and the particular, Tausk's words are deeply moving. It possibly would be wrong to use these words for retrospective inferences. They may have been the result of the utter defeat Tausk was experiencing in those hours. Correlated with the glorification of the father, Tausk turned with full force against himself. After assuring Freud that he was not suffering from melancholia, he wrote: "My suicide is the healthiest, most decent act of my derailed life. I do not accuse anyone, my heart is free of ill-feelings, I only die a little earlier than I would have died of a natural death" (Mein Selbstmord ist die gesündeste, anständigste Tat meines verfehlten Lebens. Ich klage niemand an, mein Herz ist frei von Groll, ich sterbe nur etwas früher, als ich eines natürlichen Todes gestorben wäre). A satisfactory explanation of Tausk's last deed will have to include the final stoppage of any aggression against the outer world and the consequent virtual raving against himself.

In the last paragraph Tausk sends his greetings to the Vienna Association and wishes for its "flourishing" (Gedeihen), and he sends his thanks to those who stood by him in his days of want. "Live well still for a long time, hale and vigorously working" (Leben Sie noch lange wohl, rüstig arbeitskräftig). In a postscript he asks Freud to look after his sons "occasionally" (manchmal).

This letter may sound like a manifesto of final reconciliation with the world, the final achievement of a

---

und hat die letzten 10 Jahre meines Lebens ausgefüllt./Ihr Werk ist echt und gross. Ich gehe aus dem Leben mit der Überzeugung, dass ich einer von denen war, die den Eroberungsgang einer der grössten Menschenideen miterlebt habe.

troubled mind that at last reaches peace with a world that had been experienced basically as hostile: the father is re-constituted, the debt to society is acknowledged, rivalry is abolished, and the exquisiteness of the beloved woman avowed.

Yet this appearance is specious for two reasons. The reality situation created for Hilde Loewi by the suicide was a disaster, and some sentences reflect the tragic rent in a human being who, even though not suffering from melancholia, was looking at himself with unrestrained contempt.

(4) Tausk's last will

Tausk, who had studied and practiced law, knew well how to set up a will and wrote his own. Since in Austria notarization and witnesses were not mandatory, he did not need to get in touch with any other person. The document's heading is: "My Testament. Vienna. July 3, 1919, 1:30 A.M."

It impresses one by the completeness of directions, pre-ciseness of data, and meticulous wording. The disposi-tions he made of his property are not of interest in this context (some have been presented above). The last two paragraphs, however, are of eminent importance. He wrote: "I depart from my life, which I [have] retrench[ed] systematically since my childhood and which, since I rec-ognize that I can no longer conduct it with pleasure, has now lost its meaning completely" (Ich gehe aus meinem Leben, das ich seit meiner Kindheit systematisch ab-baue[12] und das jetzt, da ich einsehe, dass ich es nicht

_____

[12]The word *abbauen*, which I have translated as "to retrench," is

mehr mit Freude führen kann, seinen Sinn vollkommen verloren hat).

Whereas in the letter to Freud the suicide act was presented—and thus justified—as one of health and decency, it is in this passage viewed as the result of a process starting in childhood, a process Tausk allegedly instituted himself. Tausk's statement must refer to his subjective feeling about his own past. It is possible that he responded excessively to the first signs of aging and that he therefore viewed his entire past as a systematic shrinkage.

In the next sentence he repudiates his "talent" (Begabung), saying that it is too small to give him a hold. It is strange that he, who was acknowledged as particularly talented by everyone, dismissed his creative potential as a worthwhile reason to continue living. Very probably his achievements were not commensurate with his ambitions. To be sure, it is questionable whether he had really made the best use of his innate and acquired talents. The need to act out and the inability to internalize aggression constructively stood in the way of the full flowering of his endowment. Thus the meaning of the statement may be that his talents did not protect him against self-destructive impulses, which would have been a correct insight. "The recognition," he continued, "that I cannot joyfully contract a marriage, that I can only hold myself

---

difficult to render in English. It was used in Austria in the context of employees being fired because of economic recession or depression. It also had the implication of what in chemistry is called catabolism: the metabolic change from complex to simple molecules, the decomposition of complex chemical compounds into simple ones. It is not probable that Tausk had the chemical implication in mind. But just the chemical implication symbolizes best the meaning of the term in the particular context in which it was used by Tausk.

and my beloved bride in conflicts and torments is the true conscious motive of my suicide" (Die Erkenntnis, dass ich nicht freudig eine Ehe schliessen kann, dass ich mich und meine geliebte Braut nur in Conflikten und Quälereien halten kann, ist das wahre bewusste Motiv meines Selbstmordes). Here to a certain extent fixation to the pleasure principle is given as a relevant factor.

One cannot escape recognition of an implied hypocrisy. There is in the statement an innuendo of martyrdom and self-sacrifice, as if he wanted to say: "I would rather kill myself than condemn the beloved to a life of torment." The anguish, however, that the woman has to suffer by virtue of having caused — even only indirectly — a death is far greater than the anguish caused by a broken engagement.

Then follows a farewell to his mother, siblings, and friends. He admonishes his sons to live better than he lived.[13] Everyone should forget him quickly. "I have deceived all of you with a life role to which I was not equal" (Ich habe Euch alle mit einer Lebensrolle getäuscht, der ich nicht gewachsen war).

It has been observed that some people shortly before their death reach a solution of conflicts that had remained unresolved until then. One may find traces thereof in Tausk's two final communications. One may also expect or assume that a human being who knows that his hours are numbered will say the truth and nothing but the truth. But the full truth which burdened Tausk's mind was not fit to be revealed.

The truth of which a mind may be certain does not necessarily coincide with reality. Tausk's full apparatus

[13]Lebt besser als ich lebe, liebe Söhne.

of denial, regression, and scotomization — in brief, his entire defensive apparatus — might have been activated in order to maintain a precarious psychic balance in his last hour.

The lengthy administrative part of his testament preceding the short confessional ending is sober, clear, and reality-adequate. But when he reached the subjective end, the subterranean excitement is felt. The letter to Freud appears to have been written with greater composure.

The final declaration of having lived a lie, of having deceived the world successfully, is again an extreme self-accusation which overshoots the mark, as did his statement to Freud that his suicide was the only decent deed of his life. These extreme expostulations about self do not sound like a last-hour enlargement of self-knowledge but rather like the effect of a last-hour collapse.

(D) Tausk's Relationship to Hilde Loewi

Tausk's statement about Hilde Loewi as well as Dr. Knopf's letter make it clear that Tausk's suicide was related primarily to his relationship to his fiancée. Therefore, it is high time to turn at long last to the little that is known about Hilde Loewi and her relationship to Tausk.

Tausk made her acquaintance when she was 24 years old; in 1934 she married. Soon thereafter she left Vienna and went abroad with her husband. She died childless in 1976 from ovarian cancer. Her husband emphasized her "unbounded selflessness, her outstanding gift as a musician and composer." He further informed me that Hilde Loewi came from a middle-class family in comfortable circumstances. Her father had been born in Northern

Bohemia. He owned a pharmaceutical company. The mother hailed from Slovakia. Hilde Loewi and her two siblings were born in Vienna. A brother died at twenty-two years of age of a cardiac ailment. Her sister, who was two years younger than she, was divorced from her first husband. The second marriage — to a musician — has been a happy one. She emigrated to the United States, where she still is living.

Hilde Loewi was also a music teacher. She became particularly popular and well known as an accompanist of Raoul Aslau, a leading Viennese actor who gave recitals. She composed some of the music for his appearances. Occasionally she also accompanied and coached the violinist Vasa Priboda, who was famous in his day. An entry concerning her in the somewhat garrulous *Wiener Jahrbuch der Gesellschaft* runs approximately as follows (Planer, 1929, p. 389):[14]

> Loewe, Hilde, a pianist, is well known to Viennese audiences: as highly endowed concert virtuoso, as sensitive accompanist of famous singers and, above all, as piano accompanist of *Burgtheater* actors when they presented chansons and melodramatic offerings. Whenever one sees the artist at the piano, one knows that the evening's musical accompaniment is in reliable hands. It may be less well known that Hilde Loewe hides behind male pseudonyms as the composer of songs known all over the world [Weltschlager]. She is occupied at present with setting to music an English libretto that probably will have its first performance in London.

[14]Hilde Loewi appeared in public under the name "Loewe." Her husband confirmed the correctness of the quoted article.

Hilde Loewe comes from a music-loving family. She was born in Vienna (birthday July 8th) and attended here the gymnasium since she wanted originally to study medicine. She gave up, however, that intention, graduated from the Academy of Music with honors, and since then has been active as teacher, concert virtuoso, and accompanist. Her interests are not limited to music . . . ; the artist participates intensely in all cultural problems of her time and is particularly interested in psychoanalysis. She is a passionate horseback rider, tennis player, and skier [my translation].

Her life story would indicate that hers was not a personality that was given to acting out. This is important, for her relationship with Tausk started on the occasion of their first meeting that was of a professional nature (Neyant-Sutterman, 1978, p. 748). As she told Olga Knopf, she was a virgin. This, despite her age of twenty-four, would not have been unusual at that time, although it may so strike a contemporary reader.

The possibility that she did not speak the truth cannot be excluded with certainty. It must be said that her case against Tausk was strong enough without having to add such a detail. Her story acquires verisimilitude by virtue of what Lea Rosen, who knew Tausk intimately, told Prof. Heinz Winnik in an interview: "Tausk was out only for young girls, if possible, for virgins" (Tausk war nur auf junge Mädchen aus, möglichst Jungfrauen). The contemporary to whom virginity has lost any meaning and value cannot imagine how highly it was prized only five decades ago. To deflower a virgin was considered the choicest tidbit of sexual entertainment. One might have expected that a man like Tausk in his mature years would know how to protect himself against complications of the sort that are alleged in Dr. Knopf's letter (see Roazen, 1972, p. 584). But in order to enjoy defloration to the fullest, the male was not to use a contraceptive, and the traditional belief that the act of defloration cannot be carried out when a condom is used was still upheld. Oddly enough, the fact of virginity would make Hilde Loewi's story all the more plausible. The photographs her husband showed me proved her to have been an exceedingly attractive, beautiful woman. Apparently when she told Tausk in her first interview that she was still a virgin, he became victimized by the temptation. It was at that time, I believe, exceptional that a psychotherapist, particularly an analyst, entertained sexual relations with a patient. Even the few instances in which an analyst married one of his patients occurred later. It must be emphasized that under any conditions, Tausk endangered his reputation as a therapist by the way he proceeded with his patient at their first meeting. It is surprising that at a time when he urgently asked to be sent patients, and despite his hard struggle to build up his practice, he risked his professional career.

At any rate, if Hilde Loewi's claim that she was seduced by Tausk in her first interview is true, this would be considered even today, when the contemporary loosening of standards of sexual behavior has contaminated the conduct of many psychotherapists, as an instance of extraordinary professional misconduct.

From the sources available, one cannot determine with certainty when Tausk and Hilde Loewi met for the first time and Tausk's transgression occurred. According to the time relations Olga Knopf recalled in her letter, it is not impossible that it took place in March, that is, at a time when Tausk was still in treatment with Helene Deutsch. The possibility was suggested (Roazen, 1969) that Tausk's acting out with his patient might have been precipitated by the premature termination of his analysis. Yet termination of an analysis is not the only factor that may precipitate acting out; the psychoanalytic situation per se may stimulate it in a predisposed subject, and Tausk's tendency to act out was characteristic of him. It remains a moot question whether he met Hilde Loewi in March or April.[15]

Tausk's dealing with women had involved acting out for a long time. The incident with Hilde Loewi would have been at best an intensification of his habitual ways.

If all circumstances are considered, one cannot assume that the beginning of Tausk's relationship with Hilde Loewi was based on love and respect. After all, he was at that time a man of mature years, engaged to Kosa Lazarević (Roazen, 1969) and in a professional situation which automatically creates a barrier to action and should arouse primarily clinical professional interests. Further, the patient who trusted his professional integrity was young, a virgin and in need of help. Thus all circumstances were stacked against starting an amorous episode. Yet against all odds Tausk dropped his inhibitions and professional standards and succumbed to a momentary arousal of drives. Such grave acting out is regularly a sign of an aggressive and destructive tendency, with instances of which Tausk's relationship to women was replete.[16] Nevertheless, the relationship may have developed soon into one of love, respect, and regard for the woman. Tausk extolled her in the two cited documents. He might have been convinced of the sincerity of

[15]If in July Hilde Loewi had been pregnant for 10 weeks, then she could not have met Tausk later than around the last week in April, and if she was in her fourteenth week, not later than in the last week of March.

[16]Cf. the previously reported avowal of Tausk to Lea Rosen.

his feelings at the moment of writing, but was it the psychological truth? As was stated before, he was exhibitionistic in his relations with women, and his love affairs were the talk of the town. But this time he was disproportionately discreet.

Neither Freud nor his colleagues were permitted to know and something stopped Tausk even from telling his son that he would marry on the following day. This is strange behavior for a man who is in love with his bride. The inescapable inference is that Tausk harbored all the time a doubt that he would marry. Even when he wrote Freud, undoubtedly alluding to the impending event, he did it in a language that steered clear of open, understandable wording.

Tausk's starting an affair with Hilde Loewi does not need any further explanation: he was a passionate man who did not succeed in taming the impetuosity of his drives. In this situation as in others he followed the usual pattern of acting out, the pleasure principle gaining the upper hand over the reality principle. Tausk's aversion to marrying Hilde Loewi is a different matter which deserves further inquiry.

(E) The Basic Mechanisms

In order to understand the situation in which Tausk found himself at the beginning of July, the basic structure of his relationship to women has to be appreciated. Women played an exceedingly large role in his life, and he had relations with a large number of them. Many of them were of high standing, professionally and culturally noteworthy personalities. One of the remarkable features, however, was that none of these associations ever resulted in mutual happiness. He deeply impressed —

even dominated—them and then abandoned them.

On the other hand, he was vulnerable when a relationship did not take the desired course and the sequence of passionate love and abandonment was upset by the woman's actions. When he was frustrated in Berlin by a woman he loved, he had a nervous breakdown and took flight into a hospital. When his fiancée betrayed him in Lublin, he became severely depressed, separated from her, and took flight to Grimmenstein.[17]

In July he found himself in the very situation he was not able to tolerate. Hilde Loewi had become pregnant, and an abortion was not possible. This time termination of the engagement and abandonment of the erstwhile loved woman were thwarted. The termination of an engagement was acceptable and not unusual in the Vienna of those days, but the reputation and status of a woman who was a member of the establishment were gravely endangered by an illegitimate child. If Tausk had refused to marry Hilde Loewi, he could have been prosecuted for breach of promise, which probably would not have happened, but to say the least, it would have become a scandal of such proportions that Tausk would have had to leave Vienna, and he would have suffered shame and humiliation in the eyes of his sons. Tausk's hands were tied; there was no alternative; he had lost the freedom of action: one of the worst psychological calamities that could befall him had taken place. Oddly enough, it must have been worse than if he had failed financially in his practice.

The request for treatment by a prominent personality contributes greatly to the psychotherapist's prestige and

[17]The psychic background of tubercular disease, such as catarrhal apicitis, from which Tausk suffered sporadically, has been often described.

has a favorable effect on his future practice. How much Tausk worried about his income and how eager he was to give his sons adequate support is known, and nevertheless he threw a promising professional opportunity into the winds for the sake of an amorous adventure. He put his pride in his virility into operation and conquered an attractive woman under the most unfavorable conditions. Initially he was the full master of the situation. But afterward the woman proved to be stronger than he by force of circumstances, and he lost all mastery. A master stroke was turned into a defeat.

To be sure, 19 years earlier he had had to face identical conditions. The woman with whom he was involved became pregnant and he had to marry her.

When he married, he was young and inexperienced, and his mother had given birth to a child only three years earlier. I imagine that he thought of marriage and parenthood as desirable narcissistic achievements. But as soon as marriage proved a burden, the bond was broken. Nineteen years later an enforced marriage had no attractive implication.

August Aichhorn made a relevant observation about the stubborn refusal of delinquent youngsters to admit the misconduct of which they were guilty and to accept the prospect of being punished for their delinquent acts. Even in the face of judge and witnesses, they remain firm and keep doggedly to their subterfuges. Aichhorn found that the delinquent harbors to the last moment the magic belief that providence will provide a miracle that will save his skin. It happens ever so often that only after it has become clear that providence will not deliver the expected rescue does denial change to repentance and confession. Tausk's behavior during the days prior to the appointed date of the ceremony reminds me of Aichhorn's observation. He behaved as if he anticipated that a sudden turn of events would liberate him from an unacceptable bondage to the woman. I do not conjecture that this anticipation was represented explicitly in his mind in the form of a well-defined event, but rather in a vague mood of undefined trust that providence would release him from the predicament.

This might have been the reason why he did not inform Freud, his colleagues, or his son of what was to happen the following day, and why he did not introduce his fiancée to any of them. Magical expectations are probably universal in the human mind. Their intensity, quality, and relevance vary.[18] They probably are the basis of optimism (Angel, 1934) and heroism (Freud, 1915, p. 296). Magical expectations may have opposite effects in those who persistently fear that catastrophe is just around the corner.

Indeed providence had up to now worked in his favor: the escape from the marital yoke had succeeded; the sons had developed favorably despite the trauma of the father's abandonment and they had been well provided for despite paternal penury; the professional switch in midstream had led to brilliant successes against all odds; friends had provided for him at an age when such favors are exceptional; women had flocked to him and he had become their idol. That he nevertheless remained unhappy and torn by conflicts does not contradict this aspect of his life. He had reasons to believe that providence would again decide in his favor and protect him.

[18]A passage in a letter written in 1905 possibly refers in a less dramatic context to dormant magical expectations in Tausk. When his financial future was most uncertain, he wrote to his former wife: "What now will come, only Freud and God alone know. I shall in the meantime study assiduously" (Was jetzt kommen wird, weiss nur Freud und Gott allein. Ich werde einstweilen fleissig studieren).

Here I must come back to another element in his coping with women. I have cited the remarkable instance in which Tausk structured the moment of separation in such a way that it entailed the greatest pain to the woman he was abandoning. Roazen (1969) cites instances of women who were deeply depressed, "crushed" for a long time, if not for the rest of their lives, after their relations with Tausk had ended. Such catastrophic effects might have been partly caused by the circumstances under which the termination of the relationship occurred. This element would explain why the suicide occurred just on the day which would have been the day of the wedding.

According to what Lea Rosen told Prof. Winnik, the rumor had it that when Hilde Loewi came to Tausk's apartment in order to join him for the marriage ceremony, she found him dead.[19] It is this maximum of anguish at the moment of highest blissful expectation — no playwright would have been able to create a more tragic situation — to which Tausk subjected his pregnant fiancée that gives rise to the idea that the motivational pressure for committing suicide on the very day was an uncontrolled urge to wreak revenge for the woman's holding him in a vise and forcing him into marriage against his true desire and intent.

Had he waited for 24 hours, the child of whose birth he was certain would have been able to carry his father's name and Hilde Loewi would have been spared the worst. Thus the final deed expressed at the same time ambivalence toward the mother and the child she expected.

[19]However, see below: according to Freud, the ceremony was to take place a week later, as was also reported by Hilde Loewi's husband. But whether the ceremony was planned for July 3 or one week later is immaterial to the reconstruction of the mechanism which I propose.

A detail intimates that possibly a delay in the suicide would have been possible. Tausk sipped cognac during his preparation for suicide. The necessity of taking alcohol proves the presence of an inhibition that had to be removed in order to make the final act possible. The question I am raising is a subtle one. It seems that the answer may provide insight into the dynamics of what happened during that fateful night. That Tausk stood under an extreme pressure to commit suicide is evident. But that pressure was not of the kind from which the melancholic patient suffers who does not need alcohol for the removal of inhibitions but has to be watched every moment as otherwise he would use the first opportunity to put an end to his existence.

The unavoidability of suicide under existing circumstances is understandable in view of Tausk's general psychopathology, but should one assume that it was equally unavoidable that he removed artificially by the use of alcohol the last constraints that stood in the way of his suicide at that moment? Knowing that a postponement of that act for only a few hours would be of decisive consequences for his fiancée and her prospective progeny, the reason that made him decide in favor of immediate action must have been potent. One is forced to assume not only that the act of suicide had become imperative but also that the determination to leave Hilde Loewi unmarried and pregnant had acquired equal urgency. To hurt the love object became again the *modus operandi* of the unconscious.

Oddly enough, Tausk had once said in a discussion (March 11, 1914) of a paper Freud presented to the Vienna Psychoanalytic Association that

Man has in general two modalities for having done

with the problem of the mother whom he has wooed in vain: (1) by turning toward the man, and (2) by over and over again representing (as a symptom) the relationship one has had to the mother, whereby one comes into contact with her after all [Nunberg and Federn, vol. 4, p. 245].

This is an extreme formulation whose correctness may be disputed. It strikes me, as it did in previously cited instances of the sort, as an avowal of processes that were valid for Tausk himself rather than the result of clinical observation.

He indeed repeated over and over again the tragic moment of his childhood when he pierced the mother's heart in her portrait. Such violence against the mother presupposed a past phase of intense love and affection. Eight times Tausk had to suffer consternation brought about by the undeniable evidence that the mother had again been unfaithful with the hated father. Thus Hilde Loewi too had to be wounded where it hurt most, and she never recovered from it, as I was told.[20]

(F) The Sequence of Events

One can approximately reconstruct what Tausk did on the second of July. In the forenoon he probably wrote the letters to his sister and to Freud. He followed the daily routine of his professional practice, as I was told by the

[20]Prof. Dr. Tausk informs me that the following words were imprinted on the bow of Hilde Loewi's wreath which was placed by Tausk's coffin: "In all love and sincerity your lonely Hille" (In aller Liebe und Innigkeit Deine einsame Hille [Tausk's nickname for Hilde]). These words are far stronger in German than they sound in English. They would not speak against the thesis I am propounding.

aforementioned patient. In the evening Tausk met his son for supper and thereafter attended Hilde Loewi's concert. Prof. Dr. Tausk does not recall that his father showed any exceptional signs of distress (Neyant-Sutterman, 1978). All that is known speaks in favor of Tausk's unawareness of his impending death throughout the last day of his life. This would not preclude the occasional momentary flash of suicidal imagery. But oné can exclude with certainty the formation of an explicit intent during that day. There is one detail that substantiates this point. It can hardly be supposed that an analyst who for some time has planned to end his life would not make certain of the way in which his patients would be apprised of the event, assuring that this is done in the least hurtful way. But Tausk's patient whom I interviewed told me that he arrived in Tausk's office at the appointed time and was told by the housekeeper of the suicide, which leaves no doubt that on the preceding day Tausk had not been aware that this would be their last meeting. The last-minute drawing-up of his will also testifies to a sudden crystallization of suicidal determination.

Something terrible must have happened to him during the last few hours of his life to unleash a storm of panic and rage that destroyed his morale and rushed him into ending his life with dispatch. A passage in a letter from Freud to Ferenczi to be presented below makes compelling the following reconstruction of the sequence of events: after the concert, Tausk went with his fiancée to her apartment and wanted to have intercourse with her but was impotent. He then rushed home, wrote the farewell letter to Freud and his last will, which gave the time of 1:30 A.M., and hanged and shot himself to death.

It was the impotence that became the last straw that felled that proud man. Tausk's veto against being forced into marriage, a long-standing worry of his, would not explain the rashness and overhastiness of his behavior during the night of July 2 to 3. Furthermore, even though Tausk's relationship to women — what I called the basic mechanism — made suicide imperative after providence did not provide any other last-minute escape route, this would not account for the loss of self-respect, the frightening reduction in self-esteem which Tausk revealed in the last two communications. Tausk could have taken the stand of a martyr; but he did not, instead deprecating himself mercilessly. His last communications display the loss of the minimum of narcissistic cathexis of self that is needed for survival. It was the self-inflicted trauma of impotence that sealed his fate.

In a letter of July 10, 1919, Freud wrote Ferenczi:[21] "Tausk has shot himself on 4/7, eight days before a scheduled marriage and left tender, conciliatory letters behind. Etiology obscure. Probably psy[chic] impotence and last act of his infantile fight with the father ghost. Despite acknowledgement of his endowment, no adequate empathy in me" (Tausk hat sich am 4/7 erschossen, 8 Tage vor seiner anberaumten Heirat mit Hinterlassung zärtlicher, versönlicher Briefe. Aetiology dunkel, wahrscheinlich ps. Impotenz und letzter Akt seines infantilen Kampfes mit dem Vatergespenst. Trotz Würdigung seiner Begabung kein rechtes Mitgefühl bei mir).[22]

[21]Roazen (1972) had surmised that Freud's letters to Abraham and Ferenczi might contain clues regarding Tausk's suicide. I had not shared that expectation. But as it turns out, Roazen was correct: something new has indeed been found, even though not of the sort Roazen expected.

[22]Published with the permission of the Sigmund Freud Copyrights, Ltd. I came upon the passage in question by accident. In trying to reconstruct Freud's income, as I have done in Tausk's case, I

Freud committed the error of postdating the tragedy by one day.[23] As a source of Freud's information, I do not see any other possibility than that Hilde Loewi told him of Tausk's impotence. After all, she was the only one who could have known about it. In view of the effect this incident had on Tausk, I conjecture that it was the first time that this ill-fortune had befallen him.

It is an almost ubiquitous lament among men that nature made their consumation of intercourse — provokingly discrepant with women's — dependent on a rather complicated interplay of biological and psychological systems which, activated by reflexes, removes the execution entirely out of the sphere of will or voluntary control. The greatest minds have deplored the way nature has organized male potency. Leonardo da Vinci complained that the penis raises itself when this is not wanted and does not raise itself when desired. Goethe devoted a

---

was able to find but one reference to it in Jones's biography of Freud (1953–1957, vol. 2, p. 216), where he indicated — allegedly on the basis of a letter from Freud to Ferenczi (Jan. 6, 1919) — that Freud's monthly income was 1,000 Kronen. This seemed highly improbable and, since Freud's letters to Ferenczi have not yet been published, I turned to Anna Freud, asking her to verify Jones's statement. Not being able to find the passage alluded to by Jones, she sent me photocopies of her father's letters to Ferenczi covering that period; in them, to my amazement, I discovered the sentence quoted above.

[23]Of course, this parapraxis can hardly be interpreted reliably. The interpretation which comes to mind would be the wish that the tragedy had occurred later, that is, never. There is still another discrepancy. As in his letter to Lou Andreas-Salomé (Pfeiffer, 1966, p. 98), Freud gives the date of the planned wedding a week later than it is stated in Tausk's letter that Nada had learned by heart. Since Hilde Loewi's birthday was on July 8, it is possible that the wedding was originally planned to coincide with that date. The rumor Lea Rosen reported would agree with the letter Tausk wrote his sister.

great poem to an incident of impotence that befell him when he was away from home and ready to be unfaithful to his wife. Fear of impotence may have been one of the many reasons why some men like Leonardo da Vinci and Newton never indulged in intercourse. Of course, the response to actual impotence varies greatly. The conclusion Goethe drew from the episode was an aphorism that contains an incredibly deep insight into pathology – an insight that by and large is still lacking its full application to science: "Illness only, indeed, bears out the healthy one" (Die Krankheit erst bewährt den Gesunden). In other words, sickness is the acid test of health. And he ends with the admonition which can be suitably quoted in this context:

> Indeed we stumble on our life's journey,
> And yet in this frenzied world [in which
>   we live]
> Two levers have much power over man's
>   hustle and bustle:
> *Duty* very much; *love* infinitely more.[24]

Carlyle, according to Frank Harris (1925), was impotent but this did not interfere with his ability to function in society or with his creativity, though it aggravated his wife's hysteria. But to a person like Tausk, whose narcissism was greatly supported by phallic pride, perhaps even centered in it, the incident was in effect a catastrophe.

Those who possibly feel shocked by the reconstruction that Tausk's destructive intent against Hilde Loewi was the principal proximate unconscious motivation of his

[24]Wir stolpern wohl auf unserer Lebensreise/Und doch vermögen in der Welt, der tollen,/Zwei Hebel viel aufs irdische Getriebe:/ Sehr viel die Pflicht, *unendlich* mehr die *Liebe*.

suicide will infer from this new information that his suicide was unconnected with his fiancée's pregnancy. They will be inclined to look at the impotence as the only etiological factor that led to an acute mental disturbance. However, one has to consider the cause of Tausk's impotence. Evidently, if it had a high etiological importance in regard to his suicide, it must have been a symptom which he never had been subject to before and for the emergence of which he was unprepared. Then the question of the causation of the symptom becomes quite pressing. Impotence, whatever its specific meaning may be in the individual instance, is the consequence of ambivalence toward a woman. Since Tausk was not impotent with other women before, a particularly intense ambivalence toward Hilde Loewi is to be postulated. This inordinate ambivalence was rooted in his rage at her pregnancy. The two complemented each other. It is here not a question of an either/or. The two are confluent.

It would be inadequate to ask whether the suicide would have occurred if Tausk had been spared that contretemps. The latter was a relevant part of his relationship to Hilde Loewi, as was his rage at her pregnancy. Thus, there are three secured facts: resistance to being coerced into marriage, impotence, and suicide. Psychological reconstruction has to bring these three data into a meaningful context.

The awareness of the final inevitability of the impending marriage led to an intensification of rage against the pregnant woman. This in turn resulted in the defiant rebuff of the woman on the very night that probably separated Tausk from becoming her husband. It is possible that he gained only in that moment full awareness that his love had reached its nadir. His impotence was a message to himself as well as to her: he no longer was enamored of her. The double aspect of the impotence was not limited to the message it carried. Impotence was an attack against the woman, her rejection and destruction on the level of psychosomatic symbolization but also an attack against himself, a maximal self-humiliation as well as castration likewise on the level of psychosomatic symbolization. (Oddly enough, there was the rumor that he had castrated himself [Peters, 1962, p. 281], which shows again that rumor and gossip may cast back a process that actually occurred in the unconscious of the person rumored about.)

The extreme consequences Tausk drew from his impotence permit the conclusion that he acknowledged the symptom, not as possibly a temporary disturbance but as a chronic one. The resulting imagery would have been that of a castrated man enslaved to a woman. Tausk's reference to joylessness, conflict, and torment with regard to the impending marriage in his last will should be recalled.

The suicide should redeem his own guilt, an attempt one can infer from his calling it an act of decency and health. Suicide was the self-inflicted punishment for past sins. In his last hour Tausk sat in judgment on himself and passed sentence. Reproaches against the world subsided and the full force of his indictment went far beyond that actually justified, as his attacks against the "father ghost" had been out of proportion. Impotence, that is, symbolic castration, made it possible to direct aggression from the outside world against the self that now had become utterly worthless and was declared to have never possessed any value. Therefore the request to be speedily forgotten, which usually is the very dread of the moribund. But here the prospect that nothing will be left of him, not even a memory, may paradoxically have served as a consolation. It was consistent with his merciless raging against himself that Tausk requested in his last will that all his papers should be destroyed.

The catalyst that brought about the redirection of aggression and the demolishment of the self was impotence. It was not only a rehearsal of death: to a certain extent it occasioned a state worse than death that made the idea of death palatable and desirable. Tausk had come close to suicide before, but the resistance to death had been vigorous. Even in the last night intake of alcohol was necessary to tear down the last barrier. The only way in which the resistance to death could be subverted was the creation of the state of castration that had become symbolic reality.

I believe the few data that have reached us explain adequately why Tausk had to commit suicide shortly before he should have gone with Hilde Loewi to the registrar's office. From the clinical point of view, the lover's pregnancy and his own impotence suffice as explanatory factors that initiated a sadomasochistic regression by which Tausk was ultimately felled on the night of July 2–3. A typology of man based on the kind of death he has suffered has not yet been fully developed, and it is intriguing to speculate what Tausk's posthumous *aura popularia* might have been if he had died in an accident and not by suicide.

Impotence, like almost no other symptom, is repudiated most vigorously by the self. Frequently, it is experienced as caused by a malicious influence coming from the outside, as the not inconsiderable number of women who were accused of witchcraft for allegedly having caused impotence bears witness. Impotence is frequently experienced like a parapraxia for which a person repudiates responsibility. Indeed, in consideration of his total situation it would have been feasible that Tausk on his way home after a passionate tryst with his lover would have suffered an accident and been run over by a car. It is well known that many a fatal accident is a camouflaged suicide. In terms of a psychology that concentrates on core events, the two would be considered identical.

It may appear contradictory that I present impotence on the one hand as the worst catastrophe that could befall Tausk and on the other as an incident he wanted and needed urgently. However, such apparent contradictions are generally found at the base of neurotic symptoms, even if not as conspicuously as in some patients suffering from impotence. A young man who had repeatedly threatened suicide because of his genital inhibition greeted me after his first intercourse saying, "You have at last succeeded in making me a beast."

The foregoing reconstruction of Tausk's last night has met several objections which I shall discuss in detail.

1. Doubts regarding the meaning of Freud's communication to Ferenczi have been raised. Did Freud convey only a conjecture about Tausk's impotence, or did he write about it as a fact? Freud, as on other occasions, wrote to Ferenczi of absence of a clear-cut etiology but added that it might have been impotence. The word "probably" was not used in the sense of uncertainty about the occurrence of impotence but about its etiological value. If his doubt had extended to the fact of impotence, he would have written *wahrscheinliche* as the adjective qualifying "impotence." *Wahrscheinlich*, as he wrote, refers to etiology: that is, the probable etiology was impotence. He felt certainty about the etiologic value of Tausk's struggle with the father ghost which loomed as

the permanent background of a life so rich in conflicts.

2. The question has been raised of whether Freud referred in his letter to previous incidents of impotence in Tausk's life. In view of Tausk's great success with women and their being disconsolate after the termination of the relationship, it is hardly imaginable that impotence might have been of any earlier relevance. Even though Helene Deutsch reported on Tausk's analysis some thirty-odd years later, it is not conceivable that she forgot a symptom that would have been most surprising in view of the patient's reputation. If medical discretion had prevented her from reporting it, she would have told Roazen, with whom she spent many hours reporting on Tausk, or me that there was something she felt averse to talking about. But she never presented a reservation and appeared to feel free to convey everything she knew about Tausk. Moreover, there is documentary proof that Freud's reference to impotence can only be related to an incident that occurred in the last few hours of Tausk's life. A man struggling with impotence would not have written to Freud on the day preceding his marriage that he is in the process of solving his life's problems and hopes to appear soon "with a minimum of neurosis." In view of his letter to Freud of July 2, and the laughing farewell to his son, there is no reason to assume that he was troubled prior to the night of July 2 by a new neurotic symptom that might have endangered the impending marriage.

3. The question has been raised of what Freud may have meant by the diagnostic term "psychic impotence." This term would hardly be used at present, but just as Freud differentiated between "actual" and "psycho"-neuroses, so he apparently differentiated in a similar way between impotence due to physical factors (alcoholism,

atony, general paresis, diabetes, etc.) and that due to psychic factors. He also used the term "psychic impotence" in his paper of 1927, where he discusses its various forms.

In orgastic impotence, the patient does not achieve full gratification. Freud did not have this type of impotence in mind when he wrote Ferenczi. He would have qualified the diagnosis by adding the term "orgastic." Furthermore, the reader may recall that incomplete gratification in intercourse was postulated by Tausk as a normal occurrence, necessitated by the biology of the process per se. I inferred earlier that orgastic impotence might have been a chronic symptom of Tausk's but not acknowledged by him as a symptom, since he was able to rationalize it by means of theory.

Another form of impotence, though relatively rare, is *ejaculatio retarda* or *deficiens*, that is, an inordinate delay in ejaculation, or an inability to ejaculate. In this instance, too, the diagnosis "impotence" is qualified usually by adding the abbreviation *"ret."* This form of impotence puts the patient under great psychic stress, but for obvious reasons it is not humiliating or, at least, not as humiliating as the following type of disturbance, which is usually meant when the clinician speaks of impotence without qualifying addition: the inability to form an erection, or the weakening of the erection at the moment of intromission to an extent that makes penetration impossible.[25]

[25]Ejaculation at the moment when intromission of the erected member is intended is rather rare, and occurs usually only under conditions of overexcitement in males who are inexperienced. Premature ejaculation after intromission will not be discussed in this context, since in clinical parlance physicians refer to this disturbance as *"ejaculatio praecox"* and not as "impotence."

Thus I infer from Freud's communication to Ferenczi that Tausk was subjected to an incident of inability to perform intercourse.

4. I shall summarize some of the previous reasoning because the certainty with which I assign the incident of Tausk's impotence to the night of July 2–3 has been questioned. Even though this allocation is made *per exclusionem*, a method which is usually looked at askance, I do not believe that it has led to erroneous inferences in this instance. The fact that an incident of impotence had occurred is established by the passage in Freud's letter to Ferenczi. Since Tausk had not reported anything of the kind in his treatment with Helene Deutsch, it must have occurred after March. Tausk's letters to Freud of July 2 and to his sister of the same date exclude the possibility that his was the mind of a man who worries about the adequacy of his potency. The failure of performance explains the sudden collapse of Tausk's morale. Hilde Loewi's secrecy vis-à-vis Marius Tausk and her insistence that her confidante must never reveal what she was told is understandable in this light: she evidently did not want to expose her late lover. Furthermore, like so many women who have had to face male incompetence, she, too, might have felt responsible for the unfortunate incident. It is probable that Hilde Loewi, like so many of Tausk's lovers, was unable to exorcise his burning image from her consciousness.

5. A strong objection to my reconstruction is raised by Prof. Dr. Tausk by virtue of a passage in his above-quoted letter to Lou Andreas-Salomé of April 30, 1920, in which he wrote her: "He [my father] parted company from her [Hilde Loewi] around 11:30 P.M. of July 2, 1919 after a concert and a walk" (Er hat sich von ihr nach einem Konzert und einem Spaziergang gegen 1/2 11

nachts am 2. Juli 1919 getrennt). He takes this passage as a proof that they had not gone to her apartment, which would be a necessary episode in my reconstruction.

However, it seems that at that time Marius himself doubted that this was the whole story, for the quoted sentence was preceded by: "About my father's really last and decisive hours only one human being is informed and that is his bride, Hilde Loewi in Vienna" (Über die wirklich letzten und entscheidenden Stunden meines Vaters ist nur ein Mensch unterrichtet und das ist seine Braut, Hilde Loewi in Wien). Hilde Loewi evidently had told the son only that they parted after a walk but she did not inform him of all the events of that night, as he himself evidently suspected.

In evaluating Marius Tausk's communication to Lou Andreas-Salomé a year after his father's death, one should consider a variety of factors.

It cannot have been otherwise than that Marius Tausk was baffled by the tragedy and eager to find an explanation of an event that had shaken the very foundation of his existence and had occurred without forewarning. The motive for his father's suicide must have desperately haunted the young man, and he rightly drew the conclusion that the decisive event must have occurred after he had left his father, since he had been in good spirits at the moment of parting. He evidently turned to Hilde Loewi, expecting an explanation from her. Further, Lou Andreas-Salomé, as the letter makes clear, had written previously to Tausk's sister Jelka but had not received an answer, and Marius Tausk, one gets the impression, tried to convey to Lou Andreas-Salomé everything he had found out about his father's last night. But what Hilde Loewi told him was surprisingly meager and bare of details. She did not tell him his father's parting words nor where she saw him last, both of which one would have expected her to share with her late fiancé's son.

My reconstruction would explain some of these riddles. Hilde Loewi's reluctance to give details would be the first consequence. Furthermore, if, as I believe is proved, an incident of impotence had occurred, Tausk must immediately have become deeply upset. Hilde Loewi would have noticed the degree of excitement with which he responded to the incident and understandably would not have let him go home alone but would have accompanied him. In Vienna one did not let lady friends walk home alone in the middle of the night, and therefore she might have preferred to leave the place they parted company unmentioned.[26] The particular time, 11:30 P.M., would not contradict my reconstruction, since evening entertainment started earlier in Vienna than in this country and usually ended between 9:30 and 10:00 P.M.

Hilde Loewi possibly wanted to draw Marius's interest away from the last hour she had spent with his father and was ready to transgress customary barriers of discretion, perhaps also in order not to be reminded herself of the last memory she had of him. She told Tausk's son quite a bit about the first hour of her acquaintance with his father (Neyant-Sutterman, 1978), even though the details she implied were osé and compromising. But in that first

[26]The colleague who was a friend of Hilde Loewi wrote me that Hilde Loewi complained bitterly about her interview with Freud. What it may have been that made that meeting so unpleasant for Hilde Loewi is quite puzzling. One of the factors may have been that Freud reproached her for not staying with Tausk through the night after she had noticed his desperate excitement. Hilde Loewi's sister, on the other hand, told me that her sister possessed a book by Freud with a personal inscription. It is also noteworthy that in the quoted write-up in the *Jahrbuch*, a positive attitude toward psychoanalysis on her part is reported.

hour Tausk appears active, self-assured, and potent.

6. In Tausk's letter to Lou Andreas-Salomé quoted above (March 26, 1919), there is a passage which gives Prof. Dr. Tausk cause for a reconstruction in essence not dissimilar to mine, but skirting the incident of impotence. Tausk wrote: "My solitude is now complete. Now I have brought my 40th year behind me and wish a companion for the evening years of my life. Do you know anyone with whom it will be worthwhile to become acquainted?" (Meine Einsamkeit ist jetzt eine vollkommene. Nun habe ich mein 40. Jahr hinter mich gebracht und wünsche mir eine Gefährtin für meinen Lebensabend. Kennst Du eine, die kennen zu lernen es sich verlohnte?). From this passage Prof. Dr. Tausk concluded that his father, on meeting Hilde Loewi, thought he had found the companion he was longing for. On that last evening during the walk with her, when discussing their future, he became aware that in this instance as in the previous ones he would not be able to form a constant, happy, mutually satisfying relationship. With this more or less sudden awareness, he plunged into a state of hopelessness and despair that forced him to end his life.[27]

To be sure, there is always the possibility that events of the past may have been different from what documents (and sometimes even eyewitness reports) would lead one

[27]What Hilde Loewi's husband told me in the second interview would speak in part in favor of Prof. Dr. Tausk's version. According to her husband, Hilde Loewi had told him that Tausk was very jealous, and, for example, did not want her to accompany the one or the other artist. He was also very nervous. His jealousy and nervousness made Hilde Loewi rather pessimistic about the impending marriage. Tausk allegedly killed himself in front of her portrait. He left a letter for her in which he wrote that he was unworthy (unwürdig) of being her husband. He committed suicide, as Hilde Loewi's husband said, because he felt that the marriage would not work out.

to reconstruct. Yet if one makes of that possibility a principle, historical research collapses, and arbitrariness becomes a guiding principle. Prof. Dr. Tausk's reconstruction is, in my estimation, an argument *ad hominem*. In Dr. Knopf's report Tausk does not appear like a man in love who intends to marry. One does not falsify a fiancée's identity without a compelling reason. There is even a possibility, faint as it may be, that when he wrote Lou Andreas-Salomé about his state of aloneness, he had already made Hilde Loewi's acquaintance. Furthermore, it appears arbitrary to postulate that just at the time of that walk during the evening of July 2, the insight dawned on him that this relationship, like the others that preceded it, would miscarry. I have enumerated the small signs that revealed Tausk's doubts about the planned marriage. But even if the improbable should have come to pass, as Prof. Dr. Tausk proposes, this would not suffice as an explanation of the ensuing fulminant burst of morbid devastation. Shattering as such a sudden recognition may have been, it would precipitate a depression rather than entail the necessity of immediate suicide. After all, Tausk knew he was not too well endowed as *pater familias*, and the recognition would not have amounted to more than his becoming certain of what he had until then been aware of as a possibility. In his letter to his sister, he spoke of a satisfying future as a hope and by no means as a certainty.

I could go on enumerating factors that make it improbable that a sudden recognition of the sort Prof. Dr. Tausk proposes was the cause, or even only a precipitating factor. It must have been an event that struck the vitals.

An event of the type Prof. Dr. Tausk proposes would have led to a separation soon after the wedding or the birth of the baby. The depressing anticipation that the painful past of aloneness will be repeated would hardly have made survival of the next twelve hours impossible.

If my reconstruction is correct, it is obvious that Hilde Loewi was in no position to let Tausk's son know the truth. If events had taken the course that Prof. Dr. Tausk has reconstructed, there would have been no reason for Hilde Loewi to be evasive. One might have expected her to tell him about his father's desperate pessimism regarding the impending marriage. Why should it have been kept from the son that his father anticipated the marriage to result in mutual unhappiness and that this was the subject of their last discourse? After all, Tausk revealed this motive without compunction in his last communication. The absence of any relevant information in her communication to Marius Tausk strongly suggests that Hilde Loewi had a powerful reason to keep the events of that last night concealed. Marius Tausk was well aware that Hilde Loewi made a secret of his father's "really last and decisive hours," and impotence would explain why she was forced to be secretive about that last night to the end of her days. Furthermore, it is hardly feasible that a man in order to spare a woman the grief and disappointment of an unhappy marriage resorts to an action that causes her a grief immeasurably more intense than even a malignant marriage would have caused, particularly in a country in which divorces were by no means a rarity.

Whichever reconstruction is correct, it must be said: in view of the history of Tausk's life, events like the lover's pregnancy and his own impotence may appear as accidental. Tausk's was a figure that could be compared to one of the heroes in Greek tragedy. He was a man torn by excessive conflicts. Endowed with an unusual creative potential, he was haunted by a search for proper channels and a medium suitable to him, but he never found them. He never came to terms with the manifoldness of creative impulses that propelled him. His discussion remarks, as recorded in the *Minutes*, are replete with great ideas which should have been elaborated by painstaking efforts. His intellect evidently was vastly superior but his passions were excessive and utterly unruly and did not permit the temporary tranquility necessary for great works. His moral strivings were of high caliber, but again his inordinate passions debarred him from a life in harmony with his morality. What makes the contemplation of his life so moving is the absence of compromise. Whereas the average man seeks subterfuges, he lived out the oedipal conflicts in full measure. All his life he faced the full brunt of his hatred of father. The many women he loved never replaced the one he must have loved passionately before the first rival was born.

Thus he may serve as an avatar of Western man perennially seeking self-fulfillment and achievement, but perennially dissatisfied and toppled by "the slings and arrows of outrageous fortune" until he is victimized by his own hubris. His life was one of great loves and great hatreds, permanently overshadowed by existential anguish.

Pregnancy and impotence may have been accidental complications that only accelerated a tragedy that was bound to occur sooner or later as, if a cliché is permitted, the result of the violent, indomitable struggle between Eros and Thanatos that had raged in Tausk since childhood.

VI. The Obituary

The obituary that was published to commemorate Tausk, written but not signed by Freud, is of secondary concern to this investigation. Yet it is of interest and deserves examination, if only for the reason that its content deviates from a letter Freud wrote Lou Andreas-Salomé on August 1.

But first the obituary (Freud, 1919): close to half the piece is an outline of Tausk's biography, who is introduced to the reader as a victim of war and as an unusually talented analyst.

The transition to the circumstances that led to suicide takes the form of high praise of his military service during World War I.

> It is... greatly to his honour that during the war he threw himself wholeheartedly and with complete disregard of the consequences into exposing the numerous abuses which so many doctors unfor-

tunately tolerated in silence or for which they even shared the responsibility [*ibid.*, p. 274].

Then the various stresses to which Tausk was exposed are enumerated: physical ill-health, mental exhaustion, the necessity of building up a new existence, the prospect of a new marriage. "He was," Freud continued, "no longer able to cope with the many demands imposed on him in his ailing state by harsh reality." The remaining one-and-one-quarter printed pages are devoted to Tausk's psychoanalytic career and the great merits he attained in psychoanalytic research. As an author, he was remarkable because of his "sharp observation, sound judgement and a particular clearness of expression." He strove toward a philosophical foundation of problems and he formulated "the whole profundity and comprehensive meaning of the very difficult problems involved." He possessed "a quite exceptional medico-psychological capacity." Psychoanalysis owed Tausk a particular debt for his activity as a lecturer: "His audiences were able to admire the clarity and didactic skill of his lectures no less than the profundity with which he handled individual topics."

Yet one discovers, notwithstanding the great praise accorded, a contradictory tendency which one cannot acclaim as an instance of the contrapuntal writing of which Freud was a true master. Some passages seem to reveal a conflictual attitude of the writer. A back-and-forth movement is visible that is rarely found in Freud's writing.[1]

Thus Freud praised Tausk for the profundity with which he grappled with philosophical problems but also declared, "Perhaps, he went too far..." (*ibid.*, p. 274).

[1]Only in Freud's brief about electric treatment of war neuroses (1955) does one discover the indication of a comparable indecisiveness.

After referring to the great attraction certain personal qualities exercised on many, he added: "...and some, too, may have been repelled by them." The meandering is conspicuous in the following: his temperament led to "sharp, and sometimes too sharp criticisms which, however, were combined with a brilliant gift for exposition" (*ibid.*, p. 275).

When Freud wrote of Tausk's "straightforward character,"[2] of his "strivings for nobility and perfection," "his honesty towards himself and towards others" (*ibid.*, p. 275), one receives the impression that Freud went out of his way and overstressed something which he did not fully believe. At any rate, no one would be able to conjecture after reading the obituary that Freud in a letter to Lou Andreas-Salomé stated that "he had long realized that he [Tausk] could be of no further service, indeed, that he constituted a threat to the future" (Pfeiffer, 1966, p. 98).

This letter to Lou Andreas-Salomé contradicts the obituary in other respects as well. There Freud wrote as if the variety of circumstances he enumerated explained Tausk's tragic end, whereas in the letter he wrote: "But what was behind it all we cannot guess."

Thus an instance is encountered in which Freud, who strove all his life toward honesty and truth to an extent scarcely ever observed in any other person's life, gave a written account which he knew did not correspond to the way he appraised the situation. Freud would not have been the first who, owing to the force of circumstances, would have been compelled to conceal in print what he really thought.

The famous *De mortuis nil nisi bene [dicendum]* — that

---

[2]The original *lauter* is even stronger.

is, of the dead only something good should be said—of which one may easily think in this context, is quoted twice in Freud's work.

In *Totem and Taboo* (1913, p. 67), Freud discussed the relation between survivors and the dead. The ambivalence of the survivor in primordial times has become diminished since then, and the unconscious hostility to the dead can easily be kept down. The conflict of satisfied hatred and pained affection of earlier times has been replaced by "a kind of scar" in the shape of piety and the demand to say nothing but the good.

In 1915, during the First World War, the same theme reappeared (p. 290). In his essay "Thoughts for the times on war and death," he described again the special attitude one adopts toward the person who has died: admiration, suspension of criticism, and overlooking of possible misdeeds. "Consideration for the dead, who after all no longer need it, is more important to us than the truth." These words imply a critical attitude toward the traditional "*nisi bene*." Inescapably, Freud must have been in conflict about the demand imposed by tradition and that of conveying the truth about Tausk, as he saw it, when writing the obituary.

It was Ernst Simon who called to my attention years ago that the Latin saying does not advise one to say nothing but the good about the dead; this would have required the word *bonum*.[3] *Bene* would refer to the way of speaking of the dead. It would not exclude the unfavorable as long as decorum and propriety are preserved, that is, a correct, honorable, creditable way.

Freud's obituary lives up to the requirements of *bene*.

[3]Mr. Strachey, Freud's translator, followed in both instances mentioned above the English tradition and quoted the sentence as saying *nisi bonum*, whereas the original wording is *nisi bene*.

If Tausk had read it, he would have been proud of it. It could well serve as a document that would assure that "honourable memory in the history of psychoanalysis and its earliest struggles" (Freud, 1919, p. 275) that Freud predicted for Tausk's activities in the service of psychoanalysis, the closing sentence of Freud's obituary. That Freud did not stray at any place from the *bene* without yielding completely to the traditional *bonum* by omitting critical references to aspects of Tausk's character makes the piece a remarkable achievement. Yet there are passages, such as, for example, the praise of Tausk's "honesty towards himself," which are contradicted by evidence which I have cited in my discussion of Tausk's general psychopathology and of which Freud must have known. A more convincing example may be the following: Freud wrote to Lou Andreas-Salomé, "I never failed to recognize his notable gifts; but they were denied expression in achievements of corresponding value" (Pfeiffer, 1966, p. 98). This value statement, indeed, seems to be discordant with the high praise Freud had extended to Tausk in print.

In view of such discrepancies, it becomes necessary to speculate about how this obituary came to be written. It must not be overlooked that it was not signed by Freud but by "*die Redaktion*," which may be freely translated as something like "the executive board," in which Freud was not included, as is learned from the byline of the obituary in memory of Anton von Freund, written by Freud in 1920, which says: *Redaktion und Herausgeber*, Freud being the *Herausgeber* (editor).

One of the difficulties Freud faced after Tausk's suicide was how to explain to the public what had happened. Common sense would take the event per se as confirming the opinion of those who had been critical of psychoanalysis and had denied its therapeutic value. How could a therapy that did not protect its own practitioners against suicide be expected to help others?

As set forth above, it is reasonable to conjecture that Freud discussed the problem with others. I think particularly of Federn and Hitschmann, two of his oldest associates, who had proved themselves as pillars of the Viennese group and were associated with the *Zeitschrift*. When the group met, each present, I assume, expressed his views on Tausk and his importance to psychoanalysis. One may be certain that there was no agreement, and that a variety of opinions was stated. Yet it was clear that an obituary had to be written, and apparently it was thought best that Freud compose it. It is probable that he asked those present what the content of the obituary would be if they had to produce it. When he accepted the assignment, he probably stipulated that he would not sign it[4] but would amalgamate the opinions expressed into a coherent piece.[5]

An objection will be raised against this reconstruc-

[4]Since writers of obituaries are as yet not held responsible for the death of the person memorialized, Roazen's (1969, p. 14) explanation of the byline, namely, that "Freud may have wanted to diffuse the responsibility for the suicide among as many people around Tausk as possible," is questionable.

[5]To be sure, Freud's feelings toward Tausk were ambivalent, and therefore he might have felt relieved by such an arrangement. The ambivalence may be inferred from the obituary's very beginning. The English translation, "Among its sacrifices, fortunately few in number, claimed by the war from the ranks of psychoanalysis, we must count Dr. Victor Tausk," does not convey it as sharply as the German beginning: *"Zu den glücklicherweise nicht zahlreichen Opfern,"* etc. It is hazardous to use the word *glücklicherweise* (fortunately) as the third word in an obituary. But such inelegance or whatever one may call it does not reduce the piece's distinction.

struction because the obituary was included in the last volume of Freud's *Gesammelte Werke*, which was published nine years later. Since the obituary was written in Freud's handwriting, the editors of the collected works did not hesitate to include it, I presume. Was Freud in a position to object? It would have meant an open disavowal of Tausk. In 1928, the anguish of the situation was a matter of the past. Tausk's reputation had weathered the storm, and the objectionable facts were the secret of a few and would never be revealed. Freud's refusal to have the obituary included would have inescapably raised an issue no one would have liked to see resuscitated.

The obituary, after all, did not contain anything that would have deserved repudiation, or else it would never have been published. Whatever Freud's motives might have been in having the obituary included in his works, the byline makes it clear that the obituary was written in the name of a group to which Freud officially did not belong. To be sure, it might have not been evident to many, if to anybody, that Freud was not a member of *die Redaktion*.

The writing of the obituary was probably facilitated for Freud by Tausk's declaration of unshakable allegiance to psychoanalysis in his farewell letter. In view of Tausk's previous behavior, Freud could not have been sure if Tausk would not leave an accusatory message, and this would have created an almost insoluble problem. By his reference to "letters which he [Tausk] left behind, in which he expressed his unreserved belief in it [psychoanalysis]" (Freud, 1919, p. 275) (a point Freud also stressed in his letter to Lou Andreas-Salomé), he made a special point that Tausk had remained a convinced analyst right to the end.

It may be worthwhile to recall a passage Freud included in his obituary of Ferenczi, who stood so close to Freud and had been so eminent in the field. Freud wrote that Ferenczi died at a time when "he kept apart, no longer certain, perhaps, of agreement with his friends" (Freud, 1933, p. 229).

This was a gentle reference to the innovations Ferenczi had introduced, mainly into psychoanalytic technique, that were not compatible with what the main body of psychoanalysis stood for. Evidently Freud thought it necessary to bring up this disagreement in the obituary, and if Tausk had parted with a declaration of dissension with Freud or psychoanalysis, I conjecture that Freud would have considered concealment of such a break dishonest.

The obituary can be taken only as a document from which one can learn how *die Redaktion* felt about Tausk. As far as Freud is concerned, one can only infer his ambivalence from it. One believes one can read between the lines that Freud was impressed and moved by Tausk's final unreserved declaration in favor of Freud and psychoanalysis, a declaration which, as a matter of fact, is striking in view of Tausk's grave father conflict.

In his letter to Lou Andreas-Salomé, Freud repeated what he had intimated already to Ferenczi: "I confess that I do not really miss him." It is surprising that it took Freud four weeks before he informed Lou Andreas-Salomé of the tragedy. She might have easily been apprised by another source. It looks almost as if Freud would have preferred not to have to write the letter. It is further unusual, in view of the grave news he had to convey, that he first wrote two paragraphs about a variety of topics before reaching the point which must have lain heavily on his mind. The tragic part is introduced with

"Der arme Tausk," a turn of phrase I have not found used by Freud on any other occasion. What he wrote to Ferenczi and to Lou Andreas-Salomé regarding his immediate reaction would strongly indicate that the mourning process was thrown out of kilter. A comparable disturbance probably occurred shortly thereafter when his daughter Sophie died. In both instances death came without warning. In both instances, I presume, Freud was stunned. It must have been uncanny to receive the news of Tausk's voluntary departure from life only twelve hours after Tausk's holding forth the prospect of a meeting in the near future. His hesitation to write Lou Andreas-Salomé — he had mentioned the tragedy earlier not only to Ferenczi but also to Pfister[6] — and particularly his *"der arme Tausk"* in the letter to Lou Andreas-Salomé — suggest a piercing reaction that had to be depersonalized.

Tausk had initially been accepted by Freud and the group with enthusiasm. Great hopes were held out for his collaboration in view of his great talents. Freud's letter to Lou Andreas-Salomé discloses that his expectations had been disappointed. The future historian might decide whether this evaluation of Tausk's psychoanalytic contributions was justified or biased.

At any rate, disappointment was a necessary consequence of Tausk's having been a troublemaker. Abrasive behavior is reported in Lou Andreas-Salomé's *Journal* and also recorded in the *Minutes*. He complained about Freud's alleged plagiarism, no doubt a source of irritation to Freud. It was also an act of ingratitude. He tried to

[6]Oskar Pfister (1873–1956), minister and psychoanalyst in Switzerland. Freud wrote him on July 13, 1919: "Dr. Tausk has committed suicide. He was a highly gifted man, but was a victim of fate, a delayed victim of the war. Did you know him?" (Freud, 1963).

seduce Federn's wife and made Freud's intervention necessary (Roazen, 1969). Or to cite a minor incident: it was probably a lack of consideration when he sent Freud a reprint and compositions and letters of his son with the request for consultation and treatment. After all, Freud was 63 years old at that time, and Tausk did not hesitate to add to the burden he knew Freud had to carry. He could have spared Freud; other analysts in Vienna were available. I summarize here incidents reported earlier because the summary shows how many reasons there were for Freud to feel annoyed by Tausk.

I also wonder how Freud must have felt on hearing that despite Tausk's financial plight, instead of treating Hilde Loewi, he started an affair with her.

At present psychoanalytic standards are rigid regarding amorous relations of analysts with their patients. I have a faint notion that Freud possibly felt less puritanical about an indiscretion of this kind. As mentioned, Hilde Loewi complained bitterly about her encounter with Freud. I conjecture that one of the reasons thereof might have been Freud's critical attitude with regard to her surrender to Tausk. It is a great loss that nothing concrete is known about the content of that meeting.

From Prof. Dr. Tausk's recollection (Neyant-Sutterman, 1978) quoted above, one learns that Hilde Loewi did not put up resistance to Tausk's advances, and it is not impossible that Freud held her responsible for the tragic situation in which she found herself, whereas nowadays one would hold the therapist entirely responsible, his duty being to withstand even a patient's open attempts at seduction. (May I emphasize that my inferences are wholly hypothetical.) There is, however, an incident reported in the exchange of letters between Freud and Jung that deserves citation in this context. In Jung's instance it had not been sexual intimacy that caused the difficulty, but apparently he had provoked erotic fantasies and expectations in his patient Sabina Spielrein (1886?–1934), who later became a well-known psychoanalyst and author of some remarkable psychoanalytic contributions (McGuire, 1974, pp. 228–233). Jung responded to her acting out in an unsuitable way. He was contrite and expected from Freud "a dressing-down more or less disguised in the mantle of brotherly love" (146J).[7] Freud's answer to Jung's letter is noteworthy, since it reflects Freud's personality in a way that is contrary to that which is now so popular:

> Such experiences though painful are necessary and hard to avoid. Without them we cannot really know life and what we are dealing with. I myself have never been taken in quite so badly, but I have come very close to it a number of times and had a narrow escape. I believe that only grim necessities weighing on my work and the fact that I was ten years older than yourself when I came to psychoanalysis, have saved me from similar experiences. But no lasting harm is done. They help us to develop the thick skin we need to dominate 'countertransference', which is after all a permanent problem for us, they teach us to display our own affects to best advantage. They are *a blessing in disguise*" [Letter 145F; Freud's italics].

Freud showed here particular understanding and tolerance. By pretending that he was 10 years older than Jung when he came to psychoanalysis, he minimized the merit

[7]References to letters contained in the Freud-Jung correspondence (McGuire, 1974) follow the numbering system used there.

of having constrained this aspect of countertransference in his own practice. This was a tactful and considerate way of handling a situation that easily could have led to Jung's humiliation. It is all the more surprising in that Freud made a concession contrary to historical truth, for at Jung's age, when transference and countertransference were not yet accepted conceptualizations of psychoanalysis and Freud was exposed to a sudden attempt at seduction by a patient, he unflinchingly converted it to insight into a psychological process unknown at that time.[8] Here Freud would have had an opportunity to demonstrate to the younger his greater strength of character. It was a problem of narcissism. Whereas Freud immediately acknowledged that the patient's behavior could not be explained by the therapist's particular attractiveness, Jung apparently took the patient's positive reaction at its face value.

Whether Freud in view of the far greater infringement of psychoanalytic ethics took the same attitude of tolerance toward Tausk as he had done toward Jung is not known. He felt affectionately toward Jung, on whom he looked as a friend, whereas Tausk was never a friend of his, contrary to Weiss's mistaken belief. Jung's transgression, furthermore, occurred in the course of a protracted treatment in a state of conflict, whereas Tausk's occurred on the spur of the moment — seemingly without inner struggle.

[8]It is worthwhile to quote the passage: "As she [the patient] woke up on one occasion [of hypnosis], she threw her arms around my neck. . . . I was modest enough not to attribute the event to my own irresistible personal attraction, and I felt that I now had grasped the nature of the mysterious element that was at work behind hypnotism" (Freud, 1925, p. 27). The incident must have taken place around 1889, when Freud was one year younger than Jung was at the time of the exchange of the quoted letters.

Yet if my reconstruction of Freud's meeting with Hilde Loewi is correct, he would have stood up for Tausk even though conditions surrounding the incident would be considered aggravating today. As a matter of fact, he added a paragraph in the letter to Jung that would favor my inference. He wrote: "The way these women manage to charm us with every conceivable psychic perfection until they have attained their purpose is one of nature's greatest spectacles. Once that has been done or the contrary has become a certainty, the constellation changes amazingly" (Letter 145F). Here Freud takes the stand of *cherchez la femme* traditionally put forward to rationalize male lapses. Particularly the last sentence insinuates that, according to Freud, in the long run it would turn out that the woman was driven by aggression and not by love.

It would be wrong to say that Freud exculpated the male outright, but he expected man to be wise enough not to be tricked by female wiles.

It is difficult to decide whether Freud still maintained that view in 1919. Possibly his alleged harshness toward Hilde Loewi served the purpose of defending psychoanalysis, which seemed compromised by Tausk's acting out. Reliable information about what went on when Freud met Hilde Loewi would greatly facilitate a reconstruction of Freud's frame of mind while writing the obituary. I am inclined to accept as correct the second-hand information that his attitude toward her was critical. Impressed by Tausk's declaration of loyalty to psychoanalysis, Freud might have decided to do his utmost in the defense of the deceased. He might have decided to draw a line between his subjective evaluation of Tausk based on the knowledge he had derived from personal contacts, on the one hand, and Tausk's *persona publica*, on the other, which was represented by the members of *die Redaktion*. In that way he would guerdon loyalty with loyalty.

It is also striking that Freud did not mention in his letter to Lou Andreas-Salomé either impotence or pregnancy and preferred to pretend ignorance of the precipitating factors of Tausk's suicide. Perhaps he did not want to disfigure the distinguished image she had of her friend. The motive may have been loyalty to Tausk.

Returning to the obituary, I should like to add that there is a particular facet of eulogies which I cannot let pass unmentioned. In his oration in honor of Thomas Mann, Oskar Maria Graf (1955) did not abstain from extremely critical remarks. From the work of the deceased, the honoring of whose memory was the function of his speech, he quoted some passages which must be called abject. Still, the oration is magnificent. The greater a mind was and the greater the work it had created, the more stricture and censure of the memorialized are compatible with a eulogy. Indeed, Thomas Mann's distinction waxes within Graf's framework of critical remarks. Tausk was not a man of such greatness that his eulogy would have been able to bear criticism of the extent found in Graf's eulogy. Veiled as Freud's critical remarks in Tausk's obituary were, and even if they should one day be proved to have grown out of his subjective feelings and are therefore only clues as to his personal relations to the dead, nevertheless the fact that Freud felt free to include them in the obituary may be a sign, however indirect, that he considered Tausk to have been a great man.

VII. Comparisons and Historical Deliberations

It is at most a minor simplification to describe the prevalent contemporary psychoanalyst as a solid citizen who belongs to several professional organizations, to whose administration he gladly devotes a significant part of his time and effort. For him an important goal is to become a training analyst, and then to be elected to administrative jobs that gradually carry him to the top positions in the administrative hierarchy. The average analyst is a personality who appears to be fully satisfied and who — at least on the surface — is on good terms with his society and in harmony with its value system; his flexibility is greater than his predecessors', as witnessed by his willingness to give up the psychoanalytic method in favor of psychotherapy, if necessary. And whereas a person who followed Freud, particularly in early times, had to have the courage of one who resides in a no-man's land for a long time, at present an analyst lives on a comfortable plantation. The differences between the early generation and the contemporary one in social position and social standing, in expectations and ambitions, can hardly be exaggerated.

Therefore, events in the history of psychoanalysis during the period prior to the 1930's can easily be misjudged and misunderstood. In considering the characteristics of contemporary psychoanalysts, one must take into account the fact that the selection of candidates has probably played a part. Around the middle twenties training institutions were organized and training candidates were selected according to strict rules. Prior to that time, almost anyone who was convinced of the validity of Freud's discoveries and who desired to be active in the field could join the movement.

As usually happens, a new movement that deviates from traditional standards and goals attracts personalities dissatisfied with the *status quo*, restless, and *novarum rerum cupidi*. For many of them joining the movement was a sacrifice, and therefore they probably expected special narcissistic compensations. A visionary romanticism strongly colored by idealistic motives could likely have been at work in most of them.

As the spectrum of personalities of those who become analysts nowadays is a broad one, by no means do I want to intimate that there was uniformity among Freud's early followers. Just the opposite. Each of them, even though many might have shared an important trait, had a strong, very distinctive personality. Tausk represented only one extreme type among those who gathered around Freud.

Yet Freud's pessimism regarding Tausk, as evidenced in his letter to Lou Andreas-Salomé, probably had been evoked in part by previous experiences with a person who though still alive at the time of Tausk's death suffered a comparable fate shortly thereafter. Tausk had something like a predecessor in the psychoanalytic movement: Otto Gross (March 17, 1877–Feb. 13, 1920).

"Gross and Tausk were two of Freud's most brilliant disciples, and their twin tragic fates mark the tragic development of that movement," wrote Green (1974, p. 65). The author did not explain why one should regard these two life histories as representative of the psychoanalytic movement, nor why their tragedies should determine the quality of the movement in which they participated. The implication seems to be that the price a psychoanalyst has to pay for brilliance would be a tragic end. But when one looks back on the lives of psychoanalysts who flourished approximately up to the Second World War, this is certainly not confirmed. That period was studded with highly gifted minds. The succeeding period, in contrast, was one in which the forefront of science moved to other areas, and the more adventurous, inquisitive spirits were drawn to sciences in which most consequential problems are at present decided: physics, biochemistry, and genetics.

OUTLINE OF OTTO GROSS'S LIFE AND PERSONALITY

I now turn to an outline of Otto Gross's history and personality, using mainly Hurwitz's (1979) recent monograph. Otto Gross was born in Austria, the only child of Hans Gross (1847–1915), who was professor at the University of Graz, Austria, and the founder of modern criminology. The elder Gross was a man of eminence and international fame in his times. He was an authoritarian, conservative person, and Otto Gross's childhood and youth were overprotected by his parents. Raised "like a prince," he attended private schools and was taught by private tutors. He was given no opportunity to evolve independence and self-reliance, on the one hand, and on the other, any of his wishes, capricious as they may have been, were fulfilled.

In 1899 Otto Gross graduated in medicine from the University of Graz. He traveled to South America as a physician in the service of a steamship company. On that trip he became addicted to morphine, cocaine, and opium; he remained addicted to these substances, except for sporadic interruptions, to the end of his life. His primary interests at the time of the trip to South America were botany and zoology, but shortly thereafter he turned to psychiatry and psychoanalysis, and he soon came to be considered by many as Freud's most eminent follower.

After thorough training in psychiatry he was accorded the honor of an appointment as *Dozent* in Psychopathology at the University of Graz in 1906, a position he resigned from two years later. He moved to Munich in 1907. There he worked for a while at Kraepelin's clinic but spent most of his time in the company of bohemians and anarchists. In the same year he defended psychoanalysis at the congress of neuropsychiatry at Amsterdam and there became acquainted with C. G. Jung. He read a paper at the International Psycho-Analytical Congress of 1908 at Salzburg, and shortly thereafter entered Burghölzli (for the second time) in order to undergo withdrawal treatment and to be analyzed by Jung. He stopped taking drugs but took flight from Burghölzli before being discharged.

The two paragraphs Ernest Jones devoted to Otto Gross in his autobiography (1959, p. 173f.) provide a vivid image of his greatness and decline:

> First and foremost in the circle [at the Café Passage in Munich] was Otto Gross. . . . He was the nearest approach to the romantic ideal of a genius I have ever met, and he also illustrated the supposed resemblance of genius to madness, for he was suffering from an unmistakable form of insanity that before my very eyes culminated in murder, asylum, and suicide. He was my first instructor in the technique of psychoanalysis. It was in many ways an unorthodox demonstration. The analytic treatments were all carried out at a table in the Café Passage, where Gross spent most of the twenty-four hours — the café had no closing time. But such penetrative power of divining the inner thoughts of others I was never to see again, nor is it a matter that lends itself to description. Shortly afterwards he was in Burghölzli asylum, where Jung did his best to help him. Jung had the laudable ambition of being the first to analyze a case of dementia praecox, and he laboured hard at the task. He told me that one day he worked unceasingly with Gross for twelve hours, until they were almost reduced to the condition of nodding automata. Gross, however, escaped from the institution and sent the following letter to Jung, which must be unique of its kind:

"Dear Jung,

> I climbed over the asylum wall and am now in the Hotel X. This is a begging letter. Please send me money for the hotel expenses and also the train fare to Munich.

Yours sincerely"

Freud wrote to Jung (Feb. 27, 1908): "You really are the only one capable of making an original contribution, perhaps except for O. Gross, but unfortunately his health is poor" (Letter 74F).

In 1913 Otto Gross was arrested in Berlin for reasons that are not clear. Green (1974, p. 66) referred to "two euthanasia cases" which "were the grounds for the Austrian authorities to judge him dangerous." According to Hurwitz, his father requested that he be declared incompetent because of drug abuse and his association with anarchists.

After his arrest in Berlin, Gross was deported to the Austrian border and interned in a psychiatric institution. An international uproar was raised demanding his release, but nevertheless he was declared incompetent, and guardianship was assigned to his father. In July 1914 he was discharged and went into analysis with Wilhelm Stekel for a short time. When war broke out, he volunteered as a physician and worked with short interruptions in various hospitals for infectious diseases.

In 1916 Otto Gross became addicted again and was institutionalized for six months. In 1917 the earlier verdict of complete incompetence was changed to partial incompetence. He died in Berlin in February 1920. Friends had taken care of him but "he eluded [their] watchfulness... he distrusted [them] because they would not help him get supplies of drugs by violence" (*ibid.*, p. 100). He was found famished and freezing in a passageway and died two days later of pneumonia.[1]

Otto Gross was an eminently endowed personality.

[1]Jones's statement (1953-1957, vol. 1, p. 30) that Otto Gross's "life came to an end through murder and suicide" before the war was over is incorrect.

As a child he displayed talents rarely observed at that age. The parents tried to prevent his becoming precocious, but he refused to read children's books. His interest was aroused by a natural history text, and after it was read twice to him he knew "every bone of a prehistorical animal, each gut" (jeden Knochen eines vorweltlichen Tieres, jedes Eingeweide) (Hurwitz, 1979, p. 51). Yet an alarming developmental imbalance could be observed from early on. At ten, he was superior to sixteen year olds in knowledge of natural history, mythology, folklore, Latin, and Greek, but at the age of fifteen he said a pair of trousers probably cost a few hundred guilders; "when he was laughed at, he recited a suitable two-page-long passage from Horace in order to console himself" (als er ausgelacht wurde, rezitierte er eine passende 2-Seiten lange Stelle aus Horaz, um sich darüber zu trösten) (*ibid.*, p. 51). His great intellectuality and his complete failure in handling even the simplest practical matters remained a characteristic discrepancy throughout most of his life. At Burghölzli he went to bed with his hat on and dropped cigarette butts everywhere. Sometimes he did not wash for a long time and went to bed with his clothes on. For many years he got up at 11 A.M. and spent the rest of the time in coffee houses discussing, teaching, philosophizing.

He was unable to handle monetary matters. His father provided him abundantly with money and only rarely refused to comply with his requests. Once Otto Gross demanded 1000 guilders to rescue a woman who had been married to his uncle but was divorced because of mental disease. She prostituted herself and ran a wine tavern that catered to low individuals. Otto Gross threatened to kill himself if his father did not provide the money. Shortly thereafter he wanted the same sum of money for the same purpose. During the Russo-Japanese war he demanded that his father send the Japanese 1000 Kronen because they had lost an armor-plated ship (*ibid.*, p. 141). He gave money indiscriminately to anyone who asked for it. What alarmed his father particularly was the fact that not only bohemians and anarchists gathered around his son but also burglars, thieves, and addicts, that is, a collection composed almost entirely of derailed existences.

In addition to his eminently impressive personality, Otto Gross evidently had unusual charisma. This is borne out by the testimony of writers who devoted chapters of their novels to his description. Only two need be mentioned: Franz Werfel (1890–1945) in *Barbara oder die Frömmigkeit* and Leonhard Frank (1882–1961) in *Links ist der Herz*. Both novels are superbly written testaments to the heart-breaking tribulations suffered by young men during the first quarter of our cruel century. Both, like many other accounts, confirm the magnetic, one may say hypnotic, effect Otto Gross had on those around him. Almost everyone who came under his spell was subjected to fascination from which he could hardly escape. Gross presented his ideas penetratingly, and his enormous knowledge provided him with comprehensive arguments which the average educated person could not disprove. Extraordinary passion went into his abstract thoughts, and he must have appeared as the initiator of a new religion and ethics, a new guru who not only perplexed his listeners by the originality of his thoughts but also stirred their innermost feelings and desires, as if he possessed the power of the Biblical prophets.

Yet from most of the eyewitness reports one gains the impression that the witnesses were aware that there was something profoundly evil, that is, destructive, in him.

His effect on women was incisive and telling. In 1903 he married Frieda Schloffer (1876–1950), the daughter of an impecunious lawyer in Graz. She suffered lifelong from headaches, insomnia, and pains in her legs. The marriage did not turn out well, and from 1911 on he let his wife live with Ernst Frick (1881–1956), an anarchist and painter with whom she had three children.[2] Otto Gross had relations with the two von Richthofen sisters, Frieda (1879–1956) and Else (1874–?) while they were married. Else Jaffé became pregnant and gave birth to a son, Peter, in 1907, the same year Frieda Gross gave birth to Otto Gross's son, who was called "Wolfgang Peter."

It may be questioned whether Otto Gross's publications match the charismatic effect of his personality. Basically, he adhered to the conceptualizations of his teacher Wernicke (1848–1907) and tried to combine them with psychoanalysis. Like his teacher, he saw in the psychoses cerebral disorders and thought in terms of brain structure and brain physiology. The result was his postulating what he called the *Nachfunktion*, or secondary function, to which he attributed great importance and which I shall not discuss because it had no further bearing on psychiatry.

His typology based on two types of consciousness, that is, the flattened-out (verflachtes Bewusstsein) and the narrowed-down types (verengtes Bewusstsein) met a similar fate, even though it had an effect on C. G. Jung's typology of extra- and introversion. As Hurwitz stated, it had no bearing on psychoanalytic research, and today it sounds like an arbitrary differentiation based on hypotheses that remain unconfirmed by research.[3]

[2] Frick, who was in prison for a short time, in turn abandoned Frieda for a younger woman. Frieda died in poverty.

[3] Hurwitz's comment that Otto Gross as well as C. G. Jung, re-

I would not go so far as Jung does, in a letter of January 4, 1935 (although I own this letter, the Jung family has not given me permission to publish it). In it Jung expressed himself negatively about Otto Gross's work as a psychiatrist and psychoanalyst. He accepted Otto Gross's work on the *Nachfunktion* and typology as valid contributions. Yet he did not observe other signs of *Genialität*, unless one looks at "clever prattle" (Gescheit-schwätzerei) and "problem wallowing" (Problemwälz-erei) as creative symptoms.

Some of Otto Gross's psychoanalytic papers, no doubt, reveal his great talents. I do not feel entitled to pass judgment, particuarly from the psychoanalytic point of view, since Otto Gross moved in many respects outside of the psychoanalytic field, to the extent that adequate assessment would require a specialist's knowledge of the history of psychiatry.

What made Otto Gross known was far less his scientific papers, whatever their quality might have been, than his ideology. To be sure, I do not want to say that he was wrong inasmuch as he was ideologue, for science may be wrong where ideology is right. But ideology pursues aims other than those of science. It sets up a system that answers all questions and solves all problems (Freyer, 1963). An ideology also sets up an enemy who stands in the way of the millennium. It is a black-and-white picture

---

spectively, needed their typologies in their struggles to overcome their father conflicts would make sense. By declaring that there are two types of personalities that perceive and experience the world in essentially different ways, the necessity of agreeing upon empirical findings and their theoretical implications is abolished. This made it possible to eschew the son's confrontation with the father, since they belonged to different types, and agreement was consequently impossible because of their basically different psychic structures.

of the world culminating in a devil and a panacea. A characteristic of an ideology is that all of its claims can never be correct, for they are born of strong wishful impulses and aim to inspire actions. To be sure, wishful impulses may accidentally lead to truth. According to a person close to him, Otto Gross himself seems to have regretted his scientific work as

> insincere, as expressing only his intense yearning to be accepted and respected by his colleagues. . . [H]e destroyed much he had written of that kind for he believed in himself. . . as a revolutionary and not as a scientist [Green, 1974, p. 42].[4]

In his ideological writings Otto Gross envisions matriarchy as the solution of all psychological and cultural problems, and patriarchy, which had established itself when the Jewish prophets turned against the cult of the Babylonian Astarte, as the arch-devil that has brought unfathomable unhappiness to mankind. Matriarchy will liberate mankind, removing such patriarchal biases as faithfulness and chastity. It will lead to real happiness, exclude conflicts, and make harmony possible. All children and adults as well live in a state of aloneness under the patriarchal system. The child is forced to accept the alien (*das Fremde*) and to give up "*das Eigene*," that is, his innate individuality. Intercourse in patriarchal society is always rape and humiliation of the woman. I shall come back to the question of matriarchy and patriarchy below. Here I stress that all this is outside of psychoanalysis, which is primarily a science.

How far away from psychoanalysis Otto Gross was

4See also Otto Gross's letter to the noted socialist, anarchist, and physician, Fritz Brupbacher (1874–1945) (Hurwitz, 1979, p. 109f.).

from the beginning—that is, how little he had grasped of what psychoanalysis essentially stood for—can be observed from his psychotherapeutic technique. Jung wrote to Freud in September 1907 (McGuire, 1974, p. 90) as follows:

> Dr. Gross tells me that he puts a quick stop to the transference by turning people into sexual immoralists. He says the transference to the analyst and its persistent fixation are mere monogamy symbols and as such symptoms of repression. The truly healthy state for the neurotic is sexual immorality.

As a matter of fact, several informants reported orgies in the group around Gross. Landmann (1973, p. 123) noted

> the orgies...[they carried out] in order to prove to each other their lacking any inhibition. For a while they retreated into a rented stable and proscribed any expression of inhibition to an unimaginable extent. In this primitive milieu incredible conditions prevailed which shared much with the mischievous behavior of the small and smallest children and with the excesses of certain 'swinish gatherings' of students.[5]

Hurwitz asserted that Otto Gross was ahead of Freud.

[5]Orgien...um sich ihre Hemmungslosigkeit zu beweisen. Eine zeitlang zogen sie sich in ein gemietetes Stallgebäude zurück und verpönten in denkbar weitesten Masse jegliche Hemmungsäusserungen. Es herrschten in dem primitiven Milieu unbeschreibliche Zustände, die viel gemeinsam hatten mit den Unarten kleiner und kleinester Kinder und mit den Auswüchsen gewisser studentischen 'Schweineabende' (quoted after Hurwitz, 1979, p. 210).

To be sure, he was Wilhelm Reich's predecessor, if anything. Hurwitz used the following incident as proof of his
thesis. When Otto Gross gave his unpublished Salzburg
lecture on "the cultural perspectives of science," Freud in
the ensuing discussion is said to have remarked: "We are
physicians and want to remain physicians" (Wir sind
Ärzte und wollen Ärzte bleiben) (Hurwitz, 1979, p. 94).
Did not Freud do the same as Otto Gross without citing
him when he later criticized society, Hurwitz asks. But
why does Hurwitz assume that Freud's remark referred to
Otto Gross's societal criticism? As a matter of fact, Freud
did not criticize society later than Otto Gross, as Hurwitz
believes, but already in 1908, when he published a
radical critique of contemporary society. Therefore, it is
highly improbable that Freud's admonition was directed
against that part of Otto Gross's lecture which contained
criticism of society. Years later Otto Gross made a short
remark about the content of his Salzburg lecture. He presented the perspective which had been opened by the
finding of psychoanalysis that the unconscious has an
effect on "the totality of cultural problems and the
imperative of the future" (Gesamtprobleme der Kultur
und den Imperativ der Zukunft) (ibid., p. 94). "Imperative of the future," one may be sure, bespeaks an ideology which always knows with certainty what the future
will bring. Freud's warning must have been directed
against that part of Otto Gross's paper in which, abandoning science in favor of ideology, he became prophet
and demanded political action, both of which do not fall
within the scope of psychoanalysis.

For a while Otto Gross tried to abjure his role as a
prophet. In an undated letter to Frieda Weekley (Green,
1974, p. 58), he wrote about a past phase in his life in
which he was a prophet. "I realized in myself that every

tendency to prophecy is an expression of self-falsification. . . . I . . . am now much further from prophecy than ever before."[6] Yet Otto Gross's good intention of abandoning the role of prophet cannot have lasted long.

Diagnostic considerations

What was the diagnosis of Otto Gross's disorder? The answer to that question must have encountered formidable obstacles, because the sorting out of the effects of addiction and drug withdrawal, respectively, from those of the basic mental disorder must have been an almost unsolvable task for those who had to diagnose him. I have reported above some of the bizarre behavior patterns that had been observed in Otto Gross: I must now enlarge on them, inasmuch as they are relevant to the question of diagnosis. When he was in Munich, he wanted to sue his chief, Kraepelin, for not using psychoanalysis in his clinics, but was detained from proceeding by Ernest Jones's intervention (Jones, 1953–1957, vol. 2, p. 29). Many a contemporary psychiatrist might take such an instance of bizarre behavior as pathognomonic of a schizophrenic disorder.

It may be worthwhile to quote an eyewitness of his last years:

> [Gross] lived. . . in a small apartment in Mariahilf [a district of Vienna], sniffed continuously cocaine and was surrounded by a small circle of cocaine addicts. . . . Their convictions were the total espousal of the doctrines of Marx and Freud. There was no

[6]The letter was probably written after the Salzburg congress and may serve as a document that gives an idea of what Freud had in mind when he emphasized the medical aspect of psychoanalysis.

property and no erotic limitation. The small circle shared the little it possessed with every member and everyone slept with everyone and all took cocaine. ...He [Otto Gross] was an extraordinary man and his principles of living by no means sounded insane, when he expounded them. He wrote an excellent article for a communist newspaper [Kaus, 1979, p. 49].[7]

It was known that he [Otto Gross] lived almost exclusively on cocaine and tried to induce all friends to sniff [cocaine]. Also he claimed the drug had awakened his productivity and he needed hardly any sleep, dozed only occasionally for a few minutes.... The group around Gross was very esoteric, and each getting together of two members was talked over, discussed and analyzed in detail.... It was impossible to help Gross; sometimes I gave him a little money but he distributed it immediately among the members of his group. A few years later, I met two of his [female] disciples in Berlin; they were as though redeemed, because the genius that had kept them under its spell no longer existed [*ibid.*, p. 85f.].[8]

[7]Er lebte...in einer kleinen Wohnung in Mariahilf, schnupfte ununterbrochen Kokain und war umgeben von einem kleinen Kreis von Kokainsüchtigen.... Die Gesinnung bestand aus der totalen Adaption der Lehren von Marx und Freud. Es gab kein Eigentum und keine erotische Beschränkung. Der kleine Kreis teilte das wenige, was er besass, mit jedem Mitglied, und alle schliefen mit allen, und alle nahmen Kokain.... Er [Otto Gross] war wirklich ein ausserordentlicher Mensch, und seine Lebensgrundsätze klangen keineswegs irrsinnig, wenn er sie auseinandersetzte. Er schrieb für eine kommunistische Zeitung einen ausgezeichneten Artikel.

[8]Man weiss, er lebte beinahe ausschliesslich von Kokain und ver-

The following three episodes are of great importance, and on their evaluation much will depend.

1. Otto Gross spent some time in Ascona, which was at that time the gathering place of those who rejected bourgeois beliefs and standards of conduct: vegetarians, cultists, occultists, reformers, nudists, long-hairs, anarchists, and what not. Among them there was a woman, Lotte Chattemer, the daughter of a North German government official, who took flight from her family and came to Ascona in 1899, not yet twenty years old (Monte Verità, 1978, p. 57). In 1906 she committed suicide with poison Otto Gross had given her for that purpose. Knowing that Lotte Chattemer was determined to end her life, he had made poison available to her, he wrote later, with the intention of sparing her a death that would involve great suffering (Hurwitz, 1979, p. 12).

2. In 1908 he took Regina Ullmann into analysis. Regina Ullmann (1884–1961) was the second daughter of Jewish parents. Her father (1842–1889), who participated as a sergeant in the American Civil War on the side of the northern states, returned to Europe and settled in Switzerland, where he became a successful merchant. After the father's death, both sisters moved to Munich. After the First World War, the older sister (1883–1929) moved

---

suchte, alle Freunde zum Schnupfen zu veranlassen, behauptete, die Droge habe seine Produktivität geweckt und er brauche kaum mehr Schlaf, döse nur ab und zu ein Paar Minuten.... Die Gruppe um Otto Gross war sehr esoterisch, jedes Zusammensein zweier Mitglieder wurde ausführlich besprochen, diskutiert, analysiert.... Es war unmöglich, Gross zu helfen, manchmal gab ich ihm etwas Geld, aber er verteilte es sofort unter seine Gruppenmitglieder. Ein paar Jahre später traf ich zwei seiner Jüngerinnen in Berlin; sie waren wie erlöst, weil das Genie, das sie in Bann gehalten hatte, nicht mehr existierte.

to California, where she married and was in charge of a private sanitarium.

Regina was described as a clumsy, slow, oversensitive child, squinting, extremely forgetful, and suffering from difficulties in learning to speak and write. One would surmise that she showed symptoms of what is nowadays called a "minimal brain damage" syndrome. She attended a private school and only later a public secondary school. Her talents in writing poetry and stories manifested themselves early. In 1906 she gave birth to an illegitimate daughter. The father was Hans Dorn, who later was professor of economics in Munich. In 1907 she became acquainted with the Richthofen sisters and with Otto Gross. In that year her only play, *Feldpredigt*, was published; it earned Rilke's admiration.[9] Otto Gross became the father of her second illegitimate daughter, Camilla, about whom I shall say more below.

From the biography of Regina Ullmann her friend Ellen Delp (1960) wrote and from her works (Ullmann, 1978), one receives the impression that she was highly talented, sensitive, utterly naïve, and even though submerged in imagery, fantasies, and daydreams, in intense contact with nature and an alert observer of human beings. A personality so little versed in coping with hard reality needed the more or less constant help and advice of friends, of whom she had a few who loyally and faithfully persevered in her care and protection. In view of her childlike naïveté one may reproach Otto Gross with particular obtuseness and lack of humaneness when he abused the authority with which a therapist is automatically endowed by a patient.

When Otto Gross was told of her pregnancy, "he

[9]See Rilke's letter in Ullman (1978, vol. 1, pp. 434–436) and Ullmann (n.y.).

apparently dropped all connection with her . . . . She even formed the impression that he was encouraging her to kill herself, by leaving poison within her reach" (Green, 1974, p. 57). "He seems to have assented to his father's refusing her the financial support to which she was legally entitled" (*ibid.*). Hurwitz (personal communication) considered the poisoning charge as unproved, because the information is secondhand. Martin Green wrote to me that he received that information "from more than one source" but cannot retrace it.[10] According to Green (1974, p. 57), "This was a major occasion for Frau Jaffé [one of the von Richthofen sisters], who had befriended Regina Ullmann, to decide that Otto Gross was pathologically irresponsible." Gina Kaus wrote to me that some members of Otto Gross's circle committed suicide. When they told him of their intention, "he never tried to stop them but firmly held their hand for a long time."

3. Otto Gross entertained a love relationship with Sophie Benz, a young painter and anarchist, who lived in Munich. In 1910 he moved with her to Ascona. She became psychotic and committed suicide by means of an overdose of cocaine he had prescribed. He reported that without warning she had suddenly become mentally sick. He devoted the subsequent months to her care and early in 1911 observed a remission: "I admit, contrary to expert knowledge, I hoped at that time for a cure. Shortly thereafter, a sudden relapse occurred and before I could grasp the turn of events the sudden end through suicide [occurred]." (Ich gebe zu, allem Fachwissen entgegen, damals auf Heilung gehofft zu haben. Gleich darauf aber kam ein plötzliches Rezidiv und ehe ich die

[10]One may infer with some certainty that the charge of leaving poison close to the patient seems assured, but that Regina Ullmann's impression of Otto Gross's intent remains open to doubt.

eingetretene Wendung noch ganz zu erfassen vermocht hatte, das plötzliche Ende durch Selbstmord) (Hurwitz, 1979, p. 240). The *Tessiner Zeitung* of March 4, 1911 reported: "In Ascona a German lady fell ill two days ago, with the signs of severe cocaine poisoning. She was moved in hopeless condition to the hospital in Locarno and died yesterday, Friday" (*ibid.*, p. 214). Otto Gross had written a prescription for several grams of the poison. The medicine was to serve as a painkiller for his lady-friend's toothaches, he told the pharmacist. "Yet instead of dropping the poison into the tooth, the unfortunate [woman] put the glass to her lips and drank it."

In view of these three rather incriminating incidents, it is not readily understandable when Hurwitz (*ibid.*, p. 123) writes that Otto Gross "was always disciplined enough...never to slide into the destructive" (noch diszipliniert genug war...nie ins Zerstörerische abzugleiten). Hurwitz called Otto Gross's mode of proceeding with Lotte Chattemer *Sterbehilfe*, which means, approximately, "euthanasia." But even those who uncompromisingly favor euthanasia will not allow a physician, particularly when he himself is addicted, to dispense poison to physically healthy patients who desire to commit suicide. Furthermore, is the incident one of euthanasia at all? The concept is applied to the act of bringing about the death of patients who are suffering from lethal, incurable disease. What was the diagnosis of Lotte Chattemer's disease? Otto Gross does not say – he only reports that she was resolved to end her life. If this resolve was caused by melancholia or severe depression, then Otto Gross's action was unconscionable, for such disorders are self-limiting. After having provided poison for her, he implored her once more to come to Graz in order to be treated by him. Thus he apparently thought her disorder to be curable: that is, he foresaw a time when she would enjoy life again and be glad that she had not been victimized by the previous suicidal impulse. One must also ask what made Otto Gross certain that no one else could have persuaded the patient to have a try at psychotherapy? Why did he not call a consultant but rely exclusively on his own therapeutic skill and judgment? A physician's arrogating the right to himself alone to decide as to whether a patient is to live or die presupposes a belief in his own omnipotence and his superiority over all his colleagues. The presence of a predisposition to megalomania in Otto Gross can be inferred from other instances, too.[11]

His problems with Regina Ullmann cannot be justified from any point of view. He would not have been able to supply a rationalization. His making her pregnant flew in the face of any conception of medical ethics and was in utter disregard of the human consideration a physician is supposed to feel for his patient. If it is true that he attempted to induce the suicide of a patient who evidently did not wish to die, it would have been an act of outright criminality.

The third instance, the suicide of Sophie Benz, should have been investigated by the courts, as the local paper

[11]Jung wrote in his letter of 1935 that Otto Gross suffered from unbounded megalomania; he always thought that he was treating the therapists who were treating him. Stekel (1920) ended his obituary of Otto Gross with a statement that possibly also implies the megalomaniacal aspect: "His [Otto Gross's] mind resisted every deeper insight into itself and the opium served to narcotize this self-knowledge. His was the tragedy of all neurotics who would analyze themselves. They arrive at an impasse, and no amount of learning takes them beyond." From this one may infer that Otto Gross's addiction magnified the megalomaniacal attitude.

demanded. From Leonhard Frank's autobiographical novel *Links ist das Herz* it is known that he and Sophie had a passionate love affair, both of them apparently falling in love for the first time, when Otto Gross enticed her away. She became addicted to cocaine like Otto Gross, evidently under his influence. In 1915 — that is, at a time when he was still an ardent admirer and follower of Otto Gross — Franz Jung (1888–1963) published a novel about Sophie's last hours with her lover (F. Jung, 1915). This novel, very likely, was composed of episodes Jung himself observed or was told of by Otto Gross. From that novel one would have to infer that both Gross and Sophie were under the acute influence of drugs at the time she committed suicide. One passage (*ibid.*, p. 59) would also indicate that she wanted "to conquer the world" with Leonhard. "He had such a strong will power," but Otto Gross apparently interfered with their relationship.

In any event, what was Sophie's diagnosis? Otto Gross only said: "Sophie Benz has poisoned herself because of the psychosis by which she was attacked" (Sophie Benz hat sich wegen der Psychose, von welcher sie befallen war, vergiftet) (Hurwitz, 1979, p. 12f.).

It is strange to hear such a diagnosis from a psychiatrist as experienced as Otto Gross, for psychosis is not a sufficient diagnosis. Why, as in the case of Lotte Chattemer, did he not communicate a diagnosis?[12] There

[12]Hurwitz (personal communication) stated that Otto Gross had used the term "psychosis" in a communication to laymen — that he wanted to be given the possibility of justifying his actions before a court but was prevented from doing so by being declared incompetent. However, if he seriously had wished to make an appearance before a court (the incident with Sophie Benz occurred two years before he was declared incompetent), he would have had an op-

is also the question of whether society can permit an addicted physician to treat his psychotic lover. It stands to
reason that it was Otto Gross's duty to provide his unfortunate mistress with treatment by a competent colleague. After all, there was the chance that Sophie Benz
had developed a psychotic reaction to cocaine from
which she might have recovered if she had been hospitalized. But Otto Gross wrote: "One will raise the reproach against me that I did not bring her into a psychiatric institution. That I have not done this is for me
the only idea that consoles" (Man wird mir zum Vorwurf
machen, dass ich sie nicht in eine psychiatrische Anstalt
gebracht habe. Dass ich es nicht getan habe, ist mir das
einzige Bewusstsein, welches tröstet) (*ibid.*, p. 13).

Otto Gross upon his lover's death took refuge with a
lawyer. It is chilling to read that he himself voluntarily
entered a "psychiatric institution" (Mendrisio)[13] three days
after his lover's death, but found consolation in the fact
that he had not granted Sophie Benz the same privilege.

He was discharged from Mendrisio with the diagnosis
of psychopathy. This diagnosis is nowadays in disrepute,
but it makes no difference by which less harsh term it is
replaced. There is no doubt that there is a group of patients who suffer neither from a psychosis nor a neurosis
nor an organic mental disorder but are highly deranged

---

portunity since he was informed that he would be arrested upon his
reentry to Switzerland. Only through his father's intervention did he
escape prosecution. Furthermore, since he knew that he would not
have to face a court (which apparently would have sentenced him unless a plea of insanity had been made), one would expect him to have
been eager to publish the facts that would exonerate him.

[13]It is possible that like Tausk, Otto Gross took refuge in a hospital
after a disappointing experience with a woman, for he entered
Burghölzli shortly after he got into difficulties with Regina Ullmann.

by a perversion of their value systems. The diagnostic difficulty is to differentiate them from schizophrenics, whose value systems, too, are confused and whose barriers of repression are reduced, as in the psychopathies. That Otto Gross suffered from a severe defect in his capacity to form object relations is evident and was also recorded by some of his adherents.

Franz Jung, who until 1919 was one of the most enthusiastic adherents of Otto Gross, confessed, "I would have sacrificed myself for him without hesitation" (Ich hätte mich ohne zu zögern für ihn aufgeopfert), but knew that "For Gross himself I was perhaps not much more than a figure to be moved to and fro on the chessboard of his thought combinations" (Für Gross selbst war ich vielleicht nicht viel mehr als eine Figur auf dem Schachbrett seiner Gedanken Kombinationen, die hin und her geschoben werden konnten) (*ibid.*, p. 122). Such inner aloofness to the other person, which was noticed even in his relationship to his son, is often taken as pathognomonic of schizophrenia. But it is also encountered in the psychopathies. I conjecture that most contemporary psychiatrists in this country would diagnose Otto Gross as a schizophrenic; this would coincide with Jung's final diagnosis, after Otto Gross's flight, of *dementia praecox.*

I have gone into the question of diagnosis in much detail because Hurwitz raised a serious reproach against Freud. Hurwitz disputed the correctness of Jung's diagnosis. He was certain that Jung's shift from his initial diagnosis of "typical compulsive neurosis" (95J) to the malignant diagnosis of "dementia praecox" (98J) was not grounded in correct psychiatric reasoning and was unwarranted in terms of dynamic psychiatry as well as classical psychiatry.[14]

Hurwitz was certain that Jung's diagnosis represented his revenge for Otto Gross's abrupt flight from Burghölzli. (Jung wrote, regarding his dealings with Otto Gross, "the Gross affair has consumed me in the fullest sense of the word, I have sacrificed days and nights to him" [98J].) Jung allegedly felt humiliated in the eyes of his superior, Bleuler, whose chief resident he was, and defeated in the eyes of Freud, with whom he was entangled in a father–son rivalry.[15] Feelings of helplessness and impotence, doubts in his own therapeutic abilities, make the failing therapist shift the responsibility to the patient. Allegedly in order to rationalize the unfavorable outcome of his therapy, Jung wrote Freud (98J):

> [The infantile complexes] were . . . overwhelmingly powerful. . . drawing their affect from inexhaustible depths. . . . There is no development, no psychological yesterday for him; the events of early childhood remain eternally new and operative. . . he reacts to today's events like a 6–year–old boy, for whom the wife is always the mother, everyone who wishes him well or ill always the father.

Hurwitz may be right in his analysis of Jung's bias, but Jung's description of the difficulty he ran into with Otto

[14]The latter conclusion is particularly surprising since, as will presently be reported, two psychiatrists of the classical school reached the same diagnostic conclusion.

[15]Szasz anticipated Hurwitz's thesis that Jung's diagnosis of Otto Gross was based on rancor (1976, p. 136n). However, Szasz's claim that Freud "heartily" concurred with Jung seems to me an exaggeration, for the document he quotes establishes that Freud had doubts as to the correctness of Jung's diagnosis (see below).

Gross reminds me word for word of what one encounters in the psychotherapy of schizophrenics, particularly when the modern antipsychotic agents, which, of course, were not known in 1908, are not used. Since after some eighty years psychiatrists wrestle in vain more frequently than not with the same difficulties that Jung described in precise and most apposite terms, I can hardly agree with Hurwitz's negative statements about Jung—the mistakes one may discover in his procedure when it is evaluated from a modern point of view notwithstanding.

Hurwitz (*ibid.*, p. 183) even went so far as to look on Otto Gross's flight as the inescapable—as I interpret Hurwitz's statement—consequence of the way Jung felt about Freud. He weighed the possibility that by his flight Otto Gross wanted to revenge himself for the fact that personal differences between Freud and Jung were straightened out on his back[16] in a treatment "in which as a patient he felt no chance to be taken seriously and to be respected" (in einer Behandlung bei der er als Patient keine Chance spürte, ernst genommen und respektiert zu werden) (*ibid.*, p. 183). Hurwitz made this claim even though Jung wrote: "He [Gross] is an extraordinarily decent fellow" (95J); "For me this experience is one of the harshest in my life, for in Gross I discovered many aspects of my own nature, so that he often seemed like my twin brother —but for the Dementia praecox. This is tragic..."(98J). Nevertheless, he "would not have missed this experience for anything," in view of the "unique insight" he had gained "with the help of a unique personality." Neither is there an indication that Freud was lacking in respect for Otto

---

[16]Hurwitz used the word *Buckel* (hunchback), a disparaging vernacularism that makes Freud and Jung appear in an ugly light.

Gross. Finally, when Hurwitz wrote that the stigma of insanity imposed by Jung not only became Otto Gross's doom but "actually contributed to eliminating him from life" [dazu beitrug ihn. . . tatsächlich aus dem Leben auszustossen] (*ibid.*, p. 184), he ignored the fact that Jung was never involved in any court procedure against Gross, and that Gross was felled by his addiction, which made him resort to suicide-like actions. In view of these considerations, it is difficult to evade the impression that Hurwitz harbored a prejudice against Jung, inasmuch as Otto Gross was diagnosed as schizophrenic by two classical psychiatrists, Bonvicini[17] and Berze.[18] Both were excellently trained experts in their fields, and each had an excellent reputation as a practitioner as well as as an investigator. I do not see any reason to assume foul play in their instances, as Hurwitz assumed with regard to Jung.[19]

[17]Giulio Bonvicini (1872–1951) acquired his medical degree in 1896 *sub auspiciis imperatoris*, the highest honor a medical candidate could achieve. He was trained by Krafft-Ebing and by leading psychiatrists in Paris. From 1898 to 1902 he worked under Wagner-Jauregg at the University Clinics of the University of Vienna (Hoff, 1952). In 1911 he became *Dozent* and in 1926 professor at the University of Vienna. He lectured on addiction and mental disorders (Menninger-Lerchenthal, 1951). For forty years he was chief of the hospital for mental patients in Tulle, where Otto Gross was committed for a while.

[18]Josef Berze (1886–1957) acquired his degree in 1891 and became *Dozent* in 1902 and professor in 1921 at the University of Vienna. He did his research on schizophrenia at the Psychiatric Municipal Hospital in Vienna (Steinhof), whose director he was from 1919 to 1928. He was known internationally for his publications on schizophrenia (Stransky, 1959).

[19]The psychiatrically trained reader will agree that in Otto Gross's case many facts can be adduced that speak in favor of a diagnosis of schizophrenia. Hurwitz did not commit himself with regard to a diagnosis; he limited himself to asserting that Otto

In disagreement with Jung, Freud leaned toward a diagnosis of compulsive neurosis and toxic paranoia caused by cocaine, as is known from his correspondence with Jung.[20] It was quite natural that in view of Jung's extensive experience with schizophrenics and his past therapeutic contacts with Otto Gross, Freud granted Jung superiority of judgment. Yet in Hurwitz's eyes this concession made Freud as guilty as Jung and he held him in like measure responsible for Otto Gross's downfall.

Freud wrote Jung that he wanted "to persuade [Jung] to continue and complete my work by applying to psychoses what I have begun with neurosis" (106F). Hurwitz (*ibid.*, p. 197) reached the amazing conclusion that

the negotiators come to agreement by redefining the border of their respective territories. Otto Gross, however, perishes under these deliberations. Freud drops him and subscribes to the diagnosis of Jung, to whom authority in the field of psychosis has now been transferred. The victimization of Gross occurs

---

Gross was no schizophrenic. On this issue I am inclined to agree with him, believing as I do that Otto Gross suffered from a grave psychopathy. I have been censured by readers of the manuscript for using this diagnostic term because it carries a pejorative implication. I should not mind using a better-sounding term, but I do not think that terminology is decisive. Otto Gross's history, as far as it is known, compels the assumption that intense constitutional factors contributed to his asociability. Nowadays as then, despite the considerable progress in the intervening years, his psychopathology might be expected to be inaccessible to treatment.

[20]Stekel (1920) disputed Jung's diagnosis: "[H]e [Otto Gross] really suffered from a severe neurosis complicated with indulgence in opium and cocaine. . . . I am acquainted with no one who more terribly laid waste his powers, no one who might have done greater things."

also in the service of the psychoanalytic movement, which would anyway only have suffered severe damage through Gross. The break between Freud and Jung could, at least, be postponed for several years.[21]

Although Freud deferred to Jung's expertise in the field of psychoses, Hurwitz wrote as if Freud had falsified his diagnostic reasoning for pragmatic reasons. He described Freud as a salesman who in order to avoid strife with a competitor made an agreement of franchise. He thus ignored Freud's earlier letter (74F) to Jung, at a time when no difference of opinion existed regarding Otto Gross. "I wish," he wrote, "you would take the whole problem [of paranoia] over." Hurwitz further ignored the consideration that Freud in his research tried to follow the pleasure principle insofar as he was eager to limit his research to the field in which he felt more comfortable and competent, the psychoneuroses. Thus he hoped that Alfred Adler would take over the research into the biological foundations of the neuroses (Freud, 1914), and he expected Tausk to investigate the philosophical foundations of psychoanalysis (Freud, 1919).

Among the available documents nothing is found that would justify the following critical remark: "Neither of

21Die Kontrahenten einigen sich, indem sie Territorien gegeneinander abgrenzen.... Otto Gross geht aber bei dieser Auseinandersetzung unter. Freud lässt ihn fallen und schliesst sich Jungs Diagnose an, dem ja die Kompetenz für das Gebiet der Psychosen nun übertragen ist. Gross' Opferung geschieht auch im Dienst der psa. "Bewegung," der Otto Gross doch nur schweren Schaden zugefügt hätte. Der Bruch zwischen Freud und Jung konnte wenigsten fr einige Jahre hinausgeschoben werden.

them [Freud and Jung] had the greatness to admit later that injustice had been done to Otto Gross" (Die Grösse hatte keiner später einmal einzugestehen, dass Otto Gross Unrecht geschehen war) (Hurwitz, 1979, p. 301). What Hurwitz could have had in mind with such a statement is a mystery. As other biographers nowadays do, he evidently tried to move the psychopath into a favorable light at the expense of a genius.

Freud's actions, however, had no bearing on Otto Gross's fate. Moreover, in this instance Otto Gross's actions left not much choice: he either had to be declared incompetent or he had to be prosecuted, which would have almost certainly led to a prison sentence. No civilized society can suffer physicians who provide poison for those who are disgusted with life, or who treat their psychotic girlfriends without minimal protection against the consequences of the disease. According to Hurwitz, it was his father to whom Otto Gross owed the fact that he was not prosecuted (*ibid.*, p. 213). Still he severely reproached the father for pursuing the declaration that his son was incompetent, even though Otto Gross himself finally admitted that "the fact of my commitment per se has been of saving consequences" (. . . dass die Tatsache der Internierung an sich ein rettendes Moment für mich gewesen ist) (*ibid.*, p. 235).

Tempting as it may be to go into the details and problems of the Freud-Jung relationship as it becomes clear in their correspondence (which has not yet been adequately analyzed and evaluated), I shall, for obvious reasons, restrain myself here. An unprejudiced reader of the Freud–Jung letters will agree that Hurwitz greatly inflated the importance of the Gross episode and misinterpreted the meaning it held in the interrelation between Freud and Jung. A passage in one of Freud's subsequent letters — which one, I do not recall — quoted by Hurwitz demonstrates this. When Freud was obliged to straighten out the consequences of Jung's acting out with his patient, Sabine Spielrein, and Jung was contrite about the mistakes he had committed, Freud wrote (149F): "When I think that I owe your intimate conversion and profound conviction to the same experience with Gross, I cannot possibly be angry and can only marvel at the profound coherence of all things in the world." Furthermore, it becomes evident that Freud was little influenced by Jung's diagnosis, since he wished (179F) Otto Gross to be invited to the next psychoanalytic Congress in Nuremberg (i.e., that of 1910). At any rate, in 1908, when the Gross affair took its inception, the Freud–Jung relationship was in its ascendancy. Freud was, as he remained almost to the bitter end, fascinated by Jung's creativity, vigor, charm, and devotion to the psychoanalytic movement. A controversy about diagnosis and treatment of a patient could never have endangered Freud's closeness to his "friend, helper and heir" (304F). Even when a far greater difference of opinion arose years later, Freud vigorously stated that disagreements about scientific matters must never touch upon their friendship, which he not only hoped but anticipated would last a lifetime. From the beginning he was aware of "the resentment that is bound to accumulate in the course of a year between two persons who demand a good deal of each other. . . ." (106F).

One receives the impression that the sporadic disagreements about scientific matters which are part and parcel of a cooperative undertaking between two original and hard–working minds drew Freud, if anything, closer to Jung. Both of them were aware, as references in their correspondence prove, of Jung's "father complex," about whose strength and interference Jung complained to

Freud from time to time. But Freud never doubted that Jung would be able to master that source of irritation. Hurwitz strengthens the impression of affinity between the Gross episode and the final break between Freud and Jung by making it appear as if the ripple of the initial episode had become an undercurrent surfacing in the end as a renewed controversy about schizophrenia (dementia praecox). This attempt at tightening his reasoning fails, since the difference of conceptions that gave Jung the opportunity to enforce a break with Freud derived from an entirely different context.[22]

[22]Jung felt incensed by Freud's disagreement with his opinion about the meaning and function of the incest motive frequent in mythology. Freud repeated "that personal variations are quite justified and I still feel the same need to continue our collaboration. I must remind you that we first made friends at a time when you had gone back to the toxic theory of Dem[entia] pr[aecox]" (324F). He delineated in sober terms that which he did not mean to be a refutation of Jung's theory but "should be taken merely as expressions of doubt" (314F). Shortly thereafter (316F), he tried to promote a further calming of the threatening storm: "I don't expect you to explain this difficult matter more fully in letters; I shall be patient until you publish your ideas." Although, as is evident, he did not agree with Jung, he made a concession that should have instantly calmed the atmosphere. "I value your letter for the warning it contains and the reminder of my first big error, when I mistook fantasies for realities. I shall be careful and keep my eyes open every step of the way." In vain. Jung (318J) was "grieved to see what powerful affects you have mobilized for your counteroffensive against my suggestions."

After their meeting in Munich, Freud again praised Jung, even though he interpolated a reservation. He wrote (329F) "that you have brought us a great revelation, though not the one you intended. You seem to have solved the riddle of all mysticism. . . ." Jung's reply (330J) carried nothing but scorn: Freud's opinion convinced him that Freud greatly underestimated the value of his work, for the insight for which Freud had praised him "has been self-evident for us for years."

Whatever the historian's final evaluation of the meaning of the Gross episode in relation to Freud and Jung, from Otto Gross's case history one can learn what shock-

---

In the preamble to that rude letter Jung himself called it an "impudent [unverschämt] attempt." Understandably, after Jung had had a "good laugh" [kräftig ausgelacht] at him on that occasion, Freud "dare[d] say no more about your libido innovation now" (334F).

In reference to his fainting spell in Munich, Freud (329F) wrote to Jung of "a bit of neurosis that I really ought to look into." Jung in a supercilious manner advised Freud that "'This bit should. . . be taken very seriously" and indecently added a classical quotation, saying that "it leads to the semblance of a voluntary death." When Freud (337F) called Jung's attention to a *lapsus calami* in a previous letter (335J), Jung replied with an outpouring of invective that forced Freud to "propose that we abandon our private relations entirely" (342F). Oddly enough, the use of *lapsus calami* for psychological insinuations had been initiated by Jung in their correspondence. He had pointed out "with diabolic glee your slip of the pen" (126J). Ironically, Freud had not made the alleged *lapsus* at all, as the facsimile of the letter (125F) shows.

What is even more surprising than Jung's hitting Freud over the head whenever the latter suggested a compromise or made a conciliatory gesture is Jung's almost obscene language in their discussion of incest, in which he claimed that a mother's body, in view of her pendulous belly [Hängebauch] and varicose veins, could not possibly have been attractive to primitive man. The mother is so worthless for the adult "that he hurls it with a few kicks of the foot into the bush" [dass er's mit ein paar Fusstritten in den Busch schmeisst] (313J). Jung's raging against the body of the aging mother and his insistence on breaking with Freud become understandable when one takes notice that at that time (as is commonly repeated by those with relevant information) Jung had started a relationship with a woman 13 years his junior. Understandably, he had to deny the psychic reality of incestuous wishes, rave against the waning attractiveness of aging women, and attack the man who for years had functioned as a father substitute. Some details may find further clarification after the publication of Freud's letters to Bleuler, which, I have been told, contain many references to Jung.

ing situations Freud had to face. The claim that Otto Gross was Freud's most gifted and original pupil — as Freud himself initially thought — was promulgated widely; it can be imagined how embarrassing this must have been for Freud, since psychoanalysis was not only suspected but even accused of immorality, and Otto Gross's way of treating patients seemed to confirm this. Nevertheless, Freud never took a public stand against him, but only "removed Gross's titles from the bibliography of psychoanalysis" (Green, 1974, p. 43).[23] Yet despite his discretion and limited contact with Otto Gross, Freud did not escape Hurwitz's castigation. (For another perspective on Otto Gross, the reader is referred to the Appendix.)

Comments on Patriarchy and Matriarchy

Martin Green had the felicitous idea of tentering Otto Gross's life history within the framework of patriarchy and matriarchy. Ambiguous answers are not the only responses historians make when asked regarding the history of matriarchy. Some doubt that it ever existed as a historical entity. Others attribute to it a well-defined and highly consequential phase in mankind's history. The decision one way or the other is immaterial in this context. There is no doubt, in my estimation, that matriarchy is psychologically represented in almost every member of contemporary occidental society, and possibly this is true as far back as human history is documented.

The subjective representation of matriarchy in man's unconscious is the natural, that is, unavoidable, consequence of the fact that every human being goes through a phase that Freud called preoedipal. In it reigns a mother

[23]The author was not able to give me the source of that information.

endowed with limitless power, unencumbered by any rivalry with a father. It is a world in which no trace of a father or even of his shadow can be discovered. It is the world when mother nursed the child; his whole existence depended on her wisdom, willingness, and love, and he was entirely enveloped in the nurture, warmth, and affection that came from her. Such incredible delights as these leave ineradicable traces in a human being's unconscious. And despite the fact that the unconscious representation of this primordial phase may be overlaid by the subsequent phase, in which paternal authority assumes ever-increasing relevance and significance, the preoedipal traces can be brought to silence only under special circumstances. Even though Freud considered the father's death "the most important event, the most poignant loss, of a man's life," as he expressed himself in 1908 in the Preface to the Second Edition of his *Interpretation of Dreams* (Freud, 1900), he wrote in a letter (1929), "The loss of a mother must be something very strange, unlike anything else, and must arouse emotions that are hard to grasp. I myself still have a mother, and she bars my way to the longed for rest, to eternal nothingness" (E. Freud, 1960, p. 392). In another letter after his mother's death (1930), he wrote:

It [the mother's death] has affected me in a peculiar way, this great event. No pain, no grief, which probably can be explained by the special circumstances — her great age, my pity for her helplessness toward the end, at the same time a feeling of liberation, of release, which I think I also understand. I was not free to die as long as she was alive, and now I am. The values of life will somehow have changed, noticeably in the deeper layers [E. Freud, 1960, p. 400].

In a moving way Freud here articulated sentiments and associations that intimate a primary bond to the mother who bound him to life and whose disappearance freed the way to "longed-for nothingness," which is, after all, a return to the initial stage of life. The aliveness of the "matriarchal" layer, however, neither aroused conflicts nor interfered with the rules and exigencies of the patriarchal world in which he was living and creating.

I wonder to what extent Martin Green, in describing the particular constellation in Germany at the turn of the century — the conflict between the North, represented by Bismarck, a typically patriarchal figure, and the intelligentsia concentrated in the South and Rhineland, the thinking of part of which was directed toward a matriarchal world — has presented a special instance of a general pattern. Is the conflict between patriarchy and matriarchy one that runs quite generally through man's history and is one of the many motors, a general *movens agens*, that drive history on, one of those conflicts that can never come to rest? Since the conflict between psychological matriarchy and psychological patriarchy is found, even though to a varying degree and with varying consequences, in every individual, it could easily be projected into external reality and basically contribute to the reactions of elitist groups (and consequently of the masses) to economic and political conditions.

Be that as it may, according to Martin Green, the Bismarckian patriarchy incited a passionate countermotion in other parts of Germany, particularly in the South. Munich became its center, as symbolized in its suburb Schwabing.

Otto Gross was a prominent representative of that movement in opposition to his father, a high-profiled representative of patriarchy. It is fascinating how the contrast between the principles colored Gross's conceptualization of psychoanalytic technique. His therapeutic stance, which anticipated some of Wilhelm Reich's work, was not a late development but was displayed a decade earlier. The reader will recall the letter to Freud of September 1907 in which Jung told him of Gross's method of avoiding the transference and of the latter's advocacy of "sexuality immorality" as "the truly healthy state for the neurotic." Shortly before his death

> he called for sexual revolution in order to save the world in our day. . . . [H]e demanded a state ministry dedicated to the liquidation of the bourgeois — that is, patriarchalist — family and of bourgeois sexuality. The limitation of sexual life to the orthodox forms of "decent" genital monogamy he regarded no less a tyranny than marriage itself. Pleasure is the only source of value. Only by entering into the Paradise Lost of polymorphous perversity can man renew himself. He believed in, and practiced, an orgiastic therapy which he called the cult of Astarte [Green, 1974, p. 44].

I believe that Martin Green overvalued Otto Gross's contribution to the great movement of expressionism, which also rejected patriarchy. He did not consider Frank Wedekind and his great plays, in which, as I shall show, Otto Gross's ideas were anticipated and brought most forcefully to public attention. As the reader will see, there is another reason for turning attention now to Wedekind, namely, that he recognized a powerfully potent conflict in the male psyche which might explain the conflicts neither Tausk nor Otto Gross were able to solve and which led them ultimately to disaster.

WEDEKIND

In my consideration of Frank Wedekind, the great

German playwright, I do not intend to present a psycho-analytic study. I shall limit myself mainly to those data which may permit an overview of his biography and shall delve into his work chiefly for the purpose of presenting a special character of woman which he created and which is relevant in this context.

Benjamin Franklin Wedekind (1864–1918) was conceived in the United States but born in Hannover, in the north of Germany. His father, Friedrich Wilhelm (1818–1888), born close to Göttingen, lived a rather restless life. After he graduated as a medical doctor in 1839, he traveled extensively in Germany. In 1843 he went to Turkey, where he worked as a physician in a mine and participated in an expedition into Asia Minor. After his return in 1847, he was employed by various newspapers to report on the *Deutsche Nationalversammlung* in Frankfurt–am–Main, where Germany's political future was to be decided. When he was disappointed by the defeat of the liberal cause, he emigrated in 1849 to the United States and settled in San Francisco as a general practitioner. He acquired a large fortune but lost it as the result of embezzlement. He played a central role in the German community and became president of the German Club. In 1860 he became acquainted with the woman who was to become his wife, Emilie Kammerer (1840–1916).

She was born in the vicinity of Zurich. Her father, Jakob Friedrich (1796–1858), was an uneducated man who acquired considerable wealth by improving the production of matches. He had a choleric temperament, hated princes and clergy, but felt warmth for his neighbors. For his political activities he was arrested but escaped imprisonment by flight, leaving Germany to settle near Zurich.

Emilie's mother was Jakob Friedrich's second wife. She died when Emilie was still a small child. Jakob Friedrich remarried but Emilie was treated badly by her step-mother and sent to a boarding school, where she received an excellent education. Her older sister, Sophie (1834–1858), had a remarkable career as a singer, securing a position at the Vienna opera. Once she had done so she felt responsible for her younger sister. She refused to become the mistress of an archduke, left the Vienna opera and moved to Nice, where she married a young French officer whose family was of the old nobility. They moved to Valparaiso.

Emilie followed them, and thus the life of Wedekind's mother was even more adventurous and colorful than his father's: sixteen years old, she was the only female pas-senger on the sea voyage which took her after 101 days to Valparaiso (Kutscher, 1964, p. 13). The family lived in Chile under straitened conditions. Both sisters were forced to earn their living. Emilie, too, had musical tal-ents, and both sisters sang in the opera. They made their appearances in major cities of Chile, Peru, and Central America.

In 1858, Emilie's situation again changed suddenly. The family decided to go to San Francisco. During the sea voyage, Sophie died of yellow fever. When Emilie arrived in San Francisco with her brother-in-law and Sophie's daughter, "the hard-working girl who was not spoiled by fortune and never discouraged by indulgence, supported the little family by concerts, singing in churches, and theater play" (*ibid.*). Emilie's was a chaste nature (Kutscher, 1922–1931, vol. 1, p. 16), meaning that she did not fall prey to the temptations of a career which forced her to appear in music halls. Yet her acting in vaudeville got her into disrepute with the German community in San Francisco. She had become engaged to a wealthy German merchant in Valparaiso, but she broke off the engagement because she did not love him enough. In San Francisco she married an old singer out of compassion; as an innkeeper her husband had lived a solitary life. Her husband's peculiarity and way of living were disappointing to her, and when it turned out that she would be held responsible for large debts he had incurred and concealed from her, she separated from him.

At twenty, in 1860, she was again alone and had to depend on her ability to earn a living. She fell sick and was treated by Dr. Wedekind. Since both of them felt lonesome, they drew closer together. At first they felt only friendship for one another. He offered her the affection and devotion of a brother, which she accepted. Soon they fell in love with each other. Nevertheless, he resented her life as an artist. In particular, her appearances in music halls were a source of embarrassment to him. He traveled to Southern California in order to forget her, but fell sick. After his return he was ready to let her be trained, at his expense, as a singer, but she decided in favor of marriage. They were legally joined in 1862.

These details concerning the lives of Frank Wedekind's parents, particularly his mother's, are important because, as I believe, the parents' restlessness and adventurousness, as well as the perils to which they were exposed, penetrated his dramatic opus.

In 1863 Wedekind's older brother was born in Oakland. Wedekind's father, despite his enthusiastic preference for the political institutions of his new homeland, named him Armin, after Germany's liberator. Apparently this was the expression of his unease in the West. As he wrote in his diary, "One does not find anything there that forms and lifts the mind" (was geistig bilde und erhebe) (*ibid.*, p. 18).

Shortly after their return to Germany, the second son was born and named Benjamin Franklin, in honor of the country of liberty, thus expressing the conflict of the father's political convictions. In 1866 the third son, William Lincoln, was born; in 1868, Erika, who became a famous singer; in 1871, Donald, who later committed suicide; and in 1876, Emilie. None of the sons was baptized, but the daughters were, at the mother's insistence.

Wedekind's father discontinued his medical practice after his return to Germany and turned toward politics. He put his American experiences in the service of his fight for a true democracy against the dawning Prussian absolutism. When the war of 1870–1871 brought a limited unification of Germany and instead of democratic liberty the reign of a *Kaiser*, he who considered George Washington to have been the greatest statesman of all time (*ibid.*, p. 21) decided to leave Germany. He settled with his family in Switzerland. He bought Schloss Lenzburg, whose foundation goes back to the eleventh century. It was a picturesque castle, situated on a hill looking down on a small town of two thousand inhabitants. Wedekind's father had wanted to retire but was kept busy by the demands of caring for his extensive property. He had time, however, for his avocation as art collector, gathering a small museum, full of paintings, coins, sculptures, and lithographs.

Schloss Lenzburg must have deeply impressed the boy Wedekind. It was mentioned often in his letters, and he visited it frequently for relaxation after moving out of his parents' household. Thus, the boy's early environment was most suitable for the formation of a romantic author who indulged in the pursuit of medieval beauty and the praise of rural life. Yet Wedekind's demon took him into far-off regions. A story, "one of the most precious narrations of our times" (gehört zu den wertvollsten Erzählungen unserer Zeit) (Kutscher, 1922–1931, vol. 2, p. 31), used a tale a prisoner told his father in the presence of the fourteen-year-old boy. The protagonist of the story was a prisoner who had fallen madly in love for the first time in his life but found himself impotent when at last the beloved girl granted him a tryst. Thereupon he set fire to the village in order to prove his virility to her. We notice here how early the youth's imagination was incited by, and drawn to, sexual complexities, the female being the male's ominous destiny.

Wedekind was a poor student who barely made his way through gymnasium. The professor in whose house he boarded wrote that "his boundless laziness, indifference and the dabbling in poetry which obviates any healthy development and discipline baffle description" (seine grenzenlose Faulheit, Gleichgültigkeit und die jeder gesunden Entwicklung und Disziplinierung um Wege stehende Poetaserei spotten jeder Beschreibung (Kutscher, 1922–1931, vol. 1, p. 31). However, his open and friendly behavior, his rich talents, his maturity of judgment and intelligence were acknowledged. The absence of interest in his studies was determined by his above-average endowment in, and devotion to, poetry. He spent great energies in the service of this devotion and hoped to avoid the need to study laboriously, as was expected. Discipline and interest in the sober and sobering subjects he should have studied were certainly not favored by the parents' colorful pasts and their thirst for liberty, individuality, and independence.

Early on he joined a group of students who felt as he did. Tragedies, stories, and poems were written. An important subject of disputation was, of course, love, about which he "however could not speak from his own experience" (allerdings nicht aus eigener Erfahrung sprechen kann) (*ibid.*, p. 33). Sex would remain the preoccupation of his life and the principal subject of his plays. Noteworthy is a statement in an early letter (1881): "I love more than anything else roaring, unrestrained passion, the heart's tumults, perhaps just for the reason that I am most bereft of them" (Ich liebe die brausende, zügellose Leidenschaft, die Tumulte des Herzens, über alles, vielleicht gerade darum, weil sie mir am meisten abgehen) (F. Wedekind, 1924, vol. 1, p. 28). Here is the inception of what possibly would prevail during the rest of his life, his passions being attached to the figures he created and their sufferings rather than to the living. Thus he discovered that the figures of his fantasy aroused greater love in him than the girls of Lenzburg (letter of June 1882, *ibid.*, p. 20), as was expressed in an early poem:

> My waking eye never saw you,
> I see you only in dreams.[24]

He soon recognized the narcissistic root of his poetic endeavors:

> I sang of the fiery heat of love
> Of rosebuds and moonshine,
> I sang of radiant sunlight —
> Beauty I achieved in plenty
> As happened with the most beautiful poem
> I have celebrated myself in song.[25]

24Mein waches Auge sah dich nie/Ich seh dich nur in Träumen (Kutscher, 1922–1931, vol. 1, p. 80).
25Ich sang von feuriger Liebesbrunst,/Von Rosenknospen und Mondschein;/Besang der Sonne strahlendes Licht —/Viel Schönes

And in one of his last poems he made the general statement:

> For my poem. . .
> Was always first destined only for me.[26].

This, however, was hardly true of his plays, for he spent a considerable part of his energy in fights with producers and censors. The prospect that his plays would not be performed was unacceptable to him.

A general outline of Wedekind's life may suffice. He went through the pretense of studying law, as his father requested. When he could no longer conceal the fact that he had deceived his father by studying literature, a serious argument broke out. As a consequence, he was forced to earn a living and worked for a while as advertiser for the well-known manufacturer of Maggi's soup cubes. Later a new showdown occurred with the father, and Wedekind attacked him physically. A disparaging remark that his father made about his mother precipitated the outbreak, which Wedekind deeply repented. He attained a reconciliation by pleading for it. After the father's death, Wedekind was financially independent for a while. He spent two years in Paris and half a year in London.

For many years Wedekind's main worry concerned his upkeep. He had to beg friends and relatives for money as he was practically destitute. He found relief transitorily when he was an itinerant singer in Munich's famous "Die elf Scharfrichter" (The eleven executioners). After the

---

ist mir gelungen./Jeweilen mit dem schönsten Gedicht/Hab ich mich selber besungen (1883; F. Wedekind, 1920–1921, vol. 8, p. 30f.).

26Denn mein Gedicht. . ./War immer zuerst nur für mich bestimmt (F. Wedekind, 1920–1921, vol. 8, p. 172).

turn of the century, when his plays found increasing acceptance, he acquired moderate wealth. But for most of his life, and certainly through the decisive years, his fight for survival was all-consuming.

Wedekind spent seven months in prison because of a political poem published in *Simplicissimus*,[27] in which he satirized Kaiser Wilhelm's journey to Palestine. This episode was all the more embittering to Wedekind since he had written the poem at the request of his publisher, Albert Langer (1869–1909), who had promised that it would be published only after consultation with a legal authority and that Wedekind's hand-written manuscript would be destroyed upon receipt. Oddly enough, the poem was published despite the fact that the authority had warned against it, and the original was not destroyed but found its way into a copy of *Simplicissimus* that was handed to the police detective who searched the publication's premises.

Wedekind was greatly hampered by an unending fight with censors who repeatedly prohibited publication and performance. He was ready to make compromises and changed his original manuscripts in order to make performance of the plays possible. Since the various versions he prepared to appease censors have not been published, a reliable analysis of his works is greatly impeded.

Wedekind's struggles were not restricted to fights against censorship, for most critics rejected his work violently and accused him of immorality and decadence. Some of Germany's greatest literary minds recognized his outstanding contribution to literature during his lifetime, as is documented by *Das Wedekindbuch* (Friedenthal,

[27]*Simplicissimus* was a famous political periodical whose publication began in Munich in 1896, was suspended in 1942, and resumed in 1954.

1914), commemorating his fiftieth birthday. And yet, by and large, his works were rejected for a long time, perhaps even to the present.

The bare facts of the Oedipus complex can be easily discerned in Wedekind's life history, as is to be expected. The father himself, an unsettled, conflictful personality, was not free of tyrannical traits, but they were not of an extreme intensity. However, one of the areas where he was unready to compromise caused his son great unhappiness. The father insisted that Wedekind, prior to becoming a poet, had to acquire a profession in order to be able to support himself. Only then should he follow his literary mission; otherwise, the father would not support him. Yet despite Wedekind's rebellion against the father, his love of him never ceased. At the age of 20, he discussed the opinion that children cannot be raised without religion and wrote: "[T]he father could and should be for his children strictly speaking the highest being and might in his relation to the children refer the first Commandment of the Decalogue very well to himself" (Der Vater könne und solle seinen Kindern eigentlich das höchste Wesen sein und dürfe seinen Kindern gegenüber sehr wohl das erste der 10 Gebote auf sich selbst beziehen) (F. Wedekind, 1924, vol. 1, p. 49).

His relationship to his mother was despite ambivalence a loving one. From his letters one notices that the decline and death of the father were correlated with progress in maturation, with an increase in his actively sharing of his mother's worries and guiding her by advice. As so often, the oedipal guilt was displaced to the sister. In an early verse drama (*Elins Erweckung*) he presented a priest who was preparing to give his first sermon but was torn by scruples caused by an erotic dream about his sister in which he desecrated the wafer.

The gravity of Wedekind's conflicts with the parents was expressed in two remarkable letters. The first (Sept. 28, 1887, — *ibid.*, p. 178) was written shortly after his assault against his father, and the second (Feb. 8, 1890, *ibid.*, p. 207) after his father's death, when he disagreed with his mother about the way she treated his youngest brother Donald, whose suicide he predicted. There he wrote of her having been on the verge of "losing her mind" (am Verrückt werden warst) and of the parents' never having achieved a half-way bearable *modus vivendi* (zu keinen einiger Massen verträglichen *Modus vivendi* gebracht). "As for what concerns me, I consider such circumstances based on scandal to be the most terrible that can exist, breeding places of crime" (Ich meinerseits halte derartige auf Skandal gegründete Verhältnisse für die schrecklichsten, die es gibt, für Brutstätten des Verbrechens). These mysterious passages do not reveal the nature of the stresses to which the children were exposed.

Seehaus's (1974, pp. 21–23) inferences seem convincing. He referred the tensions between the parents to their age difference: "The mother's maturation coincided with the weakening of the father's vitality" (Das Reifen der Mutter fiel zusammen mit dem Nachlassen der Spannkraft des Vaters). Both had chosen a life that differed from traditional bourgeois conventionality, and thus their marriage did not follow the usual patriarchal pattern in which the wife's submission was enforced. Wedekind's mother was not ready to adjust to such requirements, and her "energetic striving for self-assertion" (energische Selbstbehauptungswille) was one of the causes of tension. Yet the parental conflicts were not concealed but openly carried out. The children's opinions were respected by the parents.

Seehaus saw in this set-up signs of emotional strength and vitality. The boy apparently was dealing with parents endowed with passionate temperaments tied to each other by unsolvable conflicts. Wedekind wrote on one occasion of his parents' self-destructive discord (Kutscher, 1922–1931, vol. 2, p. 65): "I lack in every respect the mental equilibrium that comes to fruition in a human being from a family home befitting humans" (Mir fehlt eben das seelische Gleichgewicht, das dem Menschen aus einem menschenwürdigen Familienheim erwächst). One can easily imagine the intensity of emotional arousal to which the boy was exposed over long periods of time. The effect of that loaded atmosphere can be observed in two aspects of Wedekind's personality that also emerge in his work: impetuous *joie de vivre* and deep pessimism. The synthesis of both was perhaps his greatest accomplishment. "Thus jubilation grows out of pessimism," wrote his biographer (Kutscher, 1922–1931, vol. 3, p. 267). Wedekind once noted: "Happy is he who never was happy" (Kutscher, 1922–1931, vol. 1, p. 41), and in 1881 he wrote to a friend: "According to my view, only a pessimist can be truly happy, since he has disabused himself of all hope..." ([M]eines Erachtens kann nur ein Pessimist wahrhaft glücklich sein, da er doch alle Hoffnung... verlernt hat) (F. Wedekind, 1924, vol. 1, p. 28). Pessimism was the guiding principle in his philosophy of life.

That Wedekind as a young man evolved the theory which he upheld for the rest of his life might have been an outgrowth of this pessimism. This theory held that egoism is the only driving force in man: "[I am] convinced that man does not do anything without commensurate reward, that he does not know any other love but egoism" (Überzeugt, dass der Mensch nichts tue ohne angemessene Belohnung, dass er keine andere Liebe kennt, als Egoismus) (*ibid.*, p. 29). He denied values such as love, faithfulness, and gratitude (Kutscher, 1922–1931, vol. 3, p. 258), thus coming close to Otto Gross's views.

Under the psychologically stressful conditions of his parental environment, Wedekind had developed his *Realpsychologie*, as he rightly called it, a parallel to the *Realpolitik* that evolved on the German political scene. That he was an unusual human being was noticed early, and his father introduced him, even as a boy, with the statement "This is the thinker" (Kutscher, 1922–1931, vol. 1, p. 39), signifying a boy who did not take the world the way others did but rather formed his own views, extreme and wrong as they may have been.

Wedekind had intercourse for the first time at the age of 20. His partner was a mature women who became his preceptor in amorous matters (*ibid.*, p. 36). Subsequently he had a large number of girlfriends. Some of these relationships lasted relatively long, coming close to marriage. He did not marry, however, until 1906, when he was 42 (only a few years younger than his father when the latter married). He married Tilly Newes (1886–1970), an actress twenty-two years his junior, which was close to the age difference of the parents. With her he had two daughters. (Previously he had had two illegitimate sons, one with Strindberg's second wife.)

What really went on between him and women is, of course, not known. It seems that a new world of eroticism was opened to him during his years in Paris through extensive contact with cocottes. This new horizon of sex and eroticism found its literary expression in *Sonnenspektrum*, a substantial fragment of an erotic play in prose about which more will be said below.

There are two aspects to Wedekind's literary opus: his erotic poetry and his plays. The two are almost antipodes. In some of his erotic poems Wedekind is charming, seductive, mellifluous, and irresistibly graceful. The poems, immediately captivating and thrilling, take full possession of the reader without any effort on his part. Poems like "Ilse" (I was a child of 15 years) or "Under the Apple Tree," to menion just two, impress me as peaks of erotic poetry which certainly exceed any others of their kind in German literature and possibly are unmatched by anything in any other language. It would be important to know how Wedekind came to have his incredible freedom of uninhibited eroticism without ever falling into the pitfall of pornography.

Remarkable as Wedekind's erotic poetry was, it was his plays that made him famous and permit one to look on him as a literary great. The world of his erotic poetry is not an esoteric one. It is the one that is shared by all sensuous beings that find pleasure in the attraction of the human body. It is a healthy, sane, natural eroticism, uncomplicated by conflict and tragedy. Some poems refer to perversion — for example, "Chastity," in which a masochistic chaste girl becomes so intensely attached to her seducer that she loses all willpower. He exposes her to the cruelest humiliations until he tires of her and orders her to commit suicide, which she promptly does.

Poems of that sort were inimitable satires. They bring us closer to his plays, which contain a cataclysmic aspect of sexuality. Despite forerunners that historians of literature are prone to find in whatever is written (Rothe, 1960), I believe that Wedekind created a new world, in the center of which stands a new type of woman, as exemplified in Lulu.

According to Kutscher (1922–1931, vol. 1, p. 362f.),

Lulu is not a human being; indeed, she is not an individual of any type.

> She is an appearance of transreality, a phenomenon, an allegory, but not 'the' woman and something other than a type, . . . a force of nature, a mystical being . . . a personification of the female sexual drive that stands in the center of life, a spirit of the earth that drags one down, a destroying demon. Egotism is her foundation and finds just here its most uncompromising expression.[28]

Kutscher responded here to a particular aspect of Wedekind's literary art that hardly will be found handled with equal mastery by another playwright: the intermingling of different existential layers, that is, crass realism, symbolism, and unrealism. The reader may often be in doubt as to whether Wedekind is satirical or serious, praising or castigating, presenting the world as it is, should be, or will never be but exists only in our nightmares. It is a supreme accomplishment when all this is condensed into one character like Lulu.

One may look at Lulu as a type, the uninhibited impulse-ridden woman overwhelmed by sexual desires which she must serve without consideration of consequences, or as the victim of anxiety who, traumatized and seduced, after growing up in the slums revenges her

---

28Sie ist eine überwirkliche Erscheinung, ein Phänomen, ein Gleichnis, aber nicht etwas 'das' Weib, auch etwas anderes als Typus, sondern eine Naturgewalt, ein mystisches Wesen . . . Personifikation des weiblichen Geschlechtstriebes, der im Zentrum des Lebens steht, Geist der Erde, der herabzieht, ein vernichtender Dämon. Der Egoismus is ihr Fundament und findet gerade hier seinen härtesten Ausdruck.

frustrations and humiliations until she is crushed by society's ultimate penalty, death. One may find also traces of an unresolved oedipal conflict. Yet the deepest psychological meaning, I believe, is that in Lulu, Wedekind created a new version of a mother goddess, a link in the long chain of matriarchal representatives. Lulu is *au fond* a mythical figure (see Seehaus, 1974, p. 68). Whether as noted above there actually was a matriarchal phase in historical development is not relevant in this context.

Owing to deeply repressed early experiences, man is forced to believe in the matriarchate as a historical entity. Each historical period creates its own version of matriarchal deities. To me Wedekind's outstanding achievement was the creation — with mythopoeic genius — of a new version of a matriarchal deity that fits our times. The woman who devours men, who consummates and then throws them aside, who becomes the undoing of men in some way, is a frequent theme in literature, opera, and folklore. Lulu is not that. By her existence alone she attracts men, all men; she does not need to be active and strive toward them. What she really wants from men is left unclear. Men are fascinated simply by seeing her: an irresistible promise of what is hidden behind her appearance makes them addicted to her. Their destruction is not her fault, as Kutscher remarked, but is caused by their utter unfitness to deal with that untainted *vis viva* of nature. When she is felled ultimately, it is by a monster representing the evilness of society. She does not fall by virtue of her weakness but because patriarchal society contains no existential space for her. Just as Christ's martyrdom cannot be interpreted as a sign of weakness, no more can Lulu's being butchered. Despite her fear and will to take flight in the end, she predicted and desired her final martyrdom, and thus shares another characteristic with Christ.[29] Wedekind characterized Lulu's slayer with raw realism resulting in egregious imagery. Perhaps it was too much for him, for he used the English language on that occasion. It is contained in the first version of the play and had to be dropped because of censorship:

> I would never have thought of a thing like that. — That is a phenomenon, what would not happen every two hundred years. — I am a lusty dog to find this curiosity. . . . When I am dead and my collection is put up to auction, the London Medical Club will pay a sum of three hundred pounds for that prodigy I have conquered this night. The professors and the students will say: 'That is astonishing! —' [Kutscher, 1922–1931, vol. 1, p. 361].

Jack the Ripper in his final outburst expresses man's contempt for, and admiration of, the female genital: his voyeuristic-exhibitionistic pleasure, the victory over archaic fears, the abasement of science to an inhuman destructive force hostile to life, the unmasking of the paternal power as assaultive and violating, the nonhuman exclusion of any kind of love, and its refutation by untainted narcissistic destruction. On the other hand, that only a beast of that sort had the ability to fell her, that no man could integrate her almost preternatural sexual intensity, amounts to an elevation of Lulu.

There are passages that can be cited as objections to my thesis. I shall not discuss them here. It must be kept in mind that Wedekind did not intend to write a murder mystery or a picaresque play. He wrote a play whose

[29]Paradoxical as it may sound, Lulu is a matriarchal Christ, a statement I cannot discuss further in this context.

meaning went far ahead of his time but was set in contemporary society. For a great playwright it is not of decisive relevance whether he has a correct psychology at
his disposal. I do not agree with Kutscher (1922–1931,
vol. 1, p. 368f.) when he considers it a deficit in Lulu that
she possesses only half of the female qualities. He post-
ulates that the missing half is required "for the sake of the
totality which nature, the vital feeling, demands" (. . . um
der Totalität willen, welche die Natur das Lebensgefühl
verlangt). Certainly Wedekind saw the world most one-
sidedly, probably already from his boyhood days on,
but just this onesidedness makes his work great and
unique, and certainly superior to the contemporary pro-
ductions of naturalism, such as those by Gerhart Hauptmann, who was so much more successful than he.

It is clear that if it were possible to put on the stage
characters identical to those extant in reality — that is, if
the difference between created protagonists and real beings, between art and life, was reduced to zero — then art
would not exist. On the other hand, it would be a fallacy
to measure the greatness of creative achievements in de-
grees of deviation from reality.

As is well known, an exact reproduction of reality is
scarcely possible. There is not only the fact of transposi-
tion from one medium into another, but also the obvious
factors of selection and subjectivity. Even a photograph
conveys personal elements. At any rate, there are people
in reality, a mankind that, of course, is ever changing. In
addition, there is an undetermined number of potential
human realities, some of which are realized in the products of creators of literary works. Shakespeare's plays
form a cosmos in themselves. The great creator wrenches
open human reality as it is and fills the opening with the
reality to which he has given birth in his imagination.

The two realities, the real one and the newly created one, must have something in common, or the latter would lose the quality of being understood or even being understandable. Both share language, patterns of action, and many more characteristics. The secret of the great literary creation is its double aspect: it is essentially different from "real" reality, and at the same time it predicates something about it. If nothing or little of the latter is contained in a literary work, it becomes esoteric and has validity only for a few initiates. In accordance with these considerations, one may grade the greatness of literary works by following a scheme that assigns the highest score to the work which shows a maximum of difference from "real" reality but predicates the maximum about it. (This aspect omits the value of form, that is, the aesthetic aspect.)

Wedekind succeeded in creating on the stage a new world that no one before him had conceived or even imagined, however dimly. It differed so much from the real world which his contemporaries perceived — or pretended to perceive — that he had to be rejected. Only later was it recognized how much his world overlaps with *realiter* existing humanity.

One episode from his play *Schloss Wetterstein* is especially pertinent. The Comtesse d'Armont, who became by her own decision a prostitute, accepts a millionaire's challenge that he find in her arms the peace of mind to commit suicide. When she wants to disrobe, he rejects her attempt at enticing him but demands that she tell him the saddest experience of her life, how her father died, what the earliest recollections of her parents were, whether she recalled how "they railed at each other, beat and cursed each other" (Wie sie sich schalten, schlugen, sich verfluchten).

When he asks her what she had done since the time of the morning (it was on the last day of the year) when her father lay in his coffin, blazing passion is aroused in her (Wedekind undoubtedly is referring to a father transference). When her client pretends he is about to drink the poison prepared for his suicide, she drinks it in his stead. The millionaire has succeeded in the same maneuver several times before with prostitutes; he wonders why no strumpet feels herself superior to her parents, even though children regularly do so, and why it is that no strumpet can hold out against talking about her relationship with her parents. It is surprising to find such implications in a play written in 1910 by a man who had no knowledge of psychoanalysis to speak of.

In accordance with prevalent trends in literary criticism, the critique of capitalistic society allegedly contained generally in Wedekind's plays is pointed out also in *Lulu*. No doubt, Wedekind himself, although a bourgeois at heart, castigated the bourgeoisie, but societal critique is not the motor of a play like *Lulu*. Lulu would perish in any society, corrupt or incorrupt, noble or mean, just or injust, unless it were matriarchal.

Wedekind presented a fundamental feature of the relationship between male and female. For him the act of procreation contained a mystery and a secret that was beyond understanding and integration. I have the impression that basically he found it to be unfathomable. The female body had a religious value for him, perhaps the highest value in the whole cosmos. Every infringement of that value, any inhibition that might limit the unfolding of the potential and triumphant ecstasy of which the female body is capable was a deadly sin. In the plays whose center is the female a subordinate function is assigned to the male universe. Man exists only to activate female existence. Only in one play, *Sonnenspektrum*, is there peace and harmony between the sexes. There the balance between man and woman is established in a bordello. Women exhaust their lives in lovemaking independently of who their objects are, and men are unrestrained by obligations. Both parties are satisfied and happy with what they are doing and receiving.

Wedekind coined the term "spirit of the flesh." It is the pinnacle in the value pyramid, an equivalent of the Holy Spirit, but it seems it descends only on women.

A remarkable feature in Wedekind's philogyny is the absence of the procreative factor as a relevant element in the psychology of his female characters. Only in a later play, *Franziska*, does he let the protagonist find salvation in motherhood — and only after she was permitted to live for two years as a man.

In his personal life Wedekind showed those little bizarrenesses that are so frequently observed in the hypercreative: his study was decorated in a gaudy red color; the slightest noise disturbed him; those around him had to wear rubber heels; he hated "tinkering" on the piano. He suffered from inhibitions despite his passionate eroticism and urge to enjoy life in its fullest depth. He was not free of almost pathological sentimentality and his temperament was melancholic. He was exposed to sudden gloomy mood swings, even spasms of weeping. Hypochondriacal fears were not alien to him but do not seem to have been of great importance. However, his distrust in his feelings created conflict, and reason was used and needed as a defensive barrier.[30]

[30]Things got so bad that in 1908 he had to seek medical help from a nerve specialist (Richard Cassirer, 1868–1925), "because I was so afraid that a screw might be loose. He calmed me, everything is still

Following Kutscher (1922-1931), I have pointed to some randomly selected personal traits of Wedekind's. I have done this to indicate the rich panorama of intense psychopathology that is characteristic of him. If one considers the deep disappointments he had to bear, the decades of professional failure, the exposure to penury, an undeserved prison sentence, one has to admit that his psychic apparatus was exposed to strains and stresses which must be called excessive. Yet he escaped severe acting out. The creation of literary works remained the center of his existence, besides the staging of, and acting in, his plays. The central point I have in mind is the absence of gross aggression and destruction against others when his life is compared with those of Otto Gross and Tausk.

Wedekind's psychopathology would have entitled him to act out in the wildest possible way. Perhaps being an actor reduced the potential for acting out.

Yet this should not indicate by any means that there was anything saintly in him, or that his personal life was bare of aggressivity. As reported above, he may have hurt some women whom he loved and intended to marry, but did not. His relationship to his wife was marked by pathological jealousy which caused her great heartache. Her own sometimes very severe depressions were apparently only secondarily caused by the marital stresses, for her mother suffered from depressions and then "played with ideas of suicide" (und spielte dann mit Selbstmordgedanken) (T. Wedekind, 1969, p. 15), which she finally carried out. One sister committed suicide at the age of 25. At the age of 20, Tilly Wedekind jumped

---

solid" (. . . weil ich fürchtete, es sei eine Schraube los. Er beruhigte mich, es sei noch alles fest) (F. Wedekind, 1924, vol. 2, p. 201).

into the Spree. It seems it was not a serious attempt but rather for the purpose of making Wedekind marry her. The second attempt at the age of 31 was more serious.

Probably one of the principal factors that made her marriage difficult — and possibly that of everyone who lives with a great writer — can be discovered in the following paragraph (*ibid.*, p. 188): "How well could Frank grasp all the sentiments of those he created. And how little was he able to comprehend the person closest to him!" (wie gut wusste Frank alle Regungen seiner Geschöpfe zu beurteilen. Und wie wenig konnte er den ihm am nächsten Stehenden begreifen!). For a playwright the focus of primary interest moves from the living person to the persons to whom he gives birth. In Tilly Wedekind's case the situation was aggravated because her husband was strictly opposed to her acting in any plays but his, even then agreeing to her participation only when he played the role of the protagonist.

Thus Tilly was in danger of losing her autonomy. That this did not occur can be seen after she lost her husband at the age of thirty-two. She found other spouses and lived a full life, dying only after she had attained old age. She rejoiced when contemporary drug therapy freed her of her depressions.

Wedekind's relationship to his two daughters was generous and kind. To all external appearances it was unambivalent. Both left memoirs in which they reported on their father (Kadija Wedekind, 1931, 1964; Pamella Wedekind, 1967). His relationship to two illegitimate sons — conceived before he married — was of a different character. Tilly Wedekind wanted to take the two boys into their household, but Frank opposed her plan. In the early years Wedekind occasionally visited his son by

Strindberg's second wife. Later, the contacts seem to have been slightly more frequent. The son made "a very noteworthy career. Our relations with him were good" (eine sehr besichtliche Karriere gemacht hat. Wir standen gut mit ihm) (T. Wedekind, 1969, p. 151).

Wedekind's relationship with his other son was more dramatic. This son was born before his mother was legally separated from her husband, a Belgian diplomat of some wealth. At the age of ten, the son attended a military academy with his half-brother. His mother was a beautiful woman, clever and gifted. She was the only woman in Wedekind's life of whom he did not speak well because, as he claimed, there was something destructive in her character (ibid., p. 150).

When he was ten, the boy was told who his natural father was, and he read all the plays his father had written. Six years later he met his father and stayed with him and his stepmother for a while. Unfortunately, Tilly lent one of her husband's neckties to the youngster, and this provoked a strong reaction of excessive jealousy in the father. Tilly succeeded in appeasing him. But a few weeks after that visit, a manuscript written by his son arrived. The plot was shattering. The protagonists were an aging father, his young wife, and the father's son by a previous marriage. The father is a querulous person who torments his young wife, goes to taverns at night and entertains a relationship with a waitress. The wife and son meet accidentally in the library and a love scene follows. "The son had hit with sure instinct his father's fatal wound" (Der Sohn hatte mit sicherem Instinkt die Todeswunde seines Vaters getroffen) (T. Wedekind, 1969, p. 156).

Wedekind could not forget the incident, and he up-

braided Tilly for the rest of his life. The episode is important because it reveals the intensity with which the
oedipal conflict was still alive in him. He was haunted by
the fear that a younger man would alienate his wife from
him. As so often, he behaved, if anything, in a way that
would have favored such alienation. "Just as he could
raise one up into heaven one day, so he could thrust one
into the deepest abyss the very next day. One lived with
him as though on a keg of powder. Explosions were constant" (Aber ebenso wie man von ihm in alle Himmel
gehoben wurde, konnte er einen schon am nächsten Tag
in den tiefsten Abgrund stürtzen. Man lebte mit ihm wie
auf einem Pulverfass. Ständig gab es Explosionen) (*ibid.*,
p. 89).

Thus Wedekind's ambivalence toward Tilly can hardly
be disputed. But once he had married her, she became a
part of his life from which he could not—despite occasional threats—break away. Her attempts at suicide, certainly favored by his irrational behavior, evidently had a
constitutional basis. She grew at his side and was not deprived of her autonomy, and he left her intact to be able
to live a full life into old age.

The lives of men like Gross and Tausk who possess a
magnetic attraction for women are harder to manage
than those of men who are spared that endowment. The
latter encounter fewer temptations and therefore, one
may assume, are not as strongly incited to act out. On
the other hand, one ought not to overestimate the external factor.

OTHER GENIUSES IN RELATION TO WOMEN

Oskar Maria Graf (1951) wrote an instructive essay on
Rilke and women. His essay ends with a quotation from

Rilke that is autobiographical:

> He has loved and loved again in his solitude, each
> time with the abundance of his total nature and with
> an unspeakable anxiety about the freedom of the
> other. . . . How intensely did he then summon up the
> memory of the troubadour who does not fear any-
> thing more than that his adjurations be heeded![31]

Rilke, despite his physical ugliness, was wooed and
courted by a large number of women. But no instance of
exploitation or rough treatment seems to have been recorded.

Over and over he must acknowledge the icy solitude
by which he is possessed, in which "twosomeness" must
become an irritant. The form his marriage took was an
achievement of wisdom with regard to the conduct of
life. "In true freedom, two human beings associate, separate from each other often for months and years, and
meet only sporadically; each of them goes his own way
without constraint but the spiritual and human connection perseveres without blurring" (In echter Freiheit
gesellen sich zwei Menschen zueinander, trennen sich
monate- und jahrelang und treffen sich nur sporadisch,
jeder geht ungehindert seinen eigenen Weg, aber der
geistige und menschliche zusammenhang bleibt ungetrübt)
(*ibid.*, p. 205). Rilke's attitude toward women apparently
was not constructed primarily around his own gratifications — erotic-sexual or narcissistic; rather, it embodied

[31]Er hat geliebt und wieder geliebt in seiner Einsamkeit, jedesmal
mit Verschwendung seiner ganzen Natur und unter unsäglicher
Angst um die Freiheit des anderen. . . . Wie jedachte er dann des
Troubadours, der nichts mehur furchtet, als erhört zu werden!
(Graf, 1951, p. 210).

respect of women and probably was a factor in the growth of his creative potential.

Freud's relationship to women evolved around a primary chasteness which has erroneously been equated with Victorianism; rather, Freud's attitude was based on devotion, loyalty, and primary care of the love object. Only one incident of meanness to a woman is known, one in which at the age of 19 he composed a satirical, demeaning epithalamium (Freud, 1967) when a girl he had loved for a short while married. The missive was sent only to a friend and never reached its target. After four extraordinary years of passionately wooing his fiancée — years that almost defeated him but did not infringe on his creativity — he married. No further conflicts centering on a woman are known. The rumors about involvement with his sister-in-law have not been confirmed.

In Wedekind, Rilke, and Freud one observes the primary impulse toward creativity in comparison with which acting out and aggression toward the world are rendered insignificant. Internalization of conflicts leads toward series of creative acts.

FREUD, WEDEKIND, GROSS, AND TAUSK

Other contrasts in these four lives are of interest. Freud came from the lowest social background of the four, the others having fathers with relatively high social prestige. Gross's upbringing was the most favored. Both parents were deeply devoted to him. He was given all the cultural advantages of his time. Society invested far more in him than in the others. He was an only child and thus spared the conflicts related to sibling rivalry, which so often has a destructive effect on the child. The others each had many siblings. Wedekind and Freud had mothers who were much younger than the fathers, a situation which often allows optimal resolution of oedipal conflicts.

The most relevant feature that Gross and Tausk shared was their hatred of father. Like Tausk, Gross did not want to be reminded of his origin.

> There is no father, no thick legs that threateningly plant themselves [before one] and make demands. [There is] No compulsion [compelling reason] [that] I take my origin just from him, this ridiculously inflated one who disgusts me. One will no longer be someone's [issue].[32]

The impossibility of coming to terms with the father contributed greatly to their undoing, and may even have been one of the principal reasons for it.

Freud's relationship to his father was optimal; Wedekind's was marred by one episode of physical assault against his father. Such an episode is hardly thinkable in Freud's life, but one must consider Jakob Freud's mellow relationship to his son, and particularly the fact that Jakob Freud hardly ever imposed the invocation of express authority on his son. Thus his direct bearing did not incite much of an aggressive response in the boy, who under these circumstances had to cope mainly with the aggression inherent in his genuine Oedipus complex, which remained almost untainted by aggravation brought about by external reinforcement. I also infer that his father was not seductive enough to cause a negative Oedipus complex in the boy. The evolvement of a strong

---

[32]Es gibt keinen Vater, keine dicken Beine, die sich drohend aufpflanzen und fordern. Kein Zwang, gerade von dem da soll ich sein, dem lächerlich Aufgeblähten, der mich ekelt. Mann wird nicht mehr von einem sein (F. Jung, 1915, p. 38).

superego, even though the father was mild and un-authoritative, may create, if anything, a particularly favorable constellation. Perhaps the effect of the superego is optimal when it is derived less from reactions to external impositions than from the child's own structural and genetic conflicts.

It should also be noted that Freud's father was a failure in his enterprises. Oddly enough, this was true of Albert Einstein's father as well. It is possible that a genius of a certain type flourishes under the auspices of a failing father — as if the child were incited to accomplish something which the father had been unable to achieve. (The resulting feeling of guilt has been described by Freud.) On the other hand, the great social successes of Gross's and Tausk's fathers were of no apparent benefit in relation to their sons' maturation. It may be relevant to recall that Freud in his formative years sought guidance from a strict authority but "found rest and full satisfaction" (Freud, 1925, p. 9) only after he had gained refuge in the physiological laboratory of Ernst Brücke (1819–1892), whose "terrible blue eyes" (Freud, 1900, p. 422) haunted Freud in his dreams even when he was a mature man. This should be compared with Tausk's and Gross's enduring fights with authority.

At any rate, in Freud and Wedekind one observes a great ability to keep conflicts in a state of suspension and to bear displeasure without resorting to the pleasure principle, whereas in Tausk and particularly in Gross a quick activation of the pleasure principle is noticed. Tausk and Gross suffered severely from feelings of aloneness. In Rilke that feeling was perhaps even more haunting, if anything. Wedekind also felt often that way. In Freud, on the other hand, I see no indication that aloneness troubled him. His object relations appear to have been particularly strong. Despite conflicts with the "world" he seems to have been intensely *in* the world. The conviction that the meaning of the world is death, an opinion he held for a while, did not affect his feeling of being deeply rooted in the world. For Tausk and Gross aloneness was intolerable. The ability to bear this condition is a prerequisite for greatness. In Freud's years of isolation (which were not years of aloneness) the foundation of great works was laid. The constructive effect of aloneness for Rilke and his works was adumbrated before.

Gross, one can be sure, apparently tried to nullify aloneness through the fascination and thrill produced by drugs. Only through these artifacts was he able to burst through the frontiers of self, which apparently held him with iron prongs and gave him the feeling of being in prison. Tausk's addiction, if I may say so, was apparently deep attachment to women. Whether he was able to step out of aloneness when he was in love is not known. The instance reported of his calling a lover "it" makes me surmise that infatuations did not interrupt the inner alienation which was then projected onto the love object. Yet he was able to produce fascination in his lover, a fascination which he was unable to experience himself. Rilke in his humbleness and pious deference to God probably took aloneness as man's destiny; he did not rebel against it but built poems on it. For Rilke the created work was probably the only bridge to the world beyond the self.

Lastly, the ability to bear aloneness without rebellion or the fear that a moral collapse might be approaching may be the mark of genius. In general, one may say that solitude does not necessarily lead to aloneness, and aloneness is not bound to solitude. In the state of aloneness, whether combined with solitude or not, the creative mind will feel closer to his creator, the universe, or his mission in life, depending on the existential frame of reference to which he is attached. Therefore, in the state of aloneness he may be readier to be thrust toward the creative process.

In order to draw specific inferences, it would be necessary to know the causation of the feeling of aloneness in the particular instance. In minds like Wedekind and Rilke the feeling of aloneness might not have been the result of a defect, as it probably was in Gross and Tausk, but rather the effect of what I would call a hyperproliferation of personality. The growth of functions may be stunted in some people; in others it may lead to excess but still optimal growth, just as the countenance of some people is more clear-cut, articulate, categorical, in bolder relief than the faces we are accustomed to seeing. Personalities whose functions are of categorical boldness possibly find in their aloneness their natural habitat and therefore do not fight it off or try to abolish it.[33]

TAUSK'S AND GROSS'S PSYCHOPATHOLOGY VIS-A-VIS WOMEN

In the following I shall try to reconstruct the basis of Tausk's and Otto Gross's psychopathology in their rela-

[33]Much has been written about solitude and aloneness. Here I want to quote what Theodor Herzl has written about Paul Heyse (1820–1914), a poet illustrious in his day but now forgotten, even though he was the Nobel laureate of 1910: "He did not know the fierce and pure mountain joy of the lonely. Those who are alone grow thereby and harden themselves for extreme tasks. In that his life and works were lacking. He was too little alone" (Er kannte die grimmige und reine Bergfreud der Einsamen nicht. Die Einsamen aber wachsen dabei und härten sich für die äussersten Aufgaben. Das hat seinem Leben und seinem Werke gefehlt. Er war zu wenig allein) (Herzl, 1900, vol. 1, p. 305).

tionship to women. As a preliminary, more must be said about patriarchy and matriarchy. Martin Green (1974) presented the problem constellation of patriarchy versus matriarchy as it pervaded German culture at the turn of the century. As a protest against, or an antithesis to, the dominance of Bismarck and the cultural changes associated with his rise, a countermove formed in Bavaria and the Rhineland, a part of which consisted of an extolment of matriarchy. Green wove individual vicissitudes into the framework of the collision between these two seemingly irreconcilable aspects of culture.

The patriarchal principle insists on law and order — on logical subordination of passions to discipline; that is, the course of passions should be approved by reason. The principle of matriarchy is organized around the emotions and affects. An intuition is acceptable when it grows out of strong feelings and does not need verification by a cognitive process. The voices of the great priestesses, such as that of the priestess at Delphi, were accepted as truth. St. Mary was the leading intermediary of mercy between man, weak and sinful, and God, whose patriarchal consistency may otherwise condemn him. Matriarchy wants growth and propagation, closeness, and unending love. These remarks are a superficial outline of the two principles that are also encountered in the Apollonian and the Dionysiac.[34]

In Wedekind's tragedy *Samson* lines are found that uncompromisingly extol female superiority:

> Hail to you Delilah, mentor of mankind
> Praised be your art of transmuting

[34]Recent brain research opens up the possibility that the biological roots of the two principles may be found in the prevalence of either the right or the left cerebral hemisphere.

Us from dirty human beings into most
innocent[35] animals.[36]

One's preference for patriarchy or matriarchy can be
based only on subjective value judgments. A harsh reality seems to have enforced a patriarchal principle in early
phases of cultural development. How deeply civilization
is rooted in the patriarchal system becomes evident when
the possibility is considered that science is patriarchal.
This may have a relevant deep biological root. Paternity
is always dubious. The unconscious root of all scientific
activity may be the quest to determine who the father is.
Science per se contains implicitly eternal opposition to
illusion and myth, even though science itself may in the
final analysis turn out to be an illusion. Man's mythical
predisposition may, after all, be the principal agent in
science. It is significant that Otto Gross regretted having
written scientific papers, and Tausk very early in his psychoanalytic career, before he had had an opportunity to
test the psychoanalytic tool, expressed doubt in the scientific method "for illuminating a personality; art is often
better suited for that purpose" (Nunberg and Federn, vol.
2, p. 388). Otto Gross, at one point, seemed to have
equated the drive with the matriarchal, and the ego with
the opposite. It would be an error to deduce an equation
of superego with patriarchy and of the drive with
matriarchy. The proper confrontation is that of social
meaning and function of drives and superego in matriarchal and patriarchal systems. To be sure, in matriarchy
the ego's general attitude toward the drive will be signifi-
cantly different from that in patriarchy. Another error

35Or "chaste."
36Menscheitserzieherin, Delila, Heil!/Gelobt sei dein Kunst, aus
schmutzigen Menschen/Uns in die reinsten Tiere zu verwandeln.

would be to equate matriarchy with femaleness and femininity and patriarchy with maleness and masculinity. These pairs each contain independent variables. There are, of course, women — and they are probably the majority in patriarchal society — who integrate the patriarchal aspect, and men who — in their rebellion against father and in turning toward instituting mother in her full glory — integrate or try to realize matriarchal aspects. Needless to say, such processes are steered by the upsurge of highly cathected unconscious conflicts of infantile character.

The central problem that haunted the large group of which Gross was one of the representatives, and to which, to a certain extent, Tausk belonged, was the revolt against patriarchy, as Green convincingly asserts. Gross went so far as to describe "the expulsion of women from religion by Jews, Greeks, and Mohammedans, as the World's first White Terror" (Green, 1974, p. 44) and for this execrable crime he held patriarchy fully responsible. The matriarchal revolution should end the innately corrupt and cruel patriarchal world. This revolution "would have led to no state at all. All compulsion to work and to sublimate one's energies would be removed" (ibid., p. 63). "[P]sychoanalysis was called upon to make men capable of freedom to create a ferment of revolt within the psyche against the dominant ego. . . . The coming revolution is the revolution for matriarchy" (ibid., p. 63). The question must be raised why this passionate intercession for women was combined with so much aggression against women. One of Otto Gross's former lovers wrote that he almost had destroyed his wife's life, "that he's not able to constrain himself even for a quarter of an hour, whether it be for a person or for an objective value" (ibid., p. 53).

We see Tausk at his best when he resorted to actions against opprobrious outgrowths of patriarchal society, defended the victims of society against a merciless court, or interfered with brutal arrests, but he, too, failed in love of women.

Psychoanalytic common sense would ascribe the revolt against patriarchy, directly evidenced by lifelong discord with the father, as happened in the lives of Tausk and Gross, to a provocative, authoritarian, sadistic father. However, this is only one of the possible variables. The decisive factor in many instances of this sort will be the depth of disappointment which the child experienced as a consequence of the father's behavior. The latter need not have been necessarily harsh; but the discrepancy between the child's original affectionate and tender impulses and fantasies, on the one hand, and the actual measure of their gratification later on, on the other, will often be decisive. Whether the phase of rebellion is regularly preceded by a benign, affectionate one I should not like to decide. At least in one instance of my observation in which a son as an adult uncompromisingly rejected his father, I learned that until early in the latency period, their relationship had been tender and mutually affectionate. Then, as it seems, the father withdrew, and the son never forgave him for this. That the patient's hatred and contempt for the father were of a reactive nature can be deduced from the fact that as an adult he once dreamed that the father had intercourse with him. If this genetic element should be generally present, one may call the passionate opponents of patriarchy disappointed lovers.[37] After the disappointment by the

[37]The age at which the child engaged in strong feelings of love for the father is traumatically disappointed by him must be considered and will have a bearing on the form the psychopathology takes in adult years.

father, a child of this type withdraws totally from him.
The remarkable process is the ensuing substitution of the
father by the mother and the development of a maternal
superego. The woman is endowed with insuperable qualities. As girls are overawed by the penis (Greenacre,
1956), boys are overawed by the mother, and the woman
becomes for the boy an object of immense envy.

It is noteworthy that Wedekind, Tausk's and Gross's
contemporary, expressed man's envy of women with a
radical frankness that hardly will find its equal. Seven
strophes of his rarely quoted "Confession" read as follows:

> Joyfully I swear with every oath
> Before Allmightiness that can chastise
>   me!
> How much more would I like to be a
>   whore
> Than the man most rich in glory and in
>   fortune!
> World, you lost in me a woman,
> Purified from all impurity and bare of all
>   inhibitions.
> Who was born for the market of love
> As I was born for it?
> Would I not live faithfully devoted to
>   love
> As others are to their craft?
> Would I love only once in life
> Any particular human being?
> To love? — On each it never brings
>   delight
> To love brings degradation and envy.
> But to be loved with frenzy many times
>   and vigorously

That means life and blissfulness!
Or should shame arrest me
When early youthful power wanes
To soothe a pain that boldest fantasy
Imagines and desires?
Shame—I felt it often;
Shame that follows noble deeds;
Shame in front of laments and of
     wounds,
Shame when one receives rewards.
To feel shame about one's body
That is overrich in delights
Such ingratitude has been alien
Since I was delighted by the first kiss.[38]

One must ask, in awe, where Wedekind had obtained
that knowledge? What gave him the audacity and cour-

[38]Freudig schwör' ich es mit jedem Schwure/Vor der Allmacht,
die mich züchtigen kann!/Wie viel lieber wär ich eine Hure/Als an
Ruhm und Glück der reichste Mann!/Welt, in mir ging dir ein Weib
verloren,/Abgeklärt und jeder Hemmung bar./Wer war für den
Liebesmarkt geboren/So wie ich dafür geboren war?/Lebt ich nicht
der Liebe treu ergeben/Wie es Andre ihrem Handwerk sind?/Liebt
ich nur ein einzig Mal im Leben/Irgendein bestimmtes Menschen-
kind?/Lieben?—Nein, das bringt kein Glück auf Erden,/Lieben
bringt Entwürdigung und Neid./Heiss und oft und stark geliebt zu
werden,/Das heisst Leben, das ist Seligkeit!/Oder sollte Schamgefühl mich hindern,/Wenn sich erste Jugendkraft verliert,/Jeden
noch so seltnen Schmerz zu lindern,/Den verwegne Phantasie
gebiert?/Schamgefühl? Ich hab es oft empfunden,/Schamgefühl
nach mancher edlen Tat,/Schamgefühl vor Klagen und vor
Wunden;/Scham, wenn endlich sich Belohnung naht./Aber
Schamgefühl des Körpers wegen,/Der mit Wonnen überreich
begabt?/Solch ein Undank hat mir fern gelegen,/Seit mich einst der
erste Kuss gelabt.

age to write and publish these enraptured verses in which male wishes which in the heterosexually oriented are always submerged in deepest repression are glorified and fully acknowledged?[39] It is all the more puzzling, since they were Wedekind's own wishes, as will presently be seen, although he apparently never indulged in manifest homosexuality.

In a fantastic short story, "Mine-Haha"[40] — named after the main female character — Wedekind set forth how young girls should be raised, but in 1894 or the following year he earned his living under the name "Cornelius Mine-haha" by reciting dramatic works by Ibsen. Wedekind's bordello play, *Das Sonnenspektrum*, which was finished in 1894 (Kutscher, 1922–1931, vol. 1, p. 26), starts with a dialogue between Gregor, who is visiting the establishment for the first time, and Franziska, who became a prostitute because she felt bored when living with her mother:

> GREGOR: Does not love, after all, also become boring?
>
> FRANZISKA [shakes her head].
>
> GREGOR: Of course, you are not permitted to say that.
>
> FRANZISKA: Does love bore you?
>
> GREGOR: Unfortunately, I am not a pretty girl.
>
> FRANZISKA: The more one loves, the more one wants to love.
>
> GREGOR: If I could only say that also of myself.
>
> FRANZISKA: You are not very friendly.
>
> GREGOR: I envy you. If I had been born a pretty

[39]For an entirely different interpretation of Wedekind's "Confession," see Friedenthal (1914, p. 25).

[40]Completed in 1895. See Kutscher (1922–1931, vol. 1, pp. 1, 30, and vol. 2, p. 3).

girl, I think I, too, would have chosen your profession.

It turns out that Gregor is a writer. Whether this documentation suffices as a proof of Wedekind's own sexual fantasies, as I believe, is not decisive. At any rate, Wedekind was one of the few, or perhaps the only one, who positively and forcefully revealed a male wish that usually is kept as a secret from others and oneself.

The boy's envy of women has been the topic of psychoanalytic papers. Freud has been criticized for not having discovered this content of the male unconscious, and only emphasizing the equivalent female wish. However, he seems to have known of this male wish, too. In a paper he presented to the Vienna Psychoanalytic Association (October 30, 1912), he said: "As the result of the castration complex, there develops in the man almost regularly the wish to be a woman" (Nunberg and Federn, vol. 4, p. 110). Perhaps Freud dropped this generalization and limited the wish to be a woman to instances of masochism (Freud, 1924).

I should be inclined to assume that in conjunction with the matriarchal layer in man's unconscious there exists in every man the wish to be a woman. The wish to give birth is sublimated with relative ease into the longing for creations of cultural values (Kris, 1939). If the feminine quality of these longings is too pronounced, crisis and inhibition may follow. The integration of feminine wishes is an important prerequisite of creativity in men. Man's wish to obtain the sexual gratification which women experience is far more dangerous for males than is penis envy for women. Strong active strivings and rivalry with men may, in women, lead to considerable cultural achievements and subjective happiness. The male desire for passive sexual gratifications is less suited for sublimation and amounts often to a severe narcissistic injury. Strong reaction formations are built against that desire, and, occasionally, indeed, one discovers an inordinate longing for passive gratification behind male over-creativity.

As Loewenstein (1935) showed, a developmental phase of phallic passivity is possibly the rule, but in this context it is not only a matter of gratified passivity but rather of the female orgasm. Whether the female orgasm is generally more intense than the male's is still debated, but much speaks in favor of its superiority in intensity. Clinically, one sometimes finds simple defenses against male envy of female orgasm. Men with compulsive personality and reduced orgastic strength who marry women with strong and intense orgastic responses are not rare. Here envy is abated if not satisfied by partaking in the pleasure of the love object. Identification is not necessary. One lets another person expose herself to the danger of ecstasy. The narcissistic compensation is evident, inasmuch as the ecstasy is produced by the phallus.

However, there seem to be males for whom this delight in effigy does not suffice, and they long for the experience of the female orgasm — that is, they are under the more or less constant pressure of an urge for an ecstasy that requires penetration. Nevertheless, they are not trans-sexuals. I am inclined to assume that during their childhood they did not evolve a strong enough castration complex. This complex, as Freud exemplified in the Wolf Man's childhood history, initiates and activates strong defenses and leads to an overemphasis on phallicity.

I assume that some boys evolve a wish for a female genital (equivalent to the girl's desire for a penis). It might be perhaps more correct to say that they wish to have a genital like mother's, which would not necessarily include the image of loss of penis. It struck me that Otto

Gross shared his parents' bedroom up to puberty. In reconstructing the etiology of Gross's psychopathology, Hurwitz was inclined to attribute great relevance to the inferior status of women in a patriarchal family and to a lack of maternal affection. As a matter of fact, nothing certain is known about Otto Gross's mother. She evidently was a caring mother, for she is reported to have spent much time with her son in childhood and she called for him when he was discharged from hospitals. Otto Gross also lived with her occasionally after his father's death.

In general, the status of Victorian women at the head of upper-middle-class households is underrated. To be sure, their activity was of a kind that did not necessarily leave documentation, but in many instances — and as I surmise, even in the majority — they were family life's pilots and held the steering wheel in firm hands. But even if this was not the case in Otto Gross's family, I do not see why the image of a degraded mother would give rise to the conviction of absolute female superiority that signifies Otto Gross's ideology. However, if a child should hear even only once (and Gross might have heard it repeatedly) his mother's orgastic outcry, this experience may become the core of a traumatic fixation that will haunt him for the rest of his life. That outcry will overawe him; mother will become something like a supernatural figure; and secretly or even consciously he will be driven by the desire to experience an ecstasy that may live up to what that ecstatic cry made him expect. In that moment he may feel averse to being a boy and wish to develop into something like mother.

Girls when suffering from penis envy hold their mothers responsible for their own failure to possess a phallus. I suggest that boys sometimes have the feeling that they owe the phallus to the father.

At least some Jews, in their daily prayers, offer their thanks to God that they are males. This is also adumbrated by the Bible when it says that the male was made in the image of God, who therefore was of male gender. In contrast, a state unlike that of God was apportioned to the female, who evidently was not created in the image of God. Is it possible that some boys hold their fathers responsible for their own situation as boys and hate them for it? In these instances the penis would unconsciously be considered a liability and a burden. Indeed, one encounters — not too rarely — the attitude that masculinity necessarily carries the obligation of performing special deeds. Women under this aspect are loved for themselves, for just what they are, but men have to vindicate their existence by achievement, heroism, activity, and what not. Male pleasures are to be earned, whereas female existence per se gives the privileged status of yielding the highest pleasures, which are reaped as one's due. Under this aspect it makes sense that Yevtushenko won wide applause in 1979 at the gathering of poets in Castelporziano with a poem in which he expressed the wish that "every man should have a chance to become a woman once to find out what it means" (*New York Times*, July 5, 1979). This request was born, not from intellectual curiosity, but from intense physical desire. If this wish becomes widespread and its repression weakens, it would spell the collapse of a patriarchal system, which then would necessarily turn into a matriarchate.

Otto Gross's father reportedly believed that his son's addiction was due to the fact that he was several times "caught by girls" (von Mädchen gefangen) who got him to the point of promising them marriage. He did not love them and was desperate until the parents succeeded "in

making him free" (loszumachen) (Hurwitz, 1979, p. 53).[41]
He married in 1903. He never divorced his wife but separated from her. For a while he traveled with her and the
man with whom she had three children and to whom he
had assigned her "as better for her erotic needs than himself" (Green, 1974, p. 253). The matriarchally oriented
man will be brutal and cruel to women because he envies
(and fears) them. But under suitable conditions his vener-
ation and adulation may become manifest and lead to extravagant, inordinate imagery. In one of the Richthofen
sisters, Frieda Weekley, who later married D. H. Law-
rence, Otto Gross found the ideal woman. As he wrote her:

> My most paralyzing doubts about mankind's future
> and my own striving... can no longer find a vulner-
> able spot in me — now I know that I have seen and
> loved the woman I dreamed of for coming genera-
> tions.... I *know* now how people will be who are
> no longer stained by all the things I hate and fight — I
> know it through *you*, the only person who *today*
> has stayed free of chastity as a moral code and
> Christianity and Democracy and all those heaps of
> nonsense.... How have you... you golden child —
> kept the curse and the dirt of two gloomy millennia
> from your soul with your laughter and love?...

[41]If an incident as reported by Franz Jung (1915, p. 45f.) is a correct account of what he had been told by Otto Gross (which it
probably was), Hans Gross had considerable responsibility for his
son's inability to cope with women. A 16-year-old girl cousin of
Otto Gross came to visit the family. Once, when he was walking
behind her, she turned around. Otto Gross did not dare at first to
approach her, but then he ran after her, kissed her, and took flight.
When he later entered the house in great excitement, his father
"looked him over" and called him, in the girl's presence, "a stupid
lout" (dummer Lümmel), who deserved to have his ears boxed.

The art of bestowing happiness in the greatest simplicity and at the same time in the knowledge that you are giving an invaluable gift.... And an incomparable rich and passionate, exuberant giving of oneself and so much nobility and majesty... — you are so exquisite, Beloved...so marvellously new — forever new and new again...a wonderfully pure soul in you, one kept pure by a genius for *insisting upon* yourself....You are the *confirmation* of my life of the flower and fruitful *yes* — the future which has come to me...you *free one from the past*[42] [*ibid.*, pp. 47-60, italics Green's].

To my mind this quotation can reflect but little of the real Frieda Weekley and must contain the projected image of a cherished fantasy. Apparently Otto Gross had found in her the symbol of the Mother Goddess he was searching for and was in need of.

There is a high probability that by the intake of drugs Otto Gross tried to reach a state of ecstasy (*Rausch*) equivalent to that which he believed as a child he had observed repeatedly in his mother. The state of ecstasy, envy, and excitement this observation must have aroused in him would explain both the idealization of women, as observed in his relationship to Frieda Weekley, and the aggression against them, as observed in other instances.

Prof. Dr. Tausk called to my attention a passage in his father's poetry that indirectly would refer to a belief in the superiority of women. In the verse dialogue quoted

[42]Yet Frieda Weekley lost her faith in Otto Gross, although she had once thought, "Where you stand is sacred ground" (Green, 1974, p. 61). Possibly she and her sister, both of whom were loved by Otto Gross and loved him, were shocked by the way he treated Regina Ullmann.

above, Spinoza advises: "Give as a woman that loves, gives. The fruit of giving remains in her womb" (Gib wie ein Weib gibt, welches liebt, Die Frucht des Gebens bleibt in ihrem Schoss). Here the male is advised to integrate femaleness as part of the superego, which is the other aspect of matriarchy. It may seem like an injustice to Tausk to set up a parallel between him and Otto Gross. It goes without saying that Otto Gross's psychopathology exceeded Tausk's by far. Tausk's psychopathology never reached that degree of destructiveness. If there were addictive trends in him, they never reached a manifestly relevant degree,[43] whereas addiction became the bane of Otto Gross's life.

Yet by and large, one may say that one possibly detects Otto Gross in minutiae in Tausk. They had in common cruelty against women and negligence of progeny — the latter enormously enlarged in Otto Gross. Otto Gross begat three children, and there is no report that he showed any interest in them. Peter, his illegitimate son, died at the age of seven, and Peter, his legitimate son,

> died still young, of the tuberculosis he had long suffered from, a very gifted and troubled boy. He had learned Russian by himself from books, but failed exams which more ordinary students passed. He suffered from crises of identity and took cocaine like his father [Green, 1974, p. 254].

Camilla Ullmann grew up with foster parents in Feldkirchen, close to Munich. Richard Graf Du Moulin Eckhart, professor of history in Munich, became her and her sister's guardian. She attended parochial schools and

[43]I suspect he might possibly have had a tendency to alcoholism whose expression apparently never exceeded the limits of so-called social drinking.

graduated at the Baliol School in Sedbey (Yorkshire) and was trained as a nurse in England. In 1929 she returned to Germany and worked as a governess and as a nurse. In 1959 and 1960 she took care of her mother. At present she is retired (Kemp, 1978). She was kind enough to respond to my inquiry: Evidently she never met her father. It is remarkable that she apparently does not harbor feelings of resentment against him, despite the deprivations and crises which he caused in her mother's as well as in her own life. It seems that she possessed sufficient strength and courage to compensate for the traumatic experiences of the past and found equilibrium in a religiously oriented outlook on the world.

Tausk, as described earlier, showed great concern for his two sons, but his actions did not live up to what his words would make one expect. In Otto Gross the ambivalence to progeny was outstanding. To be sure, the cruelty to women is understandable as a reaction to envy and the unfulfilled desire to enjoy a bliss granted them, but what is the root of the increased ambivalence toward the children? I assume that the child reminds a man of this type once again of woman's superior creativity. Progeny reminds him of the other outstanding privilege of women. Thus progeny reminds him of what is denied him forever.

Contemporary history is again full of signs of a revolt against patriarchism. All kinds of authorities are assailed. The necessity of work and duty is negated, and the immediate realization of pleasure demanded. The majority has not yet been seized by that revolt, but the number of its adherents is substantial and gives color to contemporary history. The decline of our language, as marked by the virtual prevalence of substandard usages, is one of the many glaring manifestations. It could not be otherwise but that representatives of patriarchy are violently attacked.

This is also the fate of the Freud image that has been presented to the public by would-be biographers. In the introduction, I cited an author who states that Freud participated in the murder of one of his most talented pupils. But Freud is also described as a plagiarist, as tyrannical and intolerant, as indifferent to his children because he never changed their diapers, as greedy for money, as hating his Jewish origin, as a corruptor of morality and ethics, as not having been original, and as one who created legends about himself. Recently it was even claimed that the goal of his scientific endeavors was not to find truth but to conceal and obscure it. His family could not escape derogation. One is reminded of the ancient myth of the curse of the house of Atreus when one reads that allegedly Freud's family lived on forged money; that his stepbrother had a sexual relationship with the boy's mother and that the little boy knew about it; and that his father was a sexual pervert who seduced the boy by indulging in his sexual aberration in the boy's presence. At one point, an author openly stated that Freud wanted his pupils to be castrated. If one adds the horror one author expressed about Freud's having analyzed one of his daughters, as if this had been an act of incest, one can hardly escape the inference that some biographers look on him as the primal father in the primal horde — as hypothesized by Darwin and taken over by Freud himself when he reconstructed the beginning of culture (Freud, 1913).[44]

[44]The fashion of debunking Freud was bound to falsify the judgments of some psychoanalysts as well. Thus a British psychoanalyst recently considered it probable that Freud was *fraudulent* in his research. Without going into the details, this abstruse conjecture

In writing about the psychology of the primal father, Freud stated that

> ...the father of the primal horde was free. His intellectual acts were strong and independent even in isolation, and his will needed no reinforcement of others. Consistency leads us to assume that his ego had few libidinal ties; he loved no one but himself, or other people in so far as they served his needs. To objects his ego gave away no more than was barely necessary [1921, p. 123].

This is exactly the way authors increasingly want Freud to be understood.

Stekel was the first to ascribe to Freud the character of the primal father. He spoke of Freud's "primal horde complex" (Urhordenkomplex) (Wittels, 1924).[45] In this country, Puner (1947), I believe, introduced this idea. I shall take up only one point of Puner's biography, the twelfth chapter of which, by the way, is titled "Old Man of the Horde." Puner holds as "hopelessly contradictory" Freud's feelings about ancestry and progeny:

---

was based on the erroneous identification of Irma, as Freud called the principal person in his famous specimen dream (Freud, 1900, pp. 106–130), with Emma Eckstein. Irma, as Freud let us know, was a young widow (*ibid.*, p. 116) (Emma Eckstein never married), and her last name resembled the German word *Ananas* (*ibid.*, p. 115). Both qualifications — recent widowhood and similarity of names — would fit Anna Hammerschlag, who was Freud's favorite patient (Jones, 1953–1957, vol. 1, p. 223) and in treatment with Freud at the time the dream occurred.

[45]Wittels (1933) disavowed this and other critical statements about Freud, but almost no author took cognizance thereof.

...in one section of the book [*The Interpretation of Dreams*] Freud says brusquely, "It is nonsense to be proud of one's ancestors."... And despite his dismissal of pride in ancestry, there runs throughout his self-revelation the theme of his pride in his own children [*ibid.*, p. 100].

The dismissal of pride in ancestry, of course, was strongly determined in Freud's mind by his awareness of the ridiculousness of two trends in his cultural environment: aristocracy and racism. Both aristocrats and racists demand privileges and respect, not for personal merits and achievements, but primarily because of their ancestors. Yet a father of children who develop well and might achieve signally has, aside from the act of begetting them, contributed to their upbringing, and thus the children's satisfactory development in general reflects parental assets. Of course that pride may take on gigantic proportions in the unconscious.[46] In the unconscious, no doubt, irrationality and absence of logical thinking are the rule, but Puner constructed a contradiction in logic in Freud's ratiocination by declaring Freud's refutation of pride in ancestry to be incompatible with the pride in progeny. In this way she succeeds in calling his six children "the hostages he has created for that purpose [the guaranty of his own immortality]" (*ibid.*, p. 101). The purpose of this wrong inference becomes clear when the arbitrary claim of irrationality in Freud's conscious thinking is used to imply a selfish, unloving attitude in Freud toward his children reminiscent of the primal father.

Thus Otto Gross and also Tausk became symbolically tragic heroes who tried to free the world from the tyranny

[46]Freud wrote in the course of an analysis of one of his own dreams of "the suppressed megalomania of fathers'" (1900, p. 448).

of the father of the primal horde but succumbed to the latter's merciless insistence on his all-powerful position.

Another way of diminishing Freud and his world has become fashionable. Biographers and critics tend to attempt to prove the incorrectness of his discoveries by arguing that they grew directly out of his psychopathology. In reading such attempts, I always rejoice that Freud never dreamed, as Einstein did, that he cut his throat with a razor blade (Speziali, 1972, p. 133). For some this would have proved the inaccuracy of the theory of the death drive, whereas the theory of relativity has not yet been doubted despite its author's self-destructive dream.

The Problem of Aggression in the Lives of Talented Persons and the Genius

To live means to destroy. That is the essential problem of ethics. Goethe's Werther was right in his heart-breaking lament that when he takes a walk, he inescapably destroys a mass of life, small as it may seem.

At the bottom of the problem is the tragic truth that man cannot live by forming the higher chemical compounds on which life rests out of inanimate inorganic elements alone. Every act of eating presupposes the destruction of life—the lives of plants or animals, as the case may be, but in every instance destruction of what was previously flourishing life.

Aside from this primary, preordained destructive aggression on which life per se depends, there is contingent aggression, whose degree varies from individual to individual. It is one of the many paradoxes of human existence that man possibly can go through life without love but never can reduce his contingent aggression to zero. There are human beings who devote their lives to charitable actions and succeed in going through life with a minimum of contingent aggression. They come close to ethical sainthood. Others indulge freely in the gratification of the crudest aggression and hardly miss an opportunity to cause pain and anguish to others. The subjects of the preceding essay did not belong to either type: they were neither saints nor devils. It goes without saying that each of them struggled through life to the best of his ability and to all appearances tried hard to act in conformity with his conscience. All of them belonged to the upper stratum of the cultural establishment. Tausk and Gross, being talented individuals known to small groups, left no deep traces on the cultural heritage; Freud and Wedekind, international in their fame, exercised a deep influence on their respective fields of creativity. All of them were desirous of making contributions to culture, and the creative act played a relevant role in their lives: in Freud and Wedekind from youth on, in Tausk and Gross somewhat later. In Freud and Wedekind the creative act stood at times almost in the center of their existence and became every so often all-absorbing. In Tausk and Gross it did not seem to have acquired that all-inclusive central significance, even though their coming to terms with their respective ideologies and science was of central personal importance to both of them.

The question to be raised now is whether the creative act is linked with a discharge of aggression. Objectively great creations contain an aggressive destructive seed. Shakespeare's opus debarred the rise of any future playwright of equal perfection in the English tongue, and perhaps in any language. The immediate effect of a great creation may be destructive. Thus some of Goethe's contemporaries held *The Sorrows of Young Werther* responsible for the suicides of young men that occurred after its publication, and even though Goethe and later historians disputed this on good grounds, it is striking that Goethe himself dreaded the arousal of suicidal imagery which the reading of the novel would effect in him. As a matter of fact, he read it only once, when external circumstances forced him to revise the text, and then only after having overcome intense reluctance.

All great creations, even if they were spared destructive effects in the present and for the future, have such effects retroactively. They destroy a previous style, contribute to the destruction of a previous art period, and dethrone previously famed predecessors. It is quite likely that Paisiello's *Barbieri* would still be considered eminent if Mozart and Rossini had not banished it into oblivion. New civilizations eat their way into ancient ones. Ancient buildings have been destroyed for the purpose of using the materials of which they had been constructed for contemporary edifices. Michelangelo, who owed so much to antiquity, had partially to destroy an ancient temple in order to build a church. The destruction of preceding civilizations may be compared to the vanishing of species brought about by new ones that are better adapted to the natural law of dog-eat-dog.

Parallels to some of these observations are found in possible effects of Freud's works. La Pierre (1962) like many others claims—without justification, in my opinion—that Freud undermined the traditional morality and ethics of Western civilization. There is the possibility that future historians might place Freud alongside giants like Marx and Nietzsche, under whose hammer blows Western civilization finally caved in, leading to the pres- ent cataclysmic and unsolvable crisis. To be sure, this was not Freud's intention, since he ardently adhered to traditional values and only wished to purify contemporary culture and civilization of those inclusions that stunted and hampered the growth of healthy individuality.

The degree of responsibility that an author bears for the effect of his works is an open problem. To cite an extreme example: is Christ responsible for the Inquisition? A less complicated example would be the effect Freud's popularizing of cocaine had. As early as 1886, Erlenmeyer called it "mankind's third scourge." Should one hold Freud responsible? When he did his research on cocaine, he was, of course, unaware of its destructive potential. As a matter of fact, cocaine's beneficent effect forms one of the great chapters in the history of medicine.

Wedekind's work, of course, was a thorn in the flesh of Victorian society. He laid the groundwork for the final destruction of the European classical tradition. Usually the classical style is contrasted to Shakespeare's opus and Romantic art. This is warranted to a certain extent from the standpoint of a matter-of-fact theory of styles. Heinrich Heine, however, turned against the idea that Shakespeare had broken with the principles of the unity of time and place by saying that the whole world was the place of his tragedies, and eternity his unity of time. This idea is profound and far-reaching. Only the literature of the twentieth century finally broke irreparably with the classical world. The first paragraph of Carl Einstein's (1885–1940) novel *Bebuquin*, written between 1906 and 1909 and published in 1912, runs as follows:

The shards of a yellow glass lantern jingled upon a woman's voice: Would you like to see your mother's spirit? The unstable light dripped on the delicately marked bald head of a young man who anxiously veered aside to forestall [any] consideration of the compositions of his person. He turned away from the Booth of the Distorting Mirrors, which are more stimulating to observations than the words of fifteen professors. He turned away from the Circus of Inactivated Gravity although smilingly he realized that thus he would miss the solution of his life. He avoided the Theater of Mute Ecstasy with proudly bent head: ecstasy is indecent, ecstasy disgraces our ability, and shuddering he went into the Museum of Cheap Torpor at the cash register of which sat a broad fading nude lady. She wore a bulging yellow feather hat and emerald-colored stockings with straps running up to her armpits that decorated her body with scanty arabesques. From her seal hands red rubies glared vertically: "Evening, the Bebuquin."[47]

Some historians mark that novel as the turning point in Central European literature. They may be right. The

[47]Die Scherben eines gläsernen, gelben Lampions klirrten auf die Stimme eines Frauenzimmers: wollen Sie den Geist Ihrer Mutter sehen? Das haltlose Licht tropfte auf die zartmarkierte Glatze eines jungen Mannes, der ängstlich abbog, dem Überlegen über die Zusammensetzungen seiner Person vorzubeugen. Er wandte sich ab von der Bude der verzerrenden Spiegel, die mehr zu Betrachtungen anregen als die Worte von fünfzehn Professoren. Er wandte sich ab vom Zirkus zur aufgehobenen Schwerkraft, wiewohl er lächelnd einsah, so die Lösung seines Lebens zu versäumen. Das Theater zur stummen Ekstase mied er mit stolz geneigtem Haupt: Ekstase ist unanständig, Ekstase blamiert unser Können, und ging schauernd in das Museum zur billigen Erstarrnis, an dessen Kasse eine breite verschwimmende Dame nackt sass. Sie trug einen ausladenden gelben Federhut, smaragdfarbene Strümpfe, deren Bänder bis zu den Achselhöhlen liefen und den Körper mit sparsamen Arabesken schmückten. Von ihren Seehundhänden starrten rote Rubinen senkrecht: "Abend, den Bebuquin." (Translated by Ruth S. Eissler.)

novel has been forgotten for all practical purposes, but its effect might have been a lasting one. I brought it up because I believe that Wedekind was the trailblazer of the whole movement that followed with its dissolution of logic, perversities, black humor, glorification of irregularity and chaos, seeming senselessness. In Wedekind form does not yet fall apart and there is almost always contact, tenuous as ever, with a reality, but that contact is so slight that it does not require a strong effort to plunge into dadaism. Thus one might hold him responsible for the following decadence of literature, even though his art was robust and forceful, eager to penetrate to essences.

It is noteworthy that Freud, despite the broad bonds that connect Wedekind's opus with psychoanalysis, never referred to his work.[48] Freud was characterized by Karl Bühler (1879–1963) as *Stoffendenker*, meaning that his thinking was rooted exclusively in contents (substantiality), a criticism which, I believe, overlooks important aspects of psychoanalysis. But it may have been this aspect of Freud that blocked his way to looking at Wedekind's work with sympathy. He had an aversion against expressionism and seeming senselessness. I believe it was the expressionistic flavor of Wedekind's work that held Freud back.[49] In turn, psychoanalysis does not show up in Wedekind's writings, and his contact with Freud was limited to a letter in which he asked if Freud had read Merezhkovsky.[50]

[48]The name of Wedekind appears only once in Freud's work (Freud, 1901, p. 236), when Freud referred to a series of slips of the tongue an actor had made in the same passage during three consecutive performances of Wedekind's play *Censorship*.

[49]Arthur Schnitzler, whom Freud held in such high regard, does not fall out of a classical frame.

[50]See Kutscher (1922–1931, vol. 2, p. 143n, and vol. 3, p. 249) for references to Freud.

That the playwright did not want his imagination disturbed by the science of images is quite understandable. But the absence of Wedekind among Freud's interests in literature needs an explanation. Indeed, as the above quotation from Carl Einstein's novel demonstrates, the substantiality of content is reduced by expressionism. Substance contracts and finally disappears, so much that only debris remains, from which it can no longer be reconstructed. Wedekind never went that far, but he came close to it, and the basis he established for the final burial of an ordered universe, or a universe whose order could be potentially deciphered, might have made his work repugnant to Freud, who, raised as he was in the classical tradition, needed a minimum of form in art in order to feel comfortable.

An aspect of psychoanalysis is to be mentioned that may be experienced as an irreparable loss to mankind. I was struck when Felix Braun remarked to me in a rather casual way that psychoanalysis has established conditions in which there are no "secrets" anymore. What he meant, I conjecture, was that with the science of the unconscious human beings feel entitled to talk openly about the most intimate experiences, wishes, and fantasies which previously had been veiled by secrecy. There are no recesses of the heart any longer that would deserve to be excluded from public discussion or, worse even, that a person would keep as a secret from himself.

Furthermore, with psychoanalysis the impression spread that the human psyche no longer presented irresolvable puzzles, or at least, that by means of the psychoanalytic method all remaining unanswered questions of the mind would eventually be answered. Such an attitude implies that in all respects the human psyche has become demystified. The awe-inspiring mystery and secrecy of love, religious symbols, and existential dread have disappeared. Science has had a comparable effect. Despite all unsolved problems, Western man's (often unspoken) belief is that there are no boundaries set for science, that nature is an open book. Concomitantly, Western man's experience of nature has profoundly changed. When facing an unusual, impressive phenomenon in nature, his first reaction nowadays is to ask for its natural explanation, that is, the underlying physical or chemical law. Newton believed that his discoveries proved the existence of God, and he was unaware of making a decisive contribution to the foundation of the spread of modern atheism.

Is a full human existence possible without secrets? Large segments of contemporary youth negate this and take refuge in oriental religions that abound in mysteries and secrets. Thus one may, after all, draw the conclusion that great, relevant creations, besides enriching and often facilitating human existence, inflict deep injuries that sometimes are irreparable.

Whatever the effect of created works may be, one would like to know more about the psychology of the creative act. Does it lead to a discharge of aggressive-destructive energies and thus protect the creative person against hurting and damaging his proximate environment?

The myth of Prometheus, which is the ideal type of any far-reaching creative act, answers this question. Prometheus created man and brought civilization to mankind, but all this was done as a rebellion against Zeus. Thus the Promethean act has a double aspect: he creates, that is, gives birth to man like a good mother (the aspect of love) and at the same time defies supreme authority like an aggressive son (the destructive aspect). Great creative acts bring forth new values, but in order to do so the creative person must be dissatisfied with the world as it exists, and he must be eager to replace it by a better, more satisfying one. This temporary turning away from the world or sections thereof, which is the equivalent of wanting to destroy it, is a channel of aggressive discharge. Thus great acts of creation are probably a psychological synthesis of love and destruction.

The problem of man's being the source of anguish and of achievement is intriguing. The often unverbalized expectation that greatness of achievement is combined with moral greatness is not confirmed. Michelangelo's manifest homosexuality, as claimed by many, would have shocked the Victorians but is contemplated nowadays with interest and equanimity, even though critics of given personal bent may disapprove of it on moral grounds. But here it would have been a victimless misdemeanor and, more importantly, one without which the artist might not have been able to create his unique sculptures.

Yet there are examples of aggression in the lives of geniuses which by no means can be classified as victimless. Great achievements by hypercreative personages sometimes require and impose extraordinary sacrifices on their environments. By the skin of his teeth Beethoven missed causing his nephew's death by suicide (Sterba and Sterba, 1954). The research of the Sterbas emphasized Beethoven's massive aggression against his ward and nephew, who almost paid with his life for his guardian's shocking interferences. However, Solomon (1977a, 1977b) convincingly pointed out the deep libidinal involvement in what appears to be unmixed aggression. Moreover, even if it should be assured that the Sterbas' theory is correct, aggression of this type seems exceptional, not only in Beethoven's life but in that of other geniuses.

Even if the nephew's attempt at suicide had been — most regrettably — successful, one may say that the subsequent creation of *Missa Solemnis* and the late quartets, the psychological background of whose creation, in my opinion, was ultimately connected with Beethoven's anguish and conflicts about the nephew, would have compensated for the tragedy.[51]

About Shakespeare's life, little as is known about it, one knows that at least once as a young man when he left Stratford, he probably caused severe heartache to wife and children. Retrospectively, one can say with certainty that if the young man was to acquire the greatness that was due him, both as a mature man and posthumously, he had to take that fateful step, even though it was against his moral obligation and the morality of his times. But in view of the enormity of his achievement one will say the pain he caused in terms of human relations was insignificant. Man evidently cannot live without causing pain and injury to others and often even anguish, but if biographies are compared, the proportion of pain and anguish caused on one side and the greatness of achievement on the other vary surprisingly from person to person.

What strikes me is the enormous disproportion in Tausk's life between the despair he caused versus his achievements. The development of psychology and psychoanalysis could not have been essentially different whether Tausk had or had not published those twenty papers. Of course, all those who surrounded Freud were sentenced to the status of footnotes in the history of

[51]It must also be considered that Beethoven was consciously motivated by the compelling urge to protect the youth against the dangers which he was convinced threatened him. The misfortune was that these alleged dangers were those by which Beethoven himself felt threatened.

ideas, but unquestionably an analyst like Karl Abraham will occupy a more important place in the history of psychoanalysis than Tausk, and his life was exemplary.

The same is true of Otto Gross. His acts of aggression were not limited to "victimless crimes." He brought untold sufferings to a large number of people. And again one must ask, were the achievements worth the pain he caused?

How different are Freud's and Wedekind's biographies in this respect! Their lives are filled with creative output and no acts of the kind recorded in the biographies of Tausk and Gross are known, even though both Freud and Wedekind had ample reason to act out. It is probably true not only of our times but also quite often of previous periods of declining culture that a cross-eyed value system finds a fairly large consenting audience. At such times the weak and unstable, dressed up in flamboyant colors, have a considerable chance of arousing sympathy and admiration, whereas the solid structure hardened by the struggle for survival and devoted to great purposes is looked upon askance for the very reason of its survival and success. Washouts, so the unspoken principle seems to imply, must have been good, for had they flourished, this alone would prove them to have been mean and vicious: only the mean and vicious can be strong enough to survive in a world that is in essence careless, inconsiderate, and exploitative of those who are not rapacious. In other words, the life which is short is that of the lamb, and the wolf lives long.

In reading the Sterbas' book on Beethoven and his nephew, a naïve reader may put Beethoven's nephew above his uncle, and the same may happen regarding Otto Gross and Max Weber (1864–1920), the great German economist and sociologist, who acted as one of the protagonists in Green's book. It is not probable that this was the authors' intention but it is relevant that readers may obtain such impressions. I shall cite other opinions which make a basic misunderstanding about differences between genius and talent evident. They concern alleged similarities between Tausk and Kafka. When Roazen wrote: "Kafka, whose suffering was so similar to Tausk's" (1969, p. 158), he had not, I believe, understood either Kafka or Tausk. Kafka did not "share Tausk's central conflicts" (*ibid.*, p. 118). There is the danger that the horror of marriage alone makes a man a hero or a kind of mental giant. To be sure, Kafka as well as Tausk felt strong conflicts about marriage, but Kafka looked at marriage, as Roazen indicated, "[as] the pledge of the most acute form of self-liberation and independence" (*ibid.*, p. 119), which Tausk never did. After all, he married with relative ease at the age of 21. Kafka never "disappointed women in the same way [as Tausk]," as Roazen claimed (*ibid.*, p. 119), and he found his salvation in the end in Dora Dymant.

His letters to Felice alone prove the gulf between Tausk and himself. The letters document a gigantic struggle in the service of finding a love object and establishing a viable relationship. He is addicted to the object. The struggle is fought in a realm "beyond the pleasure principle." He wants to penetrate to the innermost core of the loved person. He is insatiable in "knowing" about her. The quality and intensity of object relationship he aspires to is beyond the humanly possible. But there is no weakness of effort visible. The letters to Felice sound like a novel of morality, the message of which is that true object relations are impossible in the human world. It is one of the most tragic human documents. There is no flightiness, no lack of responsibility, but an overgrowth of a sense of responsibility toward the beloved person. Tausk would have never been strong enough to bear up under the excessive stress under which Kafka smarted when he turned with everything in him toward Felice and discovered that true object relations are not possible between man and woman when eyes are open and ready to absorb the full image of the "you." They can live together permanently only when the tie between them is moderate and one party is ready to veil part of the other's full psychic reality. Kafka was burdened by ambivalence and oedipal involvements, as all human beings are, but these were not the impediments that made the bridge to Felice collapse. I do not hesitate to repeat that he was fastened to the object with incredible intensity, inquisitiveness, and the determination of taking mental possession, of making the other human being the exclusive center of his own existence; he expected and desired from the tie to the spouse a new form of existence in which his own life, creativity, and the other's life would become a unit, undivided by palings. He demanded the impossible but was not deterred by a titanic struggle. Only when death hovered over him did he find repose in his love for Dora Dymant.

A comparison of Kafka and Tausk is most instructive. Both studied law. Both died at approximately the same age. Kafka's every day was filled with work most incommensurate with his great talent. Every day, as long as his health permitted, he dragged himself to the office of an insurance company and fulfilled his duties in an exemplary way, not expecting that his moderately wealthy father would support him. He was during his lifetime a most unsuccessful writer, only a few copies of his books being sold.

Yet his adversities did not deter him from creating literary products that, I believe, will be later regarded as unquestionably the greatest of modern times. Of course, he hurt his father's and mother's feelings, but he never caused a tragedy comparable to those surrounding Tausk. One may emphasize the difference in talents between Tausk and Kafka. But do we know the full extent of Tausk's gifts? Is not the great difference in character an even more prominent feature? Would Tausk have been able to devote himself to one great purpose that did not earn him recognition and admiration? Would he have ever been ready to bear enormous arousal in passion without having to satisfy it, as Kafka was, after he met Felice?

The same may be said about Otto Gross, who probably was even more gifted than Tausk. What is left of his works? He frittered away his life, again like Tausk tripped by the steady attachment to, and inseparability from, the dictates of the pleasure principle.

I shall bring up Wedekind once again. He must have been a man driven by powerful passions and swayed by fantasies which could not have been less irrealistic than Otto Gross's, and nevertheless he formed a durable, firm relationship to his wife, and he is not known to have engaged in remarkable acting out toward women.

All the encroachments and oppressions society imposed on him did not deter him from creating masterpieces. One may say that the societal impositions he had to bear were far heavier than those Gross and Tausk had to face. To be sure, his creations were taken as grievous provocations and assaults, but a compromise in his creating a new world would have annihilated him as a playwright. His provocations were not of the nature of personal acts. They did not fall into the category of acting out.

In Wedekind the main idea I propose here is confirmed.

He, too, was a genius who was not defeated by adversities, did not act out his pain and anguish to the detriment of others, but poured his energy into the creative act. One may be inclined to set up a general law: the greater the cultural achievement, the smaller the damage caused to others.[52] This might have been expected, since psychological deliberations would make one anticipate that the creation of great cultural achievements presupposes a high degree of internalization.[53] It is well known that geniuses show a great deal of unusual behavior — in most instances, of a bizarre nature. But this psychopathology is not directed in a primarily aggressive or destructive way at the outer world: it is in the service and expression of the creative process.

The law is certainly not generally correct. First, there is a large number of talented individuals whose achievements do not reach the unusual and in whose lives acting out plays an inferior role, and, second, there are geniuses whose acting out is excessive. Richard Wagner almost drove Bavaria into bankruptcy. Wagner's excessive acting out, however, was facilitated, condoned, and perhaps

[52]Newton's biography (Manuel, 1963, 1968) might indirectly support this thesis, since the fallow years that came after his years of highest creativity were marked by an increase of aggression against the outside world.

[53]At this point, however, the question is moot whether — at least in Tausk's and Gross's cases — the full flourishing of their talents was impeded by their psychopathology, or whether their innate endowment was insufficient for the production of great creations. The problem can also be formulated in the following way: is the ability to integrate the decisive factor which makes the genius different from the talented individual? or do the genius's extraordinary talents "absorb" innate aggression, thus facilitating integration? As so often, this dichotomy may prove misleading; in reality, both factors may operate in unison, mutually supporting one another.

even provoked by the deranged King. I should expect that within the group of creative minds the excessively acting-out type prevails among the talents but constitutes a small minority among the geniuses. This expectation should not include that of reduced psychopathology in the genius. As I have repeatedly tried to point out, in the genius one must distinguish between psychopathology inherent in the creative process, which is not only unavoidable if values of high quality are to be forthcoming but even favors the creation of such values, and on the other hand psychopathology that is not connected with the creative process but has the same structure as the psychopathology that is encountered in clinical practice.

Here I suggest another differentiation, that between alloplastic and autoplastic psychopathology. The genius's psychopathology is usually of an autoplastic structure, and the alloplastic effort is—if possible—totally bound up in the effort to create values of maximal quality.

Roazen in his book of 1969 tried to present the Tausk episode as the result of Freud's alloplasticity, that is, of destructive acting out. This would be most unusual given Freud's life style. No other instance of such acting out in Freud's life is known as acts of acting out are rather infrequent even prior to his self-analysis, and none is known of any serious damage to others.

Freud's style of life is characterized by the high degree of internalization. The destructive impulse shows up in dreams or parapraxes. Even the autoplastic psychopathology—not inconsiderable as it was prior to his self-analysis—became greatly scaled down, far more than is generally observed in persons of such gigantic mental capacity, but focused on the nicotine addiction which ultimately felled him. But in Tausk and also in Otto Gross acting out was considerable from the beginning and increased even more in the course of time until it brought both of them to their premature ends, their lives not leaving traces in the cultural panorama that could measure up to the anguish and turmoil they had caused.

REFERENCES

Andreas-Salomé, L. (1958), *The Freud Journal of Lou Andreas-Salomé,* translated and with an introduction by S. A. Leavy. New York: Basic Books, 1964.

Angel, A. (1934), Einige Bemerkungen über den Optimismus. *Intern. Zeitsch. Psychoanal.,* 20:191–199.

Benjamin, W. (1977), *Deutsche Menschen.* Frankfurt–am–Main: Suhrkamp.

Bühler, K. (1927), *Die Krise der Psychologie.* Wien: Deuticke.

Delp, E. (1960), *Regina Ullmann.* Köln: Benziger Verlag.

Eissler, K. R. (1963), *Goethe: A Psychoanalytic Study 1775–1776,* 2 vols. Detroit: Wayne State University Press.

_____ (1978), A warning to Freud biographers about Paul Roazen's methods and findings (unpublished manuscript).

Erlenmeyer (1886), Über Cocainsucht. *Wiener mediz. Presse,* pp. 918–921.

Freud, E., ed. (1960), *Letters of Sigmund Freud.* New York: Basic Books.

Freud, S. (1900), The Interpretation of Dreams. *Standard Edition,* 4 & 5. London: Hogarth Press, 1953.

_____ (1901), The Psychopathology of Everyday Life. *Standard Edition,* 6. London: Hogarth Press, 1960.

_____ (1908), 'Civilized' Sexual Morality and Modern Nervous Illness. *Standard Edition,* 9:181–204. London: Hogarth Press, 1959.

_____ (1913), Totem and Taboo. *Standard Edition,* 13:xiii–162. London: Hogarth Press, 1955.

271

_____ (1914), On the History of the Psycho-Analytic Movement. *Standard Edition*, 14:7–66. London: Hogarth Press, 1957.

_____ (1915), Thoughts for the Times on War and Death. *Standard Edition*, 14:275–300. London: Hogarth Press, 1957.

_____ (1917), Mourning and Melancholia. *Standard Edition*, 14:243–258. London: Hogarth Press, 1957.

_____ (1918), From the History of an Infantile Neurosis. *Standard Edition*, 17:147–156. London: Hogarth Press, 1955.

_____ (1919), Victor Tausk. *Standard Edition*, 17:273–275. London: Hogarth Press, 1955.

_____ (1920), Dr. Anton von Freund. *Standard Edition*, 18:267–268. London: Hogarth Press, 1955.

_____ (1921), Group Psychology and the Analysis of the Ego. *Standard Edition*, 18:69–143. London: Hogarth Press, 1955.

_____ (1924), The Economic Problem of Masochism. *Standard Edition*, 19:159–170. London: Hogarth Press, 1961.

_____ (1925), An Autobiographical Study. *Standard Edition*, 20:7–74. London: Hogarth Press, 1959.

_____ (1927), Fetishism. *Standard Edition*, 21:152–157. London: Hogarth Press, 1961.

_____ (1933), Sandor Ferenczi. *Standard Edition*, 22:227–229. London: Hogarth Press, 1964.

_____ (1936), A Disturbance of Memory on the Acropolis. *Standard Edition*, 22:239–248. London: Hogarth Press, 1964.

_____ (1937), Lou Andreas-Salomé. *Standard Edition*, 23:297–298. London: Hogarth Press, 1964.

_____ (1939), Moses and Monotheism: Three Essays. *Standard Edition*, 23:7–137. London: Hogarth Press, 1964.

_____ (1950), *The Origins of Psycho-Analysis: Letters to Wilhelm Fliess, Drafts and Notes, 1887–1902*. New York: Basic Books, 1954.

_____ (1955), Memorandum on the Electrical Treatment of War Neurotics. *Standard Edition*, 17:211–215. London: Hogarth Press, 1955.

_____ (1963), Psychoanalysis and Faith. In: *The Letters of Sigmund Freud and Oskar Pfister*. Edited by Heinrich Meng and Ernst L. Freud. New York: Basic Books.

_____ (1967), Hochzeitscarmen. *Deutsch für Ausländer: Informationen für den Lehrer*. Königswinter: Verlag für Sprachmethodik, January issue.

Freyer, H. (1963), *Theorien des gegenwärtigen Zeitalters*. Stuttgart: Deutsche Verlags-Anstalt.

Friedenthal, J., ed. (1914), *Das Wedekindbuch*. Munich/Leipzig: Georg Müller [also contains the author's monograph on Wedekind's life and work].

Graf, O. M. (1951), Rainer Maria Rilke und die Frauen. In: *An manchen*

Tagen. Frankfurt–am–Main: Nest Verlag, 1961, pp. 172–210.

––––––– (1955), Thomas Mann als geistiges Erlebnis – Totenred – New York, 1955. In: *An manchen Tagen.* Frankfurt–am Main: Nest Verlag, pp. 301–313.

Green, M. (1974), *The von Richthofen Sisters: The Triumphant and the Tragic Modes of Love.* New York: Basic Books.

Greenacre, P. (1956), Experiences of Awe in Childhood. *The Psychoanalytic Study of the Child,* 11:9–30. New York: International Universities Press.

Gutheil, E. A., ed. (1950), *The Autobiography of Wilhelm Stekel.* New York: Liveright.

Harris, F. (1925), *My Life and Loves.* New York: Grove Press, 1963.

Herzl, T. (1900), Heyses Erinnerungen In: *Feuilletons,* by Theodor Herzl. 2 vols. Berlin: J. Singer, 1911, vol. 1, pp. 296–305, 2nd. ed.

Hoff, H. (1952), In: *Die feierliche Inauguration des Rektors der Wiener Universität für das Studienjahr 1951/52.* Wien: Selbtverlag Universität Wien.

Hurwitz, E. (1979), *Otto Gross: Paradies-Sucher zwischen Freud und Jung.* Zürich: Suhrkamp.

Jones, E. (1953–1957), *The Life and Work of Sigmund Freud,* 3 vols. New York: Basic Books.

––––––– (1959), *Free Associations: Memories of a Psychoanalyst.* New York: Basic Books.

Jung, F. (1915), *Sophie: Der Kreuzweg der Demut.* Kraus reprint. Lichtenstein: Nendeln, 1963.

Kanzer, M. (1971), Victor Tausk, an autobiographical legacy. *Intern. J. Psycho-Anal.,* 52:423–440.

––––––– (1972), Victor Tausk: The creativity and suicide of a psychoanalyst. *Psychoanal. Quart.,* 41:556–584.

––––––– (1973), Victor Tausk: Analyst and dramatic critic. *Amer. Imago,* 30:371–379.

Kaus, G. (1979), *Und was für ein Leben.* Hamburg: Albrecht Knaus.

Kemp, F. (1978), Lebenschronik. In: Ullmann, R. (1978), vol. 2, pp. 412–430.

Klenner, F. (1951), *Die oesterreichischen Gewerkschaften – Vergangenheit und Gegenwartsprobleme.* Wien: Verlag des österreichischen Gewerkschaftsbundes.

Knopf, O. (1977), *Successful Aging: The Facts and Fallacies of Growing Old.* New York: G. K. Hall.

Kris, E. (1939), On inspiration. *Intern. J. Psycho-Anal.,* 20:377 [reprinted in Kris, E. (1952), *Psychoanalytic Explorations in Art.* New York: International Universities Press, pp. 290–302].

Kutscher, A. (1922–1931), *Frank Wedekind: Sein Leben und seine Werke,* 3 vols. Munich: Georg Müller.

_____ (1964), *Wedekind: Leben und Werk*. Munich: List.

Landmann, R. (1973), *Ascona—Monte Verita. Auf der Suche nach dem Paradies*. Zürich/Köln, 2nd enlarged edition [first edition 1934, Ascona].

La Pierre, R. T. (1962), *The Freudian Ethic: An Analysis of the Subversion of American Character*. Des Moines, Iowa: Duell, Sloan & Pierce.

Lesky, E. (1965), *Die Wiener medizinische Schule im 19. Jahrhundert*. Graz/Köln: Böhlaus.

Loewenstein, R. M. (1935), Die phallische Passivität beim Manne. *Zeitsch. für Psychoanal.*, 16:334–340.

Magaziner, A. (1975), Martha Tausk: Eine Grazer Frauensekretärin. *Rentner und Pensionisten*, July, p. 21.

Manuel, F. E. (1963), *Isaac Newton, Historian*. Cambridge, Mass.: The Belknap Press of the Harvard University Press.

_____ (1968), *A Portrait of Isaac Newton*. Cambridge, Mass.: The Belknap Press of the Harvard University Press.

McGuire, W., ed. (1974), *The Freud/Jung Letters: The Correspondence Between Sigmund Freud and C. G. Jung*. Bollingen Series XCIV. Princeton, N.J.: Princeton University Press.

Menninger-Lerchenthal, E. (1951), In Memoriam Prof. Dr. Giulio Bonvicini. *Wiener klin. Wochenschrift*, 101:342.

Monte Verità (1978). Milano: Electa Editrice.

Neumarkt, P. (1973), Hauptmann's *And Pippa Dances* and Victor Tausk's Commentary. *Amer. Imago*, 30:360–370.

_____ (1977), The Freud-Tausk controversy: A symphony of disharmony. *Intern. Review of Psycho-Anal.*, 4:363–373.

Neyant-Sutterman, T. (1978), Entretien avec Marius Tausk à Nimègue (mie Decembre 1978). *Révue Française de Psychanalyse*, XLII: 747–751.

Nunberg, H., & Federn, E., eds. (1962–1975), *Minutes of the Vienna Psychoanalytic Society*, 4 vols. New York: International Universities Press.

O'Malley, C. D., & Saunders, J. E. de C. M. (1952), *Leonardo da Vinci on the Human Body*. New York: Schumann.

Peters, H. F. (1962), *My Sister My Spouse. A Biography of Lou Andreas-Salomé*. New York: Norton.

Pfeiffer, E., ed. (1966), *Sigmund Freud-Lou Andreas-Salomé Letters*. New York: Harcourt Brace Jovanovich, 1972.

Planer, F., Ed. (1929), *Das Jahrbuch der Wiener Gesellschaft. Beiträge zur Wiener Zeitgeschichte*. Vienna: Franz Planer.

Puner, H. W. (1947), *Freud, His Life and His Mind*. New York: Dell, 1961.

Rank, O. (1911), Ein Beitrag zum Narzissismus. *Jahrbuch für Psychoanal. Forsch.*, 3:401–426.

Roazen, P. (1969), *Brother Animal: The Story of Freud and Tausk*. New York: Knopf.

_____(1972), Reflections on ethos and authenticity in psychoanalysis. *The Human Context*, 4:577–587.

_____ (1977), Orthodoxy on Freud: The case of Tausk. *Contemp. Psychoanal.*, 13:102–115.

Rothe, F. (1960), *Frank Wedekind's Drama, Jugendstil und Lebensphilosophie*. Stuttgart: Metzler.

Seehaus, G. (1974), *Frank Wedekind in Selbstzeignissen und Bilddokumenten*. Reinbek bei Hamburg: Rowolt.

Solomon, M. (1977a), Beethoven and his Nephew: A Reappraisal. In: *Beethoven Studies*, vol. 2, ed. Tyson. London: Oxford.

_____ (1977b), *Beethoven*. New York & London: Schirmer Books.

Speziali, P., ed. (1972), *Albert Einstein – Michèle Basso Correspondence, 1903–1955*. Paris: Hermann.

Stekel, W. (1920), In Memoriam. *Psyche and Eros*, 1:49.

Sterba, E., & Sterba, R. (1954), *Beethoven and His Nephew*. New York: Pantheon.

Strachey, J. (1955), Editor's Note (Freud, 1918, Aus der Geschichte einer Infantilen Neurose). *Standard Edition*, 17:3–6. London: Hogarth Press, 1955.

_____ (1957), Editor's Note (Freud, 1917, Trauer und Melancholie). *Standard Edition*, 14:239–242. London: Hogarth Press, 1957.

Stransky, E. (1959), Prof. Dr. Josef Berze. *Wiener klin. Wochenschrift*, 70:142.

Szasz, T. (1976), *Karl Kraus and the Soul-Doctors*. Baton Rouge: Louisiana State University Press.

Tausk, Marius (1973), Victor Tausk as seen by his son. *Amer. Imago*, 30:323–335.

Tausk, Martha (1930), *Fernambuk und Anderes*. Zürich: Genossenschaftsbuchhandlung.

Tausk, V. (1913), Zur Psychologie der Kindersexualität. *Intern. Zeitsch. für ärztl. Psychoanal.*, 1:444–458.

_____ (1916a), Diagnostic considerations concerning the symptomatology of the so-called war psychoses. *Psychoanal. Quart.*, 38:382–405, 1969.

_____ (1916b), On the psychology of the deserter. *Psychoanal. Quart.*, 38:354–381, 1969.

_____ (1916–1917), Zur Psychopathologie des Alltaglebens. *Intern. Zeitsch. für ärztl. Psychoanal.*, 4:156–158.

_____ (1919), On the origin of the 'influencing machine' in schizophrenia. *Psychoanal. Quart.*, 2:519–556, 1933 [reprinted in *Psychoanal. Reader*, 1948, 1:52–85].

_____ (1973), Victor Tausk: Paraphrase as commentary and critique on Gerhart Hauptmann's "And Pippa Dances." *Amer. Imago*, 30:340–359.

276   VICTOR TAUSK'S SUICIDE

Ullmann, R. (1978), *Erzählungen, Prosastücke, Gedichte*, 2 vols. Munich: Kösel.
_____ (n.y.), *Erinnerungen an Rilke*. St. Gallen: Tschudry.
Wedekind, F. (1920–1921), *Gesammelte Werke*, 9 vols. Munich: Georg Müller.
_____ (1924), *Gesammelte Briefe*, 2 vols. Munich: Georg Müller.
Wedekind, K. (1931), Frank Wedekind und seine Kinder. *Der Querschnitt* 11.
_____ (1964), Mein Vater, Frank Wedekind. *Münchner Merkur*, 18th July.
Wedekind, P. (1967), Mein Vater, Frank Wedekind. In: *Frank Wedekind, Der Kammersänger*. Stuttgart: Reklam Universal Bibliothek, Nr. 8273.
Wedekind, T. (1969), *Lulu. Die Rolle meines Lebens*. Bern/Munich/Vienna: Scherz.
Weiss, E. (1932), Regression and projection in the superego. *Intern. J. Psycho-Anal.*, 13:449–478.
_____ (1964), *Agoraphobia in the Light of Ego Psychology*. New York: Grune & Stratton.
_____ (1970), *Sigmund Freud as Consultant: Recollections of a Pioneer in Psychoanalysis*. New York: Intercontinental Medical Book Corporation.
Wittels, F. (1924), *Sigmund Freud, His Personality, His Teaching and His School*. New York: Dodd Mead.
_____ (1933), Revision of a biography. *Psychoanal. Review*, 20:361–374.

Appendix: A Letter by Erich Muhsam to Sigmund Freud

The context in which I wrote about Otto Gross did not provide appropriate occasion to elaborate on his great talents. The following letter, which Anna Freud has kindly allowed me to publish, contains important source material. Erich Mühsam (?–1935) was a well–known literateur and anarchist. He died a martyr's death at Oranienburg.

Hoch geehrter Herr Professor,

I owe you thanks for the cure of a severe hysteria which your pupil, Dr. Otto Gross of Graz, has performed on me with your method. I hope that the report of a patient on an exceedingly successful cathartic treatment may have sufficient interest for you to excuse this letter.

I suffered from severe pathological symptoms:

strong irritability, which led to outbreaks of rage ending in twilight states, during which I would lie there with complete control of senses immobile, without the ability to get up, the energy to move and to change the existing situation. Occasionally the attacks grew also into complete mental confusion and even into the dysfunctioning of certain senses, such as transitory complete blindness.

Dr. Gross, with whom I entertained a friendly relationship, accepted me for treatment at my request. The success was favorable beyond all expectations. I was cured completely in the course of about six weeks.

The observations which I myself made during the treatment I would not like to keep from you. My poetic talent enabled me to a special degree to find suitable word–associations and in connection [with them] I associated long thought–chains with great speed, which not only supplied me with precious insights into my method of thinking, but which gave me also exceedingly valuable knowledge about the nature of my artistic production and lifted me out of my subconscious recollections, [thus letting] me survey clearly my entire development.

I noticed gradually how the dawning ability to lead the symptoms of my illness back to their deeper foundations brought about, more and more, the disappearance of those very symptoms, and I was able to observe how sometimes through a question of the physician and the consequent answer with its associations, suddenly an entire crust of disease fell off. Also, outside of the sessions and after the termination of the treatment, the method continued to work automatically in myself by fastening spontaneously upon some object, some word, some impression, thus releasing cryptoamnesias; [I] thus experienced further relief of burdensome inhibitions.

For me as a writer, the functioning of your system was of course of particular interest. I found its value especially in the fact that the task of the physician would be mainly to make the patient himself the physician. The patient is induced to diagnose his sickness. On the basis of the diagnosis discovered by himself, he therefore carries out his own cure. He is brought to the point where he is no longer interested in himself as a sufferer but in the suffering itself. He objectifies his condition. He does not put the importance anymore upon himself as a pitiable patient, as the emotionally martyred, as a hysteric seeking cure, but as a physician, as someone who does not feel the sickness anymore but who perceives it. This transformation of the subjective sensations into objective values is the process of cure.

I had feared lest the treatment might paralyze my productivity as a lyricist, since, after all, artistic productivity consists of the direct projection of subconscious processes into sense experiences without intellectual elaboration. I believed that the mere psychological touching on such a process would suffice in the future to activate [an intellectual] judgment about it. Today, I may state with pleasure that this apprehension did not come true. To the contrary: by the removal of numerous interfering phenomena which had laid themselves around the core of my being, my psyche has become more sensitive and reacts more easily to influences which stimulate artistic productivity. The difference from former times shows up only after production. My self–criticism is now essentially sharpened. Whereas in the past I faced my poems, even after years, as helpless and bewildered as at the hour of their origin, I now am able — retroactively —

and even only a few hours after [their] conception — to recognize the subconscious connections which tie the mood of the poem to its shaping. The events which inspired the poem thus do not live anymore in the subconscious during the process of creation and later, in appreciation of the completed product, can be lifted without difficulty to the surface.

Forgive me that I, a lay person, involve myself so deeply with the dissection of your system. Yet I believe that just my capacity to survey so clearly the method of treatment to which I owe my recovery has contributed essentially to bring it about so quickly and safely. Yet I will not fail to attribute the main credit for the success to Dr. Gross. Without his intelligent questioning, his competent response to my psychic construction, and his amiable, considerate, and discreet attitude toward the patient, who is exposed to quite a compromising. . . confession, the treatment could not possibly have been performed. However, least of all would I like to forget that my physician would not have been able to accomplish anything without your psychology [which is that] of a genius. The relief from an unending and pressing burden and the enrichment by infinitely valuable information I therefore owe to both of you.

Will you accept my sincere and cordial thanks in the form of this short report.

Very devotedly yours,

Erich Mühsam, author[1]

Munich, 28/5/1907
Türkenstrasse 81. II

[1]Translated by Ruth S. Eissler.

The German text reads:

Hoch geehrter Herr Professor:

Ich bin Ihnen Dank schuldig für die Heilung von einer schweren Hysterie, die Ihr Schüler, Herr Dr. Otto Gross aus Graz nach Ihrer Methode an mir bewirkt hat. Ich hoffe dass der Bericht eines Patienten über eine überaus erfolgreiche Kathartische Behandlung genügend Interesse für Sie hat um diesen Brief zu entschuldigen.

Ich litt an schweren pathologischen Erscheinungen: starker Reizbarkeit, die zu Wutausbrüchen führte und ihren Abschluss meist im Dämerzuständen fand, während derer ich bei völliger Kontrolle aller Sinne regungslos dalag ohne die Energie aufzubringen, mich zu rühren und die beschämende Situation zu ändern. Mitunter steigerten sich die Anfälle auch zu gänzlicher geistiger Verwirrung und sogar zum Versagen einzelne Sinne, wie vorübergehender völliger Blindheit.

Herr Dr. Gross, mit dem ich freundschaftlich verkehre, erzählte mir viel von der kathartischen Methode und nahm mich auf meine Bitte hin in Behandlung. Der Erfolg war über alles Erwarten günstig. Ich wurde im Laufe von ungefähr sechs Wochen vollständig geheilt.

Die Beobachtungen die ich selbst bei der Behandlung machte, möchte ich Ihnen nicht vorenthalten. Meine dichterische Begabung befähigte mich in besonderem Masse, geeignete Wortassoziationen zu finden und daran anschliessend assoziierte ich lange Gedankenreihen mit grosser Schnelligkeit, was mir nicht nur einem wertvollen Einblick in meine Denkmethode vermittelte, sondern mir auch ausserordentlich wertvolle Aufschlüsse über die Art meiner künstlerichen Produktion gab und mir Erinnerungen aus dem Unterbewusstsein heraufholte, die mich meine ganze Entwicklung scharf übersehen liessen.

Ich bemerkte aumählich, wie die wachwerdende Fähigkeit, die Symptome meiner Krankheit auf ihre tieferen Gründe zurückzuführen, immer mehr das Verschwinden dieser Symptome mit sich führte, und ich konnte beobachten, wie manchmal durch eine Frage des Arztes und der sich daranschliessenden Antwort mit ihren Assoziationen plötzlich eine ganze Krankheits Krushe von mir abglitt. Auch ausserhalb der Sitzungen und nach Einstellung der Behandlung wirkte die Methode automatisch in mir weiter, in dem ich aus mir selbst heraus an irgend einen Gegenstand, ein Wort, einen Eindruck anknüpfte, dabei Kryptomnesien auslöste and dadurch weitere Befreiungen von lästigen Hemmungen erfuhr.

Mir als Schriftsteller war natürlich das Funktionieren Ihres Systems besonders interessant. Ich fand seinen Wert besonders darin, dass die Aufgabe des Arztes dabei hauptsächlich die sei, den Patienten selbst zum Arzt zu machen. Der Patient wird angeleitet, sein Leiden zu diagnostizieren. Auf Grund der selbstgefundenen Diagnose führt er dann die eigne Heilung durch. Er wird dahin gebracht, dass er sich nicht mehr für sich als Leidenden interessiert, sondern für sein Leiden selbst. Er objektiviert seinen Krankheitszustand. Er nimmt sich nicht mehr als bedauernswerten Patienten, als seelisch semarterten, als Heilungsuchenden Hysteriker wichtig, sondern als Arzt, als einen, der die Krankheit nicht mehr heit nicht mehr fühlt sondern sieht. Dieses Umwälzen des subjektiven Empfindens in objektiven Worten ist der Prozess der Heilung.

Ich hatte gefürchtet, die Behandlung könnte meine Produktivität als Lyriker lahmlegen, da ja alle künstlerische Produktion in der direkten Projerzierung unterbewusster Vorgänge ins sinnliche Geschehen bestent, ohne gedankliche Verarbeitung. Ich glaubte, das blosse psychische Berühren eines solchen Vorgangs werde künftig genügen, um sofort das Urteil darüber lebendig zu machen. Heute kann ich zu meiner Freude sagen dass diese Befürchtung nicht eingetroffen ist. Im Gegenteil: durch die Beseitigung zahloser störender Erscheinungen, die sich um den Kern meines Wesens gelegt hatten, ist meine Psyche sensibler geworden, reagiert sie leichter auf Einflüsse, die zur künstlerischen Produktion anregen. Der Unterschied gegen früher zeigt sich erst nach der Produktion. Meine Selbstkritik ist jetzt wesentlich geschärft. Stand ich früher meinen Gedichten noch nach Jahren so hilf- und ratlos gegenüber wie zur Stunde des Enstehens, so bin ich jetzt imstande, nachträglich — und zwar schon wenige Stunden nach der Konzeption — die unterbewussten Zusammenhänge zu errkenne, die die Stimmung des Gedichts mit seiner Gestaltung verbinden. Die Vorgänge, die das Gedicht bewirkt haben, leben also während des Produzierens nicht mehr im Unterbewusstsein, sondern im Vorbewusstsein, oder, wie ich mich Herrn Dr. Gross gegenüber scherzweise ausdrückte: z.D. = "Bewusstsein(?)" und sich nachher bei der Abschätzung des fertigen Produkts ohne weiteres an die Oberfläche zu heben.

Verzeihen Sie, dass ich als Laie mich so tief ins

sezieren Ihres Systems einlasse. Ich glaube über, dass gerade meine Fähigkeit, die Methode der Behandlung, der ich meine Heilung verdanke, klar zu übersehen, wesentlich dazu beigetragen hat, sie so schnell und sicher durchzuführen. Dabei will ich nicht verfehlen, Herrn Dr. Gross das Hauptverdienst an dem Erfolge zuzuerkennen. Ohne seine kluge Fragestellung, sein sicheres Eingehen auf meine psychische Konstruktion und seine liebenswürdige, rücksichtsvolle und diskrete Haltung dem Patienten gegenüber, dem doch eine recht compromittierende Ohrenbeichte zugemutet wird, wäre die Behandlung unmöglich mit mir zu führen gewesen. Am wenigsten aber möchte ich vergessen, dass auch mein Artzt ohne Ihre geniale Psychologie nichts hätte ausrichten können. Die Befreiung von unendlich drückender Last und die Bereicherung mit unendlich wertvollen Erkentnissen danke ich somit Ihnen beiden.

Wollen Sie meinen aufrichtigen herzlichen Dank in der Form dieses kurzen Berichts entgegennehmen.

Ihr sehr ergebener

Erich Mühsam
Schriftsteller

What makes this letter remarkable is that it records an impressive effect of a surprisingly short treatment on an exceedingly talented young person. His psychopathology threatened not only his mental health: his creative potential was in danger of being reduced to zero. Gross's treatment freed the patient of his neurotic symptoms and prepared the way to realization of his unusual gift.

INDEX OF SUBJECTS

(Note: "Freud" stands for "Sigmund Freud,"
"Tausk," for Victor Tausk.")

285

INDEX OF NAMES

293

COMMENTS[1]

PROF. DR. MARIUS TAUSK

I have to thank Dr. Eissler for his generosity in inviting me to have my comments on the present book included in it, just as he helped me to have those on his first book published in an American psychoanalytic journal (Tausk, 1973). At both times he knew that I had very serious objections to essential parts of what he had written or was going to write about my father.

In this book, as in the preceding one, it is Dr. Eissler's declared purpose to show that Dr. Roazen's conclusions regarding a causative role of Freud's behavior in bringing about my father's suicide were wrong. In *Talent and Genius* Eissler tried to thoroughly crush Roazen's credibility and in the process destroy the widely respected

[1]Prof. Dr. Tausk's comments are reproduced exactly as received, with the exception of minor editorial alterations. — K.R.E.

299

image of my father's personality. In the present book the immediate targets were shifted to some extent, but the author's motivation and general intention remained the same. In the period between the appearance of *Talent and Genius* in 1971 and the time of this writing (February–March, 1980) I have had a more or less ongoing exchange of letters with Dr. Eissler, who also visited me at my home (in 1978 and 1979). I have seen various drafts of parts of the present book and have made great efforts to show him what in my opinion were unfounded judgments and conclusions, but in the main my attempts were unsuccessful. I am therefore laying down many of my criticisms in this appendix, leaving the ultimate judgment to the reader. In order to keep these comments within reasonable limits, I shall have to restrict them to the most important subjects. The reader should therefore *not* assume that I agree to everything I have not specifically objected to.

During Dr. Eissler's and my exchanges of views I have repeatedly argued that his presentations of historical facts very often contain moral or moralistic verdicts. On one such occasion, during his visit at our home (on July 28, 1978) I said something to the effect that he wanted to picture my father as a bad man, to which he replied: "No, your father was not a bad person, he was seriously disturbed." This gave me hope that in the new book which Dr. Eissler was determined to write, he would give up his attitude of viewing his subject from the judge's chair (see Eissler, 1971, p. 129: ". . . one man joins in his life seeming incompatibles and acts a saint, sinner, judge and executioner") and rather take that of the physician who looks at a patient. Although the first few pages of this book seemed to bear this out, in my opinion the judge's voice is still louder than that of the doctor.

Dr. Eissler's purpose is obviously the presentation of a work of science (see e.g., his comments on Otto Gross on p. 237, and if this means that he has spared no effort to assemble as many documents and verify as many data as was humanly possible, I can only congratulate him. But, as I shall try to prove, his approach is not the one which the famous German chemist, Nobel laureate A. Windaus meant in advising his doctoral students: "Make yourself an enemy of your own theories!"

One more remark about the set-up of this book: Having established nine years ago that my father was not a genius, Eissler now ends up by comparing him with geniuses like Shakespeare and Newton — of course, to my father's great disadvantage.

There are some examples in the present book which show how far the author can be carried away in his desire to interpret small and even smallest details as symptoms or signs of my father's psychopathology. In Chapter II he elaborates on the fact that in a little verse my father wrote *Vaternamen* (not *Vaters Namen*). "...The nonce word...it makes of two elements...a configuration that cannot be disjoined...a fateful entity, like a ghost...," etc. An internationally known psychoanalyst spoke to me with reference to similar utterances of some of his colleagues of the *"furor interpretandi."* The simple truth is that *Vaternamen* is not a nonce word. It is listed in Duden's standard German dictionary (17th edition, 1973, Vol. 1, p. 719) as follows: *Vatername, Vatersname* (Familien-, Zuname).

In the same category would I place the author's remarks (Chapter II) about my father's habit of signing his letters with his surname only, without initials. "I conjecture that this practice is always [! M. T.] an external sign of an inner conviction relating to uniqueness and irreplaceability." I could easily adduce evidence to show that the habit described was by no means uncommon in Vienna in those times, but I prefer to use this opportunity for more relevant matters. Far more important is the way in which Eissler deals with my father's "Spinoza-Dialogue," in which Eissler believes he has detected "a profound depersonalizatiòn," being described "as a general quality of life's experience," and he quotes me as finding "in another part of the scene the essence of [my] father's conflict" (Chapter II). This impressive dialogue is a heart-rending revelation of my father's suffering. He accuses himself of having been busy, far too busy, with trivial things and having lost sight of the eternal truth; half blind during the day he shamefully faces frightening visions of punishment during sleepless nights. He had lost the light of the law to guide him and exhausts himself in listening to the crying of those whom he owes too much. Spinoza tells him to calm down, to quietly select what to do, to be like a pure flame. He would recognize his redemption by *the joy of living and of giving*. "Give like a loving woman: the fruit of giving remains in *her* womb." (Eissler gives a different meaning to these words when he quotes them in Chapter VII but I have no doubt that my interpretation is correct. Eissler [Chapter II] finds the "language at times obscure and susceptible of various interpretations.")

I remember a talk I had with my father in Graz in January 1918 (Tausk, 1973) when I brought up what I had heard about Schopenhauer's pessimism and he said something to the effect that what kept Schopenhauer alive was that he *enjoyed thinking* so much. I am not sufficiently conversant with psychoanalytic language to know whether this pure joy comes under the heading of the pleasure principle,[2] but I now feel sure that this was the joy my father had lost or perhaps never had had in a measure that would have sustained him in all the crises he had to go through. What strikes me in this whole book, explicitly focused on my father's psychopathology, is the little emphasis put on the patient's subjective suffering, his harmony or disharmony, as important markers of health or disease.

Eissler deals elaborately with my father's relationship to women, beginning in Chapter II, where he states that his "first choice," viz, my mother, "was a splendid one, the best he possibly would ever make." Unfortunately here already I have to contradict him, although I am of course very pleased and grateful to see in what high esteem he holds my mother. There is nothing I could add to this since my feelings of love and unending gratitude cannot be expressed in writing. Whether she was an ideal spouse for my father is another matter — if ever there was one.

The tragic ending of this and other connections Eissler puts down to the character of my father, whom he variously describes as a deserter, having a sadistic, exhibitionistic, narcissistic personality, a man who brutalized and traumatized his victims and *"structured the moment of separation in such a way that it entailed the greatest pain to the woman he was abandoning"* (Chapter V).

I have in my possession a few letters exchanged between my mother and my father in 1898 and 1899, before they were married. They show that at that very early time already my father feared that his love might not last and worried about it. They also show that their attitudes

[2]See, however, Eissler's remark on p. 125, in his discussion of my father's will.

toward certain practical duties were not the same — those of my mother definitely more in accordance with normal standards, as they remained throughout her life. Already in the summer of 1899, when my father spent some time in Dubrovnik on the Dalmatian coast because of his feeble health, he felt torn between conflicting emotions, foreboding the more severe depression of 1906, but yet he was looking forward to their marriage a year later.

My mother and my father must have been a predominantly unhappy couple right from the beginning. As I have pointed out before (1973), the conditions under which they lived in Bosnia, my mother's separation from her parents, the grave animosity between her father and her husband, the death of her beloved mother were all contributing factors to make their lives together more and more unbearable. My father did not desert my mother, they left each other, and it was with a feeling of profound gratitude that my mother returned to Vienna, well knowing how much struggle for survival lay ahead. As Dr. Eissler rightly points out, the court that divorced them put the blame on both parties.

In his discussion on the "special features" of Tausk's psychopathology in Chapter II, Eissler attaches great significance to some remarks my father made in meetings of the Vienna Psychoanalytic Association. The first two refer to an attempted explanation of the observation that the act of love may never entirely provide complete satisfaction (Nunberg and Federn, 1962–1975, vol. 3, pp. 314, 353), the third one to "anesthesia of the penis during coition" (Nunberg and Federn, 1962–1975, vol. 4, p. 111). With respect to all of these remarks Eissler "reconstruct[s] that here Tausk derived from his own subjective experience a general theory. It would have served as a rationalization of a defect in orgastic potency." The first remark Eissler quotes (it may never be entirely possible for one to be completely spent by the act of love) has obviously a far more subtle meaning than what would be covered by Eissler's term "a defect in orgastic potency." My father made the remark in connection with anxiety (fear of death in particular) and this he discussed in his paper on masturbation (briefly in the same volume on pp. 339–343, more elaborately in his paper of 1912, p. 60). These papers make it clear that he was speaking of his experience with 18 patients with complaints relating to masturbation.

My father's remark about anesthesia of the penis was not made in connection with incomplete gratification but with the existence of the castration complex and in the same paragraph he refers to "one patient or instance." Eissler states that my father's "practical experience with patients cannot have been extensive enough to warrant a law [sic!] of limitations of sexual pleasure, amounting to the assertion that anesthesia is virtually universal." This would indeed have been preposterous but Eissler's statement is clearly unfounded. I emphasize this in view of the far-reaching conclusions he draws from his "reconstruction of Tausk's relative penile anesthesia" in Chapter II. Eissler is puzzled by the sentence that "Tausk would like to claim priority for the thought that the sexual instinct is not capable of providing full gratification, in so far as professor Freud does not claim priority." The Minutes do not record the expression of such astonishment by others present at the meeting and it seems to me that my father took this simple precaution since he could not possibly know everything Freud had or might have said on the subject in the past.

One of the testimonies on which Eissler bases his judgment on my father's ways of dealing with women is a remark he quotes from a conversation with the writer Felix Braun (Chapter II): "they were the talk of the town." This gossip—just because it was gossip—suffices for Eissler to consider it an indication that "Tausk conducted his love affairs in an exhibitionistic, flamboyant way. One may be inclined to conjecture that he wanted the town to know of his many liaisons." As if even a tiny number of incidents, spread and repeated by a few talkative people in a circle feeding on curiosity, could not produce such a "talk-of-the-town" effect.

More serious are my objections to Eissler's discussion of an incident described by Roazen, when my father abruptly terminated an affair. Roazen is quoting a letter from the woman concerned in which she thanks him for his book and—and this is quoted correctly by Eissler— explains my father's act by saying: "he was just following the direction of his tormented mind." Eissler describes the farewell as "brutal and traumatic to the victim," because my father was not even courteous enough, to take her to the nearest café and prepare her politely for the bad news to come. This analysis of the event, together with a number of similar comments, shows how easily Dr. Eissler is satisfied with simple explanations that are destructive to my father's character. The physician (not the public prosecutor!) should have seen my father's act as a sign of unbearable pressure of "his tormented mind." Had he taken the girl to a café, there would have been the inevitable talking and begging, appealing and crying, and of course she would not have understood his reasons. He himself probably could not have explained why—as in other cases—he was just unable to maintain his love-relations for prolonged periods,[3] not even with

[3]From a paper by the Dutch sexologist and psychoanalyst C. van Emde Boas (1968) I deduced that psychoanalysts have recognized

his wife, whom he had loved passionately. And my father would have appeared even more cruel, had he deafened himself to the woman's imploring. In Dr. Eissler's interpretation it is all vicious purpose. "Do I go too far," he asks himself, "when I conjecture that in his narcissism he did not want ever to be forgotten by a woman he had loved?" My answer can only be: "Yes, you do indeed, Dr. Eissler."

This story in the present book is immediately followed by another one, described as analogous and typical, though it has not the slightest resemblance to it: the story of the Serbian lady Kosa Lazarević. When Austria had lost the war and my father had returned to Vienna, the Serbian scene with a temporary though endearing relationship could not possibly have been transferred into a totally different world. And again: she would not have understood.

I am now coming to the parts of the present book dealing with my father's relationship to his children, starting in Chapter II and continuing in Chapter V. Here at least I can say with confidence that I am competent to judge. To begin with, Eissler calls the fact that my father left his children desertion and a sign "of his ambivalence toward them." I do not have to repeat that the word "desert" is wrong in the present context, but I wish to emphasize that I have never detected in my father any trace of a feeling for his children, other than love and great responsibility for their education. Late in life I saw from many of his letters that he severely reproached himself for not being able to fulfill all his paternal duties. The "ambivalence" is a construction of Dr. Eissler's, introduced in his

---

a syndrome called *Liebesunfähigkeit*, i.e., inability to maintain love-relationships over prolonged periods of time.

book in Chapter V, where he also doubts the correctness of my opinion regarding the last words my father spoke to me.

When I reported (1973), as Eissler repeats, that my father teased me because I would not have a glass of beer with our supper, I was by no means suggesting that my teetotalism sprang from a "formation of ideals which could protect [me] against a widespread disorder," viz. alcoholism. I have never felt that I was in danger of becoming an alcoholic. The simple reason for my joining the "Workmen's League" (*Arbeiter-Abstinentenbund*) was that under the inspiring influence of my mother I was active in the Socialist youth movement, attending meetings of young workmen and apprentices, giving lectures, marching with them on the first of May and, as far as possible, supporting their affiliated organizations. My father never liked political systems with their hard and fast rules and would have liked his sons to enjoy life in freedom. On that last evening my father did not "tempt the son to infringe upon the very ideal the youngster had evolved." He just teased me as a good friend would tease another.

Why my "interpretation of [my] father's parting words ('kümmere Dich nicht um mich') . . . would reveal a basic contradiction" is beyond my grasp. Eissler correctly renders that interpretation on p. 111. What else could those words have meant? To me they were plain. Dr. Eissler doubts the correctness of my interpretation, but he does not offer a better one. He just calls them enigmatic! The examples that follow in Dr. Eissler's presentation as evidence of ambivalence on my father's side are equally objectionable. I would not have published the material myself, had I had the slightest doubt as to its validity as testimony to my father's serious concern about our education. I have never felt my father was "nagging" or undermining my "morale." When Dr. Eissler writes "yet despite all this unwisdom the son evolved an excellent relationship to his father," it does not occur to him that there could be something wrong with *his* interpretation of the recorded facts.

Since Eissler asks "what could be the rationale of asking the adolescent what he would have done in a pre-scientific era," the answer is — and it can be deduced from my report on that little discussion (1973, p. 332) — that my father wanted to teach me to examine critically what I am being taught and not to be simply guided by authority. This advice has been of great help in many of my activities throughout my life. When trouble occurred in the pharmaceutical works of which I was a manager, I could repeatedly show that it had been caused by somebody who had uncritically taken certain things for granted. And haven't we been told for decades that in teaching students it is more important to encourage their critical thinking than to feed them facts or theories that might be obsolete a few years later?

Perhaps the most important part of the present book is the one dealing with the events immediately preceding my father's suicide. In Chapter V, Eissler introduces as an important document the letter my father wrote to his youngest sister the day before his death. That letter has been lost but my aunt said she had learnt it by heart and since I know that she used to have an excellent memory, particularly with regard to things of great emotional value to herself, I am willing to believe that the text which she recently reproduced was more or less literally identical with the original. It contained the information "*Morgen gehen wir zum Standesamt*," which Eissler in-correctly translates as "tomorrow we are going to the civil ceremony," and he draws a number of conclusions from the timing of this communication and even more so from the planning to which it refers. *Standesamt* is the same as the British Registrar's Office. (I am not sure of the proper term or terms used in the U.S.) But you had to go to this office twice when you wanted to get married: the first time to give notice (see Eissler's remark about the banns on p. 118), the second time for the wedding. In the present context it would make a great difference and eliminate a number of questions Eissler is wrestling with, if my father in his letter to his sister actually meant the first of the two appearances before the registrar. Only now, when studying Eissler's text, have I racked my brain about this problem and a very faint memory appeared of Hilde Loewi's mentioning the word *Aufgebot* (that is, announcement of intended marriage) during the only conversation I had with her after the death of my father and before his funeral.[4] Eissler cites information that would support my memory but here as at some other places, he relegates such statements that disagree with his story to a footnote without actually taking them into account, which could have meant rewriting whole chapters or big parts of them. See the notes on pages 136, 141, and 152.

Incidentally, I do not find my father's letter to Freud of July 2 clumsy "and quite different from [his] usual style," but I would not mention this if Eissler were not drawing rather speculative conclusions from this observation of his. The farewell letter to Freud Eissler calls "clear and precise," but he sees fit to interpret one of its essential sentences in a way which in my opinion cannot be justified. My father begs Freud to assist his fiancée and he adds:

[4]Dr. Eissler kindly informed me that he had made inquiries at the registrar's office concerned and that no record of an announcement of intended marriage was found.

"She will not ask much of you because she herself has great possibilities of happiness in herself" (Eissler's translation). I call attention to the fact that my father expresses the same request in his will, where he writes, "I beg Professor Freud to assist my dear fiancée so that she may be able to properly get over the event of my suicide" ("... damit sie mit dem Ereignis meines Selbstmordes richtig fertig werden könne"). I never had the slightest doubt that what my father had in mind was psychological advice or consolation. Dr. Eissler seriously doubts that in his last letter to Freud my father wrote the "full truth. How should one interpret Tausk's telling Freud that Hilde Loewi would not ask much of him although he must have known what her main complaint and worry would have been after her fiancée's death?"

Here as elsewhere in this book Eissler refuses to take at face value what my father (should I say the defendant?) says, even when — as in this case — he has every moral claim to being trusted. And so Eissler has to resort to more and more conjectures. These are:

1. What my father could not tell Freud, although it would have been the main reason for which Hilde would have approached him, was about her pregnancy and her desire to get rid of it.

2. Hilde Loewi did in fact see Freud and this must have been between the third and the tenth of July (date of the letter to Ferenczi, see Chapter V). She must have told Freud about her pregnancy and my father's subsequent impotence. Freud had a strategic meeting with his collaborators and "someone of Freud's inner circle if not he himself established a connection with Adler and received a promise to solve Hilde Loewi's desperate plight." Eissler does not offer a conjecture as to why this very urgent business had to take two to three months, as one would

have to deduce from Dr. Knopf's letter.

I shall presently comment on Eissler's doubts as to my father's saying the full truth in his farewell letter to Freud, and I am passing over his apparent "niggling" about a truly futile grammatical error (of the sort I have often found, particularly in letters written in Dutch). But I must comment on what he considers a contradiction between my father's farewell letter to Freud and a corresponding sentence in his last will, all the more so since the atrocious word *hypocrisy* found its way into the author's discussion and since he attributes eminent importance to the respective paragraphs of the will.

The sentence in the letter to Freud (in Eissler's translation) says: "My suicide is the healthiest, most decent act of my derailed life," as contrasted with the one Eissler quotes from the will: "I depart from my life that I [have] retrenched systematically since my childhood and which . . . has now lost its meaning completely." I see no contradiction and I could without difficulty combine the two in one paragraph. What my father meant to say could be rephrased somewhat like this: *"My life was one big mistake.* [N. B.: Eissler's translation of *verfehltes* by *derailed* is not quite right. *Verfehlen* means choosing the wrong way by mistake. The German word for *derailed* would be *entgleist*, and that would apply when a train that might have run perfectly, suddenly and by accident would get off the rails.] *And so it took me downhill all the time. The healthiest and most decent thing to do now is to finish it."*

Again I may invoke the Spinoza-Dialogue, the most profound and most revealing thing my father ever wrote about himself, to sustain my interpretation. Spinoza is speaking:

*Die ganze Welt sei Dir ein wohnlich
    Haus.
Der Gipfel des Gebäudes sei der Tod.
Er ist die Krone, doch er ist kein Reich.
Doch willst das Reich Du auf die Krone
    stellen,
Das Leben auf den Tod, den Grundstein
    auf den Gipfel
Dann ist Dein Leben nichts als Tun und
    Tun,
Die schwanke Masse vor dem Fall zu
    halten.
Und Du bist immer unter Deinem Leben,
Im eignen Schatten, unter einem Felsen,
Der immer droht, Dich stürzend zu
    vernichten.
So wird Dein Tun zum Leid, das Leid
    zum Leben.
Du bist Dein Leid und stirbst, wenn Du
    nicht leidest.*

Here follows the best I could do to translate this, no
doubt below the standard of the beautiful original:

The whole world should be your friendly
    house.
Death be the vertex of the building.
It is the crown, but not a kingdom.
But if you want to put the kingdom on
    the crown,
Life upon death, foundation upon vertex,
Then restless agitation will become your
    life,
To keep the shaky mass from falling
    down.

And you will always be below your life,
In your own shadow and beneath a rock
Threat'ning to tumble down and to
    destroy you.
So all your acting will become your
    suffering,
Your suffering will become your life.
You are your suffering and you will die
    when you don't suffer.

How Dr. Eissler, who has read this poem and must know how seriously my father suffered under the burden of his repeated crises, can *construct* a hypothesis to explain my father's last confession as hypocritically feigned martyrdom is beyond my imagination.

But Eissler's need for a number of (auxiliary) constructions stems from the fact that he has to buttress a far bigger construction, his hypothesis concerning the ultimate events that led to my father's suicide and for which he has no shred of evidence. I shall now have to deal with the sections of Chapter V concerning my father's relationship with Hilde Loewi, "The Basic Mechanisms," and "The Sequence of Events."

Hilde Loewi told me during the one and only conversation I had with her that at the end of her first visit to my father's office she asked him whether she should come again (for further treatment). He then stood up, embraced her and said, "You must come again, you belong to me!" To me and to any unprejudiced reader this means that my father was overwhelmed by a passionate desire for her love. (He felt extremely lonely at that time, as I shall presently show.) Dr. Eissler feels justified in assuming that "she told Tausk in her first interview that

she was still a virgin" and that "he became victimized by
the temptation," for — as Eissler had stated in the same
context — "[t]o deflower a virgin was considered the
choicest tidbit of sexual entertainment." This interpretation alone should make the reader wary of the author's
intention or ability to present an unbiased, professional
analysis of this patient's psychopathology.

When Eissler proceeds to his discussion of "the basic
mechanisms," he seems to approach the core of the problem of my father's lifelong unhappiness and the declared
"true conscious motive of [his] suicide," viz. "that none of
these associations [with women] ever resulted in mutual
happiness." However, he eschews a deeper exploration
and stops at the assumption that also in the case of Hilde
Loewi my father would have had to abandon the "erstwhile loved woman," but her pregnancy became a practical obstacle. In his first book (1971), Eissler said "this
was the element, *evidently* [my italics], that triggered his
determination to put an end to his existence." Now he
was able to make the machinery at work a little more
complicated. (1) Magic expectations may have made him
anticipate "that a sudden turn of events would liberate
him from an unacceptable bondage." (2) The (most probably erroneous) assumption that my father wanted to kill
himself on the scheduled day of his wedding has now
become evidence of his intent to "wreak revenge for the
woman's holding him in a vise and forcing him into marriage," and "the determination to leave Hilde Loewi
unmarried and pregnant had acquired equal urgency."
(3) "Something terrible must have happened to him during the last few hours of his life to unleash a storm of
panic and rage that destroyed his morale and rushed him
into ending his life. . . . " The reader of this book by now
knows that in Eissler's strong opinion impotence was "the

last straw that felled that proud man." The way Dr. Eissler arrived at this "compelling... reconstruction" deserves careful analysis since in this essential part of his book he permits the reader to follow him closely in his deductions.

On page 140 we find the following quotation from a letter Freud wrote to Ferenczi a week after my father's suicide: "Tausk has shot himself on 4/7[5] eight days before a scheduled marriage.... Etiology obscure. Probably psy. impotence and last act of his fight with the father ghost." The unprejudiced reader will conclude that Freud wrote what he thought was probably the "etiology," in other words, the decisive motive behind his suicide. Not so the author of this book, who does "not see any other possibility than that Hilde Loewi told him of Tausk's impotence." Does he know that she had seen Freud between the third and the tenth of July? Dr. Eissler does not tell us so, but since by now he is convinced that my father *was* impotent, who else could have told Freud? And "[i]n view of the effect this incident had on Tausk I conjecture that it was the first time that this ill-fortune has befallen him." It is stupendous to see how much can be concluded from two very short, even incomplete sentences when they come from Freud and suggest a possibility.

Eissler conjectures. The word recurs with conspicuous frequency in this book. There would be nothing wrong with this, were it not that the author very often seems to forget that he used it and takes his conjectures as proved. So in this case, when he writes: "Thus there are three secured facts: resistance to being coerced into marriage, impotence and suicide."

But on page 146 the author reverts to Freud's letter, to

[5]"7/4," according to American usage.

obviate a possible objection (which in fact I have raised in my talk with Dr. Eissler at my home on July 14, 1979). "The word 'probably' was not used in the sense of uncertainty about the occurrence of impotence but about its etiological value. If his doubt had extended to the fact of impotence, he would have written *wahrscheinliche* as the adjective qualifying impotence. *Wahrscheinlich*, as he wrote, refers to etiology: that is, the probable etiology was impotence." I do not believe that anybody who knows German would have attached any significance to the use of *wahrscheinlich* (without the *e* at the end), which can mean an adjective or an adverb (in contrast to the obligatory difference between "probable" and "probably" in English). But to conclude from the absence of the *e* (1) that Freud knew my father was impotent, (2) that he had been told so by Hilde Loewi, (3) that in his scientific consciousness Freud had to make a slight reservation with regard to the question whether that established impotence was the etiological factor that made my father kill himself — this is what Dr. Eissler's argument boils down to and it is too much for me (and I suppose to other scientists as well).

When I visited Dr. Ernst Pfeiffer at Göttingen on July 18 and 19, 1979, he not only permitted me to read all the letters my father had written to Lou Andreas-Salomé (whose literary estate is under his custody), but he also gave me a present. He gave me the letter I had written to Lou on April 30, 1920, the existence of which I had completely forgotten. Eissler quotes it correctly, and he also is right in saying that I took "this passage as proof that they had not gone to her apartment." But his sentence that follows is entirely wrong: ". . . it seems that Marius himself doubted that this was the whole story, for the quoted sentence was preceded by 'About my father's really last and decisive hours only. one human being is informed and that is his bride, Hilde Loewi [I used her artist's name, "Loewe"] in Vienna.'" Although I had forgotten that I ever wrote that letter, I know perfectly well what I wanted to say, because that thought remained with me ever since. I believed and still believe that on that evening my father became tragically convinced that he would not be happy with this woman, not any more than he had been with my mother. It seemed to me probable, that this was the result of his last talk with her or perhaps just of his thoughts while he was listening to the music. Of course I could not guess and of course she would have been the one who knew or could have guessed. To this I would add today: provided she knew my father well enough to understand what really went on "in his tormented mind."

Well, again Dr. Eissler seems to know better. We read, further on: ". . . if, as I believe is proved, an incident of impotence had occurred, Tausk must immediately have become deeply upset. Hilde Loewi would have noticed the degree of excitement with which he responded to the incident and understandably would not have let him go home alone but would have accompanied him."

Dr. Eissler then repeats in his own words what I told him I had thought after I had read my father's letter to Lou Andreas-Salomé of March 26, 1919. Since he called my "reconstruction in essence not dissimilar to [his own] but skirting the incident of impotence" I wish to put my thoughts before the reader in my own words and to stress the very great differences between them and those of Dr. Eissler. The main point is that I did not try to reconstruct anything. I simply believed everything my father had said, because I never had had any reason not to do so.

The key sentence of his will (in my translation) was:

"The recognition that I can not gladly enter into a new marriage, that I can only keep myself and my beloved fiancée in conflicts and torments, is the true conscious motive of my suicide." The pregnancy was of course a most undesirable complication and this my father could not disclose, as long as there were any possibilities that it could be terminated by abortion, as indeed it was. But why should this in any way detract from the validity of my father's statement about the true conscious motive of his suicide? He felt sure he could not marry the "most precious woman who ever stepped into [his] life." She herself might even have intimated something to this effect, according to the information conveyed by her husband to Dr. Eissler and recorded by him in a footnote near the end of Chapter V.

In *Talent and Genius*, where Eissler (p. 124) said it was highly doubtful that my father was ever in love with his fiancée, he concluded (p. 127) that "the pregnancy this time made it impossible to repeat the past incidents of breaking an engagement." To this hypothetical but clearly inadequate motivation Eissler has now added a supplementary one: "an uncontrolled urge to wreak revenge. . . ."

However, from my father's own letters it is evident that in the first months of 1919 he had reached a state of complete loneliness (which I believe is a somewhat better translation of *Einsamkeit* than Eissler's "solitude"). He even wrote to his friend Lou, for whom he still felt almost boundless admiration, would she know of a woman who could be for him, late in life, a *companion*. When he met Hilde Loewi, with whom he obviously fell in love and whom he pictured in his last letter to Freud with a few endearing words, he must have fervently hoped that this was at last the fulfillment of his longing. But it was not.

Near the beginning of the present book the author writes: "It is to be expected that the historian and the loving son do not reach the same conclusions. . . ." This can, I believe, only mean that the son would be emotionally biased in favor of his father, whereas the author, guided by the principles of the historian's methodology, would by definition be impartial. It is most unlikely that Dr. Eissler wanted to say that the expected differences between his conclusions and my own would be due to *his* being biased against my father. Needless to say that for me it has become very difficult, to say the least, to admit that such bias has not become apparent in the present book. But independently of my judgment it is legitimate to ask whether and to what extent the story, as presented, stands up to the requirements of scientific historical writing. A number of things I have mentioned, in particular the numerous and far-reaching conjectures built on very scanty and, as it turns out, in part unfounded data plead against it. But leaving these serious objections aside for a moment, do we end up with at least a consistent and logically coherent story?

The character of my father, as it emerges from Dr. Eissler's elaborate descriptions, is that of a man who systematically seduced women "without giving a signal of the destructive potential that later would reveal itself." "The incident with Hilde Loewi would have been at best[!] an intensification of his usual ways." "Nevertheless, the relationship may have developed soon into one of love, respect and regard for the woman." "Hilde Loewi had become pregnant and an abortion was not possible." "If Tausk had refused to marry Hilde Loewi... it would have become a scandal of such proportion that Tausk would have had to leave Vienna... he had lost the freedom of choice." In other words, my father's concern was not the misery he wanted to spare his fiancée, but the scandal he wanted to avoid for himself. On the contrary: "It is this maximum of anguish at the moment of highest blissful expectation... to which Tausk subjected his pregnant fiancée...." "To hurt the love object became again the *modus operandi* of the unconscious." I have reasons to assume that the last three words were added to this sentence as a kind of afterthought and I do not know to what extent the unconscious according to psycho-analytic theory can be considered as capable of planning and scheming. In view of my father's letter to Freud of July 2 Eissler considers "that Tausk was temporarily determined to go ahead with his intention," viz., to marry, and he "can exclude with certainty the formation of an explicit intent" (viz. of suicide) "during that day" (July 2). So, "something terrible must have happened to him during the last few hours of his life to unleash a storm of panic and rage," and this as we have seen, thanks to Freud's sketchy note to Ferenczi, can only have been impotence. However, the panic and rage did not interfere with my father's writing his lengthy will, impressive "by the completeness of directions, preciseness of data, and meticulous wording" and a farewell letter to Freud, praised by the author for a number of qualities, including clarity and precision.

I hope that this brief summary should help the reader who has not yet arrived at a final conclusion to judge whether the author's story is — as I worded my question hereabove — at least a consistent and logically coherent one. I doubt it.

References

Eissler, K. R. (1971), *Talent and Genius: The Fictitious Case of Tausk Con-*

tra Freud. New York: Quadrangle.

Nunberg, H., & Federn, E., eds. (1962–1975), *Minutes of the Vienna Psychoanalytic Society*, 4 vols. New York: International Universities Press.

Tausk, M. (1973), Victor Tausk as seen by his son. *Amer. Imago*, 30: 323–334.

Tausk, V. (1912), In: Die Onanie, Vierzehn Beiträge zu einer Diskussion der Wiener Psychoanalytischen Vereinigung, by Datner, B., *et al.*, Wiesbaden: J. F. Bergmann, pp. 48–68.

van Emde Boas, C. (1968), Der Beitrag der Psychoanalyse zur Entwicklung der Liebesfähigkeit des Menschen. In: *Sexualität, Formen und Fehlentwicklungen*, ed. A. Schelkopf. Göttingen: Verlag für Medizinische Psychologie im Verlag Vandenhoeck & Ruprecht, pp. 79–110.